Knights of Pythias, William D. Kennedy

Official Digest of the Supreme Lodge

Knights of Pythias of the World, 1890

Knights of Pythias, William D. Kennedy

Official Digest of the Supreme Lodge
Knights of Pythias of the World, 1890

ISBN/EAN: 9783337286712

Printed in Europe, USA, Canada, Australia, Japan

Cover: Foto ©Andreas Hilbeck / pixelio.de

More available books at **www.hansebooks.com**

OF THE

SUPREME LODGE

Knights of Pythias

OF THE WORLD.

1890,

ISSUED BY ORDER OF THE SUPREME LODGE,
1891.

Entered according to Act of Congress, in the year 1891, by R. L. C. WHITE, S. K. R. S. (for the Supreme Lodge Knights of Pythias of the World), in the office of the Librarian of Congress, at Washington.

CHICAGO:
STROMBERG, ALLEN & CO.,
PRINTERS.

MANSFIELD, OHIO, January 13, 1891.

In accordance with, and by authority of the legislation had at the Biennial Session of the Supreme Lodge, Knights of Pythias of the World, held in the City of Milwaukee, Wisconsin, July, 1890—see Journal, pages 5409 and 5463—this Digest is hereby promulgated, and is the only Official Digest of the Order now extant.

The Special Committee, appointed to prepare the same, called to its assistance Past Supreme Representative WM. D. KENNEDY, of Illinois, whose recognized and known ability as a compiler of our Laws, together with his years of research, and large Pythian library, marked him specially to the Committee as pre-eminently the man to compile this work, and to him we accord the honor due.

We append the action of the Committee on Law, under the legislation above cited.

Fraternally submitted by the Committee,

JOHN C. BURNS,
Supreme Representative of Ohio, Chairman.
CHAS. A. LEE,
Supreme Representative of Rhode Island.
H. H. FRANCIS,
Supreme Representative of Indiana.

CINCINNATI, OHIO, January 8, 1891.

TO HON. JOHN C. BURNS,
Chairman of Committee on Digest:

The Committee on Law report back to your Committee, the manuscript of the revision of the Digest, with our approval of the same.

W. B. RICHIE,
Supreme Representative of Ohio, Chairman.
PHILIP T. COLGROVE,
Supreme Representative of Michigan.
JNO. H. ALEXANDER,
Supreme Representative of Virginia.

The compiler has a few words to say to the membership of the Order in regard to the best manner of consulting this Digest.

ALWAYS CONSULT THE INDEX, and if you don't find the subject under the first head, think of another and try that. Every section in this Digest has been indexed under every subject to which it refers, even remotely.

The subjects have all been placed under the departments to which each most particularly refers, and there grouped in separate classifications.

When desiring to refer to the Digest, while speaking, the syllabus at the head of each department will be found especially useful for ready reference, giving the catch line of the subject and the number of the section.

Even these few words would not have been written but that, knowing the plan of the Digest, it was thought that the readers might take the suggestions kindly from

THE COMPILER.

CHICAGO, ILL., January 13. 1891, P. P. XXVII.

AGE.

1. Every person initiated must be twenty-one years of age; nor can the Supreme Chancellor dispense with this requirement.

Jour., 1869, 26, 45, 68, 101.

2. The Supreme Lodge only fixes a minimum of age for applicants; the maximum limit is a matter for local legislation.

Jour., 1888, 4120, 1574, 1580, 1581.

NOTE.—See also constitutional provision under "Membership."

AMENDMENTS.

1. To Constitution of Supreme Lodge (3, 5, 6) and Written and Unwritten Work (4).
2. To Constitutions of Grand Lodges (7, 8, 9, 10, 11).

1—To Constitution of Supreme Lodge and to Written and Unwritten Work.

3. No alteration or amendment to the Constitution of the Supreme Lodge shall be made, unless presented at a regular session, and adopted by a two-thirds vote at the next succeeding regular session.

Const., Art. XXIX.

4. Provided, that no change shall be made in the Written or Unwritten Work, unless the same lie over from one session to another, nor then, unless four-fifths of those present and entitled to vote concur therein.

Const., Art. XXIX.

5. Provided, also, that amendments of the Constitution may be considered and disposed of at the session at which they are offered, provided unanimous consent be given for their consideration.

Const., Art. XXIX.

6. All amendments to the Constitution shall be referred to the Committee on Law for examination, and the said committee shall report on the same before they are taken up to be voted upon.

Jour., 1884, 3022.

2—To the Constitution of a Grand Lodge.

7. The power to amend the Constitution of a Grand Lodge exists in the Grand Lodge itself, and cannot be conferred upon any other body.

Jour., 1876, 1288-1292.

8. The Constitution of a Grand Lodge can only be amended as therein provided; only such Constitutions or amendments should be approved by the Supreme Lodge.

Jour., 1876, 1288-1292.

9. Where an appeal was presented to the Supreme Lodge involving the operation of a certain provision of the Constitution of a Grand Lodge, and during the pendency of the appeal the fact was discovered that the provision referred to had never been submitted and approved, as required in the case of all amendments to the Constitutions of Grand Lodges, under Art. VII, Sec. 3, Supreme Lodge Constitution, the Supreme Lodge, for the reason stated, declared the provision inoperative as against the appellants, and sustained the appeal simply on that ground.

Jour., 1878, 1558, 1619.

10. Where a Grand Lodge, by an amending clause in its Constitution, specifically provides for the manner in which its Constitution may be amended, and such provision requires that such amendments shall be submitted in a certain way, and at the next succeeding regular session acted upon, such amendments could not be legally proposed and acted upon at the same session.

Jour., 1877, 1406, 1448.

11. When a matter which, under the provisions of a Grand Lodge Constitution, is subject to a rule to "lie over" till the next session, and when considered at the next session is rejected, and its reconsideration indefinitely postponed, the latter action would not prevent the introduction of the same question, when again submitted as a proposition to "lie over"; this would not constitute a "consideration of the same subject" at that session.

Jour., 1884, 3038, 3039, 3040.

AMPLIFIED THIRD RANK.

1. Adopted (12).
2. Must be Memorized (13).
3. Lodge Determines as to Use of (14).

1—Adopted.

12. At the session of 1872 an Amplified Third Rank was adopted, and the Supreme Keeper of Records and Seal instructed to have the Rituals bound both with and without the Amplified Rank, and Grand and Subordinate Lodges were authorized to order whichever they desired.

Jour., 1872, 609.

2—Must be Memorized.

13. The Third or Knights Rank shall in no instance be conferred according to the Second or Amplified Ritual of said Rank as adopted, unless the various parts have been memorized by all the persons officiating therein, so that the same can be conferred without the use of the book.

Jour., 1872, 637.

3—Lodge Determines as to Use of.

14. A Subordinate Lodge has an unqualified right to determine for itself, and to demand the Amplified Ritual.

Jour., 1873, 718.

ANNIVERSARY OF THE ORDER.

15. The 19th day of February is declared to be and established as the anniversary of the organization of the Order.

Jour., 1875, 1131, 1149.

NOTE.—The 30th day of August has been adopted as the Anniversary of the Uniform Rank, that being the day on which, at the Supreme Session of 1878, the Rank was adopted.

ANTE-ROOM.

16. No person but the Outer Guard is allowed in the ante-room at the opening of a Lodge.

Jour., 1870, 229.
1877, 1435.

APPEALS AND WRITS OF ERROR.

1. Appeals — General Provisions (17).
   - (a) Grand Lodge—Must be from action of (18, 19, 20, 21).
   - (b) Consent—Of Grand Lodge must be obtained (22, 23), and be authenticated (24, 25, 26, 27).
   - (c) Not authenticated—May be heard, when (29) ?
   - (d) Brought in time—Must be (30); special exceptions (31).
   - (e) Bona Fide—Must be (32), and show interest (33).
   - (f) How reviewed—(34).
   - (g) Irregularities in—May (36) or may not (35) be dismissed for.
   - (h) Must be forwarded in time (37)
   - (i) Printed Copies—One hundred and fifty copies required (38).
   - (j) During recess—May be heard (39, 40, 41).
   - (k) How Heard—In Grand Lodge (42).
   - (l) How Heard—In Subordinate Lodge (43, 44).

2. Writs of Error—How brought (45, 46).

3. Additional Rules—Supreme Lodge may adopt (47).

1—Appeals—General Provisions.

17. All appeals and writs of error, taken from the action or decision of a Grand Lodge, or a Subordinate Lodge, under the immediate jurisdiction of the Supreme Lodge of the World, to said Supreme Lodge, as hereinafter provided, shall be received and passed upon by said Supreme Lodge in session, or by the Supreme Chancellor during recess; but in all cases the action or decision of a Grand Lodge, or a Subordinate Lodge under the immediate jurisdiction of the Supreme Lodge, shall be final and conclusive until reversed by this Supreme Lodge, or the Supreme Chancellor on appeal or prosecution of a Writ of Error therefrom, as hereinafter provided.

Const., Art. XVII, Sec. 1.

(a)—Grand Lodge—Must be from Action of.

18. With the consent of a Grand Lodge an appeal may be taken by any Subordinate Lodge, or member under its jurisdiction, from any action or decision of such Grand Lodge, to the Supreme Lodge of the World; Provided, however, that such consent shall not be necessary when a suspended or dissolved Lodge, after having surrendered to its Grand Lodge all its effects, books and property, appeals from such decision.

Const., Art. XVII, Sec. 3.

19. An appeal does not lie directly from the decision of the Grand Chancellor of a State to the Supreme Lodge; but the proper practice in such case is to appeal from the decision of the Grand Chancellor to the Grand Lodge, and from the decision of that body an appeal lies to the Supreme Lodge.

*Jour., 1873, 684, 685, 774.
1874, 939.
1875, 1131.
1877, 1442, 1443.
1888, 1432, 1663, 1664.*

20. An appeal from the decision of the Grand Chancellor in vacation does not lie as a matter of right, and the denial of that right does not render the Grand Lodge Constitution obnoxious to the Supreme Lodge Constitution. There is no such right guaranteed in the Supreme Lodge Constitution, and this matter is left to the control of the Grand Lodge.

Jour., 1888, 1432, 1663, 1664.

21. The subject-matter appealed must first be acted upon by the Grand Lodge, before an appeal can be taken by a Subordinate Lodge to the Supreme Lodge.

Jour., 1874, 939.

(b)—Consent—Of Grand Lodge must be Obtained, and be Authenticated.

22. Consent of a Grand Lodge to appeal must be obtained at the same session at which the action or decision from which such an appeal is sought to be taken was had, and the proper record upon such appeal must be transmitted, properly attested, to the Supreme Lodge if in session, or to the Supreme Chancellor during recess; Provided, that the Supreme Lodge may, in extreme cases, allow the appeal to be entertained at not later than its next following session thereafter. The same rules shall also apply in the prosecution of a Writ of Error.

*Const., Art. XVII, Sec. 7.
Jour., 1872, 536, 586.
1880, 1936, 2009.*

NOTE.—These latter Journal references are given because of their being cases where the direct issue came up in regard to "consent" being necessary.

23. In the case of an appeal against the action of the Grand Lodge of California, where consent that the appeal be taken was given by the Grand Chancellor after adjournment, the appeal was dismissed, it not having received the consent of the Grand Lodge of California to be brought before the Supreme Lodge.

Jour., 1873, 730, 731, 732.

24. Appeal papers from the decision of a Grand Lodge to the Supreme Lodge should be authenticated by the signatures of the Grand

Chancellor and Grand Keeper of Records and Seal, with the seal of the Grand Lodge attached.

Jour., 1871, 404.
1875, 1132.
1882, 2477, 2575.
1884, 3042.
1886, 3683.

25. The papers on an appeal from the action of a Grand Lodge to the Supreme Lodge should contain a certified copy of the proceedings of the Grand Lodge complained of.

Jour., 1876, 1309.
1882, 2575.
1884, 3042.
1886, 3683.

26. In cases of appeal it is the duty of all Grand Lodges to furnish all testimony and papers required, properly attested.

Jour., 1871, 404, 405.

27. An appeal was dismissed because it was not attested by the Grand Chancellor.

Jour., 1882, 2477, 2575.

28. A simple statement of the facts of a case is not an appeal.

Jour., 1870, 204.

(*c*)—Not Authenticated—May be Heard—When?

29. Should a Grand Chancellor, or Grand Keeper of Records and Seal, or both, refuse to sign and certify any Writ of Error, or appeal record, so as to authenticate the facts in any case in which a Writ of Error or appeal can be properly taken to the Supreme Lodge, and shall refuse to assign any reason, or shall assign an insufficient reason for such refusal (of which the Supreme* Lodge shall satisfy itself by the best evidence at its command in each case), such Writ of Error or appeal may be heard and determined by the Supreme Lodge as if the facts therein were admitted to be true and properly certified by that officer.

Jour., 1882, 2535, 2536, 2567.

*The compiler has put in the word "*Supreme*" instead of "*Grand*," as in the report, the latter being a clerical error, as will be seen by comparing the report, page 2567, with the original draft, page 2536; this correction is also necessary to make sense.

(*d*)—Brought in Time—Must be—Special Exceptions.

30. Where the Constitution of a Grand Lodge required that an appeal should be taken in a specified time, and the same was not complied with, the Supreme Lodge dismissed the appeal on that ground.

Jour., 1878, 1627, 1634.
1880, 2063.

31. In an appeal case, where the appellees contended that the appellant had lost his right of appeal, for the reason that the appeal was not taken within the time required by the Supreme Constitution, the Supreme Lodge held :

The Constitution of the Supreme Lodge (Sec. 7, Art. XVII) provides that the consent of the Grand Lodge to appeal must be obtained at the same session at which the judgment is rendered : "Provided, that the Supreme Lodge may, in extreme cases, allow the appeal to be entertained at not later than its next following session thereafter." This proviso gives the Supreme Lodge the right to entertain an appeal in certain cases, even though it may not have been taken regularly. From an examination of the facts of this case, we are satisfied it is a meritorious one, and for this reason comes within the proviso of the Constitution as an "extreme" case, and was properly in the hands of the Supreme Chancellor.

Jour., 1888, 4461-4474, 4592, 4593.

NOTE.—The numbering of the Section and Article in above are changed to comport with the numbering of the same language in the Constitution as now arranged.

(*e*)—**Bona Fide—Must be, and Show Interest.**

32. In a case presented where it appeared that the appeal was made only for the purpose of having the Supreme Lodge pass upon the matters decided, so that they might be positively settled, it was held :

The appeal is not of a character which should be entertained by this body. Whenever an appeal is made by a Representative from the action of his Grand Lodge, it must be *bona fide* made—not for the mere purpose of having the question settled, the appellant believing the law may have been correctly construed ; but the appellant must entertain a fixed belief of the *illegality* of the decision from which he appeals. Any other view of our law would subject the Supreme Lodge to long and expensive sessions, simply to determine questions of law which may come up, and be determined just as well, in each case as it arises. Whenever, by the operation of a decision of a Grand Lodge, any party interested is aggrieved, such party may appeal to this body, in proper form, and if the law or decision be illegal, it will be then so declared.

Jour., 1880, 2036, 2037.

33. Where a Supreme Representative failed to attend a session of the Supreme Lodge, and the committee appointed by the Grand Lodge to investigate the cause reported in favor of vacating his seat, which report was adopted by the Grand Lodge, from which action an appeal was taken to the Supreme Lodge by two Past Chancellors, on the ground that the Supreme Representative, whose seat was vacated, had not had a fair trial in accordance with their Constitution ; it was *ruled*, that, although *all* brothers are *entitled to*, and should be given, a *fair* trial, yet, without entering fully into the merits of the case, the only aggrieved party in the case had failed to appeal to the Supreme Lodge, the appellants had not the right of appeal, they not being directly interested in the matter, and the appeal was dismissed.

Jour., 1875, 1122.

(f)—How Reviewed.

34. Where a Past Grand Chancellor, who has never been introduced in the Supreme Lodge, or instructed in the Supreme Lodge Rank, whose certificate as a Past Grand Chancellor has been withdrawn by the body and authority that conferred it, desires the matter reviewed, the action of his Grand Lodge must be brought before the Supreme Lodge by appeal.

Jour., 1875, 1127, 1129.

(g)—Irregularities in—May or may Not be Dismissed for.

35. The action of a Grand Lodge will not be disturbed, notwithstanding that irregularities may have occurred in reaching the final result, where it appears that the final action is correct.

Jour., 1872, 447-452, 574.

36. Where it appeared, in a claim for benefits, that the committee of the Lodge appointed to investigate the matter, had made no report to the Lodge setting forth the facts of the case, and that a part of the evidence in the case was presented in an informal manner and without the regular forms of law, and a part of the evidence not presented at all, the cause was referred back, that the investigation might pursue the regular course in such cases.

Jour., 1877, 1406, 1439, 1440.

(h)—Must be Forwarded in Time.

37. All appeals to the Supreme Lodge, and accompanying papers, must be sent to the Supreme Keeper of Records and Seal at least one month previous to the session of the Supreme Lodge. And the Supreme Keeper of Records and Seal shall at that time place all appeals and accompanying papers in the hands of the chairman of the Committee on Appeals, to enable said committee to carefully review the same; also the law bearing upon them, and report fully and promptly to the Supreme Lodge at its session.

No appeal will be entertained by the Supreme Lodge if not in compliance with the above requirement, except by vote of the Supreme Lodge.

Jour., 1872, 563.

(i)—Printed Copies—One Hundred and Fifty Copies Required.

38. Provided, that appeals to this Supreme Lodge shall be accompanied by one hundred and fifty printed copies in each case. The expense of printing shall be borne by the party taking the appeal, and the pages to be of the same size as the Journal of the Supreme Lodge.

Const., Art. XVII, Sec. 2.

(j)—During recess—May be Heard.

39. During the recess of the Supreme Lodge, the Supreme Chancellor may also pass upon appeals and certify his decisions thereon to the parties in interest, and report his action thereon to the next succeeding session of the Supreme Lodge for its approval or disapproval.

Const., Art. XVII, Sec. 5.
Jour., 1886, Appendix (Errata) iii.

40. In cases submitted to the Supreme Chancellor during recess, as provided by the legislation of the Supreme Lodge in 1886, by Writ of Error or by appeal, his decision is binding upon the parties thereto unless reversed by the Supreme Lodge; the Supreme Chancellor is required, in all cases which may hereafter be submitted to him by Writ of Error or appeal, to report his action thereon, with all documents relating thereto, to the ensuing session of the Supreme Lodge, so that the same may be subject to revision by the Supreme Lodge, if demanded by either party.

Jour., 1888, 4108, 4109, 1659, 1660.

NOTE.—No provision is made here for printing, as in the case of appeals direct to the Supreme Lodge, though the fair construction would be that the requisite copies should be printed in case the losing party desired a further hearing.

41. The decision of the Committee on Appeals and Grievances, on any appeal referred to them, when reported to and confirmed by the Supreme Chancellor, shall be final, and fix the *status* of the member whose rights and privileges are in question under the appeal, until the said decision is reversed by the Supreme Lodge.

Jour., 1878, 1503, 1572.

NOTE.—Standing alone it would not be apparent what the real purpose of this legislation was, hence the ground for its adoption is given. Supreme Chancellor Davis, anticipating the injustice that might result from the long delay in the consideration of appeal cases, consequent on the change to *biennial* sessions, made the following recommendation in his report, and upon it this legislation was based, He said:

If there is to be no other session of this body for two years, I would recommend that the Committee on Appeals and Grievances be authorized to pass upon all appeals made to the Supreme Lodge in accordance with the laws, and that their decision shall be final, until reversed by this body in regular or special session. This is of great importance at this time, as the standing of members in the Endowment Rank may be affected, and by this arrangement controversy and perhaps litigation may be saved.

(*k*)—How Heard—In Grand Lodge.

42. An appeal from the decision of the Committee of Appeals of a Grand Lodge should be heard by the Grand Lodge; and it is improper to refer the action of such committee to a special committee for investigation.

Jour., 1870, 178.
1871, 400.

(*l*)—How Heard—In Subordinate Lodge.

43. When a Lodge is working in the First or Second Rank, an appeal from the decision of the chair could not be entertained, on

matters pertaining to the work, but could only be taken in the Rank of Knight.

Jour., 1884, 3037, 3038.

44. Constitutional provisions requiring that an appeal from the decision of the presiding officer can only be taken by two members, are illegal; by the language of the Ritual, the right of a brother cannot be abridged by requiring him to have some one to second his appeal.

Jour., 1888, 3992.

2—Writs of Error—How Brought.

45. Whenever a Grand Lodge, or during its recess, its Grand Chancellor, shall make any decision which would by its operation invalidate any enactment of the Supreme Lodge, the party aggrieved may demand and have issued a Writ of Error from said action, and the same shall be forwarded to the Supreme Lodge, if in session, and during its recess to the Supreme Chancellor, and the same shall be acted upon as in case of appeals. The said Writ of Error shall contain a brief statement of the facts in the case and such argument as may be deemed necessary; and, on application, the Grand Chancellor and Grand Keeper of Records and Seal shall certify the record thereof, under the seal of the Grand Lodge, and forward the same to the Supreme Lodge, if in session, and during its recess to the Supreme Chancellor, who shall render a decision thereon and certify the said decision to the parties in interest and report his action thereon to the next succeeding session of the Supreme Lodge for its approval or disapproval.

Const., Art. XVII, Sec. 4.

46. Writs of Error, as provided for by Section 4, may be issued by and upon petition to either the Grand Chancellor of the Grand Lodge, the action or decision of which is sought to be reviewed, the Supreme Chancellor or the Supreme Lodge of the World, in the case provided for in said Section, and in the order only as above named in this Section.

Const., Art. XVII, Sec. 6.

3—Additional Rules—Supreme Lodge may Adopt.

47. The Supreme Lodge of the World may also adopt such additional rules and regulations as may be deemed necessary and proper to fully carry into effect the foregoing provisions of this Article.

Const., Art. XVII, Sec. 8.

APPEALS FOR AID.

1. By a Grand Lodge—Must be approved by Supreme Chancellor (48).
2. By Subordinates—Must be approved by proper officer (49, 50).

1—By Grand Lodge—Must be Approved by Supreme Chancellor.

48. Neither Grand Lodges nor their officers can issue circulars asking aid, to be sent *out of their Jurisdiction*, without permission of the Supreme Lodge or Supreme Chancellor; and the same with Subordinate Lodges under the immediate control of the Supreme Lodge.

Jour., 1878, 1502.

2—By Subordinate Lodges—Must be Approved by Proper Officer.

49. Hereafter no Subordinate Lodge, whether under the jurisdiction of a Grand Lodge or the Supreme Lodge, shall issue a circular or request for aid from other Lodges or from brother Knights, whether to be used in their own or intended to be sent to other Jurisdictions, without first having obtained a dispensation authorizing it to do so from the Grand Chancellor or the Supreme Chancellor, as the case may be.

Jour., 1884, 2943, 3044.

50. A Subordinate Lodge under the jurisdiction of a Grand Lodge, desirous of issuing an appeal for aid to be sent to other Jurisdictions, having obtained the approval and dispensation of the Grand Chancellor of its own Jurisdiction, is not required to obtain the dispensation or endorsement of the Supreme Chancellor authorizing it to be done. Other Jurisdictions exercise their own discretion of approval or disapproval.

Jour., 1890, 4846, 5319, 5337.

ARREARS.

1. Constitutional Provision (51).
2. What Is Arrears? (52).
3. "One Year in Arrears"— Legislative enactments (53, 54, 55, 56).

1—Constitutional Provision.

51. A member who is in arrears for an amount equal to one year's dues shall be declared suspended; Provided said member is not under charges. (Obligatory.)

Const., Art. VIII, Sec. 2, Sub. v.

2—What Is "Arrears"?

52. When the dues of a member have accrued for the period designated by his Grand Jurisdiction as the limit of good standing, and the same remain unpaid, he is in arrears.
*Jour., 1878, 1568, 1606.
1884, 2989.*

3—"One Year in Arrears"—Legislative Enactments.

53. By the expression, "One year in arrears," found in Section 2, Article VIII, Supreme Lodge Constitution, it was intended to declare that a member *owing* for twelve months' dues should be declared suspended; and it is not necessary where the dues are payable quarterly to wait till the expiration of fifteen months.
Jour., 1876, 1232, 1302.

NOTE.—This question is very fully treated on by the Supreme Chancellor in 1876, page 1232, wherein he stated:

This position is taken—that a member is not in arrears until the end of the first quarter, and cannot be in arrears one year, until one year from that time, when he would be owing for fifteen months' dues.

To settle this, he made the above decision, which was approved. The present Constitution, though slightly changed in this particular, presents the same difficulty for those who view the matter from the decidedly peculiar standpoint presented by the Supreme Chancellor in 1876.

54. In 1872 the Supreme Lodge was asked the question:

As the Constitution reads that "a member who is one year in arrears shall stand suspended," is it competent for a Lodge to suspend a member for a less sum than one year's dues? To which the Supreme Lodge answered: The Article quoted, being "obligatory," a member cannot be suspended until he is one year in arrears. Again, in 1873, the following resolution was offered:

Resolved, That it is the judgment of this Supreme Lodge that its words in the Constitution, which read: "*Provided, a member who is twelve months in arrears shall be suspended*," mean that a Subordinate Lodge *may* suspend for *six months*, if they desire, or allow his indebtedness to run twelve months before suspension;

and the same being referred to the Committee on Law and Supervision, they reported that "it be not adopted," and the report was "concurred in."
*Jour., 1872, 531, 585.
1873, 683, 735.*

NOTE.—This subject is presented in detail because of the fact that owing to two of the preceding Digests having omitted the question altogether and one treating it ambiguously, many have held that "twelve months" was a maximum *below* which a Jurisdiction might go, but not *above;* in fact such ruling has obtained and an "Official Digest" erroneously quoted as authority.

While the law here presented is predicated on provisions of the old Constitution, which were known as "obligatory," there is no reason why they have not equal force under the present Constitution, since it contains the same provision, also "obligatory," and the words, "a member twelve months in arrears shall be suspended," the force of which has been construed by the above quoted law, appear in the Journals of almost every session.

55. When a member is twelve months in arrears he should be notified thereof before his suspension if his residence is known, and the fact of his suspension declared by the Chancellor Commander in open Lodge, and a record thereof made on the minutes.

Jour., 1876, 1232, 1302.
1877, 1372, 1427, 1428.
1888, 4005.

56. A member who is twelve months or more in arrears for dues, no declaration of his suspension having been made by the Chancellor Commander, his membership is not severed. The Lodge has not complied with the law. He may, at any time before the declaration is made, tender the amount due the Lodge, and it must be received, and he is restored to membership in good standing, so far as the payment of dues affects it under local laws. Should he at the same time apply for a Withdrawal Card, he would be entitled to it, if no charges were pending against him. Benefits would be controlled by local law.

Jour., 1877, 1372, 1427, 1428.

ASSESSMENTS.

1. By a Grand Lodge—On Past Chancellors (57) or members (58), illegal.
2. By Subordinate Lodges—To meet expenses, legal if so provided by Grand Lodge (59).

1—By a Grand Lodge—On Past Chancellors or Members, Illegal.

57. A Grand Lodge has no power to levy assessments on Past Chancellors and refuse to admit such as refuse to pay the same.

Jour., 1870, 197, 198, 203.
1878, 1626, 1627.

58. It is illegal to provide, by general compulsory assessment on all the members of the Order in a Grand Jurisdiction, for an "insurance," "relief" or "mortuary fund," in the nature of an insurance on lives.

Jour., 1876, 1288, 1293, 1301.

2—By Subordinate Lodges—To Meet Expenses, Legal, if So Provided by Grand Lodge.

59. A Subordinate Lodge can levy a tax on its members to meet the necessary expenses of the Lodge if approved by the Grand Lodge, that being a matter belonging to local legislation.

Jour., 1872, 625.

BALLOT.

1. Constitutional Provisions—Black balls (60, 61, 62); separate ballot (63).
2. Inspected—By whom (64); cubes allowed (65).
3. Adverse—Cannot be reconsidered (66).
4. After Favorable—How admission prevented (67, 68).
5. For Advancement—Adverse ballot cannot be laid over (69).
6. Material Rejected at Preliminary Meeting—Not considered "blackballed" (70).
7. On Application by Card— (71).

1—Constitutional Provisions — Black Balls — Separate Ballot.

60. Grand Lodges may legislate in their local law to prescribe that one black ball may reject, in cases of application for membership, but shall not increase the same to more than is prescribed in the Supreme maximum of two.

Const., Art. XXII.

61. Should two black balls appear against a candidate, the ballot shall be renewed immediately. Should two or more appear on the second ballot, he shall be declared rejected, and no other ballot shall be taken in his case for the space of six months thereafter. (Obligatory.)

Const., Art. VIII, Sec. 2, Sub. k.

62. In balloting, two (2) black balls appearing, a second ballot is ordered *at once;* two (2) or more appearing on the second ballot, he is rejected. Should three (3) black balls appear on the first ballot, it requires no other ballot to be taken at all.

Jour., 1873, Appendix 38.

63. A ballot must be had on each individual application for membership in a Subordinate Lodge. It is erroneous to ballot on more than one application for membership at the same time.

Jour., 1886, 3286, 3525 (Errata, page i).

NOTE.—This would not apply at the institution of Lodges.

2—Inspected by Whom—Cubes Allowed.

64. In taking a ballot for an applicant, *both* the Chancellor Commander and the Vice-Chancellor shall inspect the ballot, and the Chancellor Commander shall announce the result to the Lodge.

*Jour., 1876, 1227, 1296.
1882, 2275, 2465, 2466.*

65. A ballot box, provided with black cubes instead of black balls, is a proper instrument to be used in balloting for candidates.

Jour., 1880, 2036.

3—Adverse—Cannot be Reconsidered.

66. When a ball ballot has been regularly taken and the candidate declared rejected. the ballot cannot, at a subsequent period of the meeting of the Lodge, be reconsidered and a new ballot taken.

Jour., 1884. 2776, 2988.

4—After Favorable—How Admission Prevented.

67. A Grand Lodge may legislate so as to give a Lodge power to order a new ballot for a candidate for initiation, where objections are discovered previous to his receiving his first or initiatory Rank of Page, subject to same rules governing first ballot.

*Jour., 1875, 1042, 1114, 1121.
1878, 1611, 1640.*

68. If the Constitution of a Grand Lodge so provides, a member of the Lodge, whether present or not at the time a ballot was taken on application for membership, whereby the applicant was elected, has a right to enter an objection either to the admission or advancement of the candidate, provided that the law of the Jurisdiction requires only one ballot to reject, and such objection would operate as a black ball to the full extent of the law in that behalf; but where the Jurisdiction provides for two black balls to reject, it would then be necessary that there should be two objecting members of that Lodge.

Jour., 1888, 4122, 4576, 4581.

5—For Advancement—Adverse Ballot cannot be "Laid Over."

69. The laying over of an adverse ballot in the case of the rejection of an applicant for the Ranks of Esquire and Knight is illegal. The action to be taken upon a ballot in such cases should be governed by the rules provided in the case of an initiate. The ballot being had, it operates at once, but every Grand Jurisdiction has the right to say how soon the ballot can be renewed.

Jour., 1888, 3999.

6—Material Rejected at Preliminary Meeting — Not Considered "Black-balled."

70. The dropping of a name from the list of applicants for a dispensation by a ballot by all the applicants, while it virtually has the effect, among those who are interested at the time, of a rejection of the name so dropped, yet does not estop the party whose name has been "dropped" from applying in a regular way, and taking the chances of a legal ballot when or after the Lodge is legally instituted; neither does the "dropping" of the name in the first instance constitute him a black-balled or rejected party, or prevent him from applying to that or any other Lodge of the Order in a regular way, and under the local laws of jurisdiction or territory where residing.

Jour., 1873, Appendix 40.
1888, 4002.

7—On Application by Card.

71. The old Constitution being repealed, the present law requires the same ballot on an application by Card as for an application for membership by initiation.

Jour., 1875, 1042, 1114, 1121.
1888, 3994.

NOTE.—For the effect of rejection of an application by card, see "Membership."

BANNER.

72. At the session of the Supreme Lodge, of 1873, a banner for the Order was adopted, as follows:

To be composed of three pieces of silk, of color and sizes as follows: *Dark Blue*, size 18 by 30 inches; *Orange-Yellow*, size 18 by 30; *Crimson*, size 24 by 36. Colors to be placed as per accompanying diagram. The full size of banner to be 3 by 4½ feet. Shield in center *painted in white*, size 18 by 24 inches. The device on shield to be the distinction of rank of Lodge — *Supreme, Grand* or *Subordinate*.

For Supreme Lodge.—A globe, and in circle around it to be the words, "Supreme Lodge of the World, Knights of Pythias."

For Grand Lodges.—Grand Lodge or State Seal, and in circle around same, "Grand Lodge of ——, Knights of Pythias."

For Subordinate Lodges.—K. P. Cut as on accompanying diagram, with name and number of Lodge, together with location (viz., "Excelsior Lodge, No. 9, K. of P., Cincinnati, Ohio"); on edge of banner, all around, fine gold lines one and one-half inches wide; on bottom, gilt fringe three or three and one-half inches deep. Staff to be of oak or other suitable wood seven or eight feet long; on top of staff, spearhead; ball and falcon spear-heads on end of cross-piece. All marks, devices, designs, etc., on banner to be in gold or gold and black.

Jour., 1873, 687, 688, 740.

NOTE.—For some reason, an erroneous opinion has prevailed that the Supreme Lodge had adopted a "Flag"; it is true that the subject was presented (1870, 220; 1871, 399, 400; 1872, 483, 484), but either through error or intention the record fails to show that the proposition was adopted. The design is given in the pages above noted.

BENEFITS.

1. General Constitutional Provisions and Legislation—(73, 74, 75, 76, 77, 78, 79).
2. Weekly Benefits.
    (a) Probationary Period—During which no benefits are paid—illegal (80, 81, 82,.
    (b) Good Standing—Payable only to members in (83, 84, 85, 86).
    (c) Evading Payment—Lodges cannot enact laws (87, 88, 89, 90).
    (d) First Week's Sickness—Payable for (91).
    (e) On Reinstatement—Payable immediately (92).
    (f) Convalescence—Payable during, when (93)?
    (g) Reduction of—During continuous sickness (94).
    (h) Nurse Hire—Provision as to responsibility for, contracted by sister Lodge (95).
    (i) Not Payable—While Lodge is suspended (96), nor to member who has been granted Withdrawal Card, even though Card not delivered (97).
    (j) In Arrears When Reported—Not a disability, if in good standing when taken sick (98).
3. Funeral Benefits.
    (k) Full Amount—Payable though Lodge failed to bury (99, 100).
    (l) " Widow's Tax "—Payable, if entitled to funeral benefits 101).
    (m) Suicide—Payment of, in case of suicide, a matter for local legislation (102).
    (n) Not in Arrears at Death—Entitled to (103, 104).
    (o) Act of Officer—Lodge bound by, where sister Lodge expends money on telegram from officer (105).
    (p) Intemperance—Lodge cannot avoid, on plea of, if, during life, they failed to discipline (106).

1—General Constitutional Provisions and Legislation.

73. Lodges shall provide for carrying into effect the beneficial character of the Order, by providing for the payment of weekly benefits in case of disability, and funeral benefits in case of the death of a member in good standing ; and weekly benefits shall not be less than one dollar per week, nor funeral benefits less than twenty dollars. (Obligatory.)

Const., Art. VIII, Sec. 2, Sub. w.

74. The term "benefits," means all advantages and privileges.

Jour., 1872, 585.

75. By Section 2, Article VIII, of the Supreme Lodge Constitution, it is made obligatory on each Grand Lodge to require its Subordinates "to provide for carrying into effect the beneficial character of the Order"; but the nature of this "beneficial character" is declared to be the payment of "weekly benefits" to the disabled, and "funeral benefits" in case of death. Long usage in similar organizations, and in our own, has affixed a well defined meaning to the terms "weekly" and "funeral benefits"; and in this well understood sense the words were doubtless used in the Constitution. *Each Lodge* is to provide for the payment of these benefits out of its own funds, and it is not contemplated to secure the adoption of a scheme by which a combination of Lodges will pay these or any "benefits." The compulsory provision in the Supreme Lodge Constitution for a "beneficial character" of the kind specified, seems, by a legitimate inference, to exclude from the Order a "beneficial character" of a different kind, on the principle that the inclusion of the one system excludes the other.

Jour., 1876, 1288, 1289.

NOTE.—This legislation appears in a report of a committee on the legality of a system of compulsory insurance, and they took occasion thus to make a general declaration of principles as to the duty of a Lodge to do its *own* part first, and through and by the system provided within rather than without the body. This report was adopted.

76. The claim of members of the Order to a certain fixed sum, designated by law, to be paid to them during sickness or inability to procure a livelihood during such sickness, is a right, and not a charity.

Jour., 1873, 692, 753.

77. The payment of weekly and funeral benefits to sick members is a distinguishing characteristic of the Order, and may be regarded as a fundamental principle of the Order of Knights of Pythias.

Jour., 1873, 693, 753.

78. It is the duty of all Subordinate Lodges to tax their members, that they may be enabled to pay stipulated weekly and funeral benefits to sick members or the family, and that all Subordinate Lodges shall pay some weekly and funeral benefits.

Jour., 1873, 693, 753.

79. With the restrictions contained in the constitutional provisions, the subject of dues and benefits should be left to local legislation.

Jour., 1872, 466, 468, 613, 614.
1873, 692, 753.

2 — Weekly Benefits —(*a*) Probationary Period during Which No Benefits are Paid, Illegal.

80. Under the laws of the Supreme Lodge requiring the payment of sick and funeral benefits to members in good standing, a Subordinate Lodge cannot so frame their By-Laws as to deprive a Knight of such benefits for one year after attaining that Rank. This does not require full benefits to be paid; but the minimum, as designated in Clause *w*, Section 2, Article VIII, of the Supreme Lodge Constitution, at least, must be paid, for such probationary period as each Lodge may fix.

Jour., 1877, 1373, 1410, 1428.
1878, 1509, 1558, 1608, 1640,
1641.

81. Grand Lodges *may* prescribe a probationary period in their Constitution for Subordinate Lodges,i n which members may not draw full benefits; but, Provided always, that the minimum benefit of one dollar per week, and funeral benefit of twenty dollars, *shall be paid through such period.*

Jour., 1880, 1827, 2003.

82. Neither Grand nor Subordinate Lodges can enact laws which debar a member from receiving any benefits during a "probationary period." Every member who has attained the Rank of Knight, or who has been reinstated after suspension arising from any cause, is, if otherwise qualified (he not being in arrears to the extent required by local law to create a disability, nor under charges), entitled to sick and funeral benefits to the extent at least of the minimum required by the Supreme Constitution.

Jour., 1888, 3796.

(*b*)—**Good Standing—Payable Only to Members in.**

83. The payment of the minimum benefits is obligatory in the case of members in *good standing* under the local law, but the status of suspended brothers is a matter for local legislation.

Jour., 1880, 2038.

84. Where a member was suspended, on charges, and it was claimed that he would, by force of Supreme Lodge law, be entitled to receive at least one dollar per week benefits during sickness or disability, and consequently liable for dues for the limited period of suspension, it was held by the Supreme Lodge:

That the sentence was a wrong construction of the Constitution of the Supreme Lodge; that suspension for a limited period for cause other than for non-payment of dues, operates, for such time, as a suspension from the Order.

Jour., 1880, 2038.

85. The construction placed upon the constitutional provision in regard to the payment of minimum benefits was, that they shall be paid only, when in a case of sickness, to a member who, under the local provisions, is in "good standing," as provided by the legislation of 1878 (Journal, 1878, 1606); and to dependent relatives, in case of death, when the member at the time of his decease is not in arrears to the extent provided by the local law (Journal, 1876, 1318).

Jour., 1888, 4121, 4575, 4576, 4581, 4502, 4591.

86. If a Knight fails to pay his dues on the last meeting night in June, also fails to do so on or before the last meeting night of the Lodge in September, but on the last meeting night in December he pays his dues, together with all arrearages, and in January is taken sick, and is incapacitated for several weeks, he is entitled to weekly sick benefits.

Jour., 1890, 4845, 5319, 5337.

NOTE.—This is the exact language of the decision of the Supreme Chancellor; it was evidently based on some specific case, and in its *general* application only reaffirms the legislation contained in Sections 210, 436 of this Digest.

(*c*)—Evading Payment—Subordinate Lodge cannot Enact Laws.

87. A brother in good standing who leaves the country in impaired health, and who continues so after his departure, so that he is incapacitated from gaining a livelihood, is still entitled to benefits from his Lodge.

Jour., 1875, 1147, 1148.

88. And the fact that after the brother's departure, referred to in the preceding Section, the following By-Law was incorporated in the laws of the Subordinate Lodge —" A sick brother, while under the care of this Lodge, shall not leave the jurisdiction of the Relief Committee without forfeiting his weekly benefits, unless he shall have obtained the consent of the Relief Committee and the approval of the Lodge " —cannot affect his right to benefits.

Jour., 1875, 1147, 1148.

89. In a case where a brother in good standing took sick, and during his sickness his Lodge adopted a resolution " suspending the payment of all weekly benefits for six months," and on the strength of said resolution said Lodge refused to pay said brother any weekly benefits; and further, on an appeal to his Grand Lodge, that body sustained the action of his Lodge in the refusal to pay benefits, under said resolution; on appeal to the Supreme Lodge, the appeal was sustained, and it was held: That while they neither did nor could adjudicate as to the sum claimed as benefits, yet they enunciated the principle, that the brother was entitled to benefits within the limits of the paramount law, viz.: That weekly benefits "shall not be less than one dollar per week."

Jour., 1878, 1558, 1640, 1641.

90. A Lodge cannot avoid the payment of a sick benefit of one dollar a week to a sick brother in good standing as long as his disability continues. He is entitled to receive it week by week, and no change can be made in the manner or time of payment without his express consent. If the By-Laws of a Lodge provide for a greater benefit, he is entitled to receive it according to their terms, and no amount paid him under the By-Laws can be offset against the dollar a week to which he is entitled for any time not covered by the By-Laws.

Jour., 1886, 3286, 3526, 3555.

NOTE.—This ruling arose out of a decision of a Supreme Chancellor on a query from a Lodge, as follows:
If a Subordinate Lodge pays four dollars a week, for thirteen weeks ($52), does this payment discharge its entire obligation to the brother?
The Supreme Chancellor ruled that, to the extent of fifty-two weeks, the payment stated, complied with the law requiring one dollar per week, but, on review, the Supreme Lodge decided as above.

(*d*)—First Week's Sickness—Payable for.

91. Enactments providing that benefits shall not be paid for the " first week's sickness " are illegal; a beneficiary member is entitled to be paid for *every* week's sickness, at least to the extent of the minimum provided by law.

Jour., 1888, 3995.

(e)—On Reinstatement—Payable Immediately.

92. Every member, who is not in arrears to his Lodge, is entitled to the minimum benefits, both weekly and funeral, required by the provisions of the Supreme Constitution, and the simple fact that a member regained his membership after suspension for non-payment of dues does not create a disability which can debar him from receiving all the benefits of the Order immediately upon his again becoming a member in good standing.

Jour., 1888, 4001.

(f)—Convalescence—Payable during—When?

93. A brother who is convalescent, but unable from weakness to resume his daily vocation, is entitled to benefits, and his case would come within the law that prescribes that a brother who is unable to attend to any business whereby he may gain a livelihood is entitled to benefits.

Jour., 1882, 2274, 2465.

(g)—Reduction of—during Continuous Sickness.

94. Where it is evidenced that a sickness is continuous, notwithstanding the fact that a brother declared himself off the sick list, a Lodge has the right to consider the sickness continuous; and if, by its By-Laws, the Lodge provides for a reduction of benefits after a certain number of weeks, commencing with the sickness, it is justified in applying the rule to the case, and may reduce the benefits just as if the member had not been declared off the sick list.

Jour., 1888, 4122, 4123, 4579, 4581.

(h)—Nurse Hire—Provision as to Responsibility for—Contracted by Sister Lodge.

95. When a brother is placed in charge of a Lodge other than his own, the Lodge so accepting him is bound to give him the same care and general aid as it would to one of its own members; but unless the Lodge to which he belongs has a provision for furnishing a nurse, the Lodge caring for him would not be justified in providing a nurse and then claiming additional payment on that account; Provided, that in no case shall a Lodge be bound to furnish financial aid to an amount greater than the benefits allowed by the Lodge of which the brother is a member.

Jour., 1888, 4120, 4574, 4580, 4581.

(i)—Not Payable—While Lodge is Suspended, Nor to Member Who has been Granted Withdrawal Card, even Though Card Not Delivered.

96. In the case of an appeal of a widow of a deceased brother against the Grand Lodge of Maryland on a disputed claim for benefits, it showed:

The widow claims sick benefits for seventy-four weeks, or from May 10, 1871, to October 10, 1872. From the printed proceedings of the Grand Lodge of Maryland it appears that the aforesaid Lafayette Lodge, No. 25, was suspended nearly all the time mentioned above.

Even on the day of the death of the brother the Lodge was not recognized by the Grand Lodge of Maryland. *Held*, that the deceased brother was not entitled to any benefits during such suspension; also, he being notified the Lodge was about being organized, and not paying any attention to the notification, he should not be considered a member of the aforesaid Lodge. The case was accordingly referred back to the Grand Lodge of Maryland to audit the accounts of the said Lafayette Lodge, No. 25, with directions that if any benefits were found due, prior to the suspension of the aforesaid Lodge, and he entitled to them, that the Grand Lodge order it paid, without interest.

Jour., 1874, 944.

97. Where a Past Chancellor, who at one time was a member of a Lodge, asked for a Withdrawal Card, which was delivered to him, but improperly filled out, and he refused admission to membership in a Lodge until the error was corrected; and, further, where, pending his admission he became ill, and continued so for a period of five weeks, the question was presented: Is the Lodge, which issued the Card irregularly, responsible for the benefits he would have received on account of his sickness had the Card been properly issued by the Lodge to which he formerly belonged? And the Supreme Lodge decided:

When a member asks for and is granted a Withdrawal Card, the act of granting the Card severs the membership, whether the Card is taken or not; though under the circumstances, while some hardship may have resulted from the ignorance of the officer of the Lodge, no responsibility in regard to paying benefits existed after the application had been made, and the Card had been granted.

Jour., 1888, 4123, 4579, 4580, 4581.

(*j*)—**In Arrears When Reported—Not a Disability, if in Good Standing When Taken Sick.**

98. A member was suspended from Mechanics Lodge, No. 33, of Maryland, for non-payment of dues, and was reinstated to membership on November 28, 1873, and on May 29, 1874, was reported to the Lodge as sick. On this night he would owe the Lodge $2 (or one quarter's dues), and had been reinstated six months, and had been sick for nine days. He applied to his Lodge for benefits. The Chancellor Commander declared that he was not entitled to benefits, because he had not been reinstated six months. From this decision he appealed to the Grand Lodge, stating the Lodge had no By-Laws fixing the time required to pass before a brother who had been reinstated becomes beneficial. This appeal was referred to the Committee on Appeals and Grievances (Grand Lodge). This committee decided that the brother had complied with all the laws, and was entitled to benefits, which action was sustained by the Grand Lodge. *Held*, on appeal to the Supreme Lodge, that the decision of the Grand Lodge was correct.

Jour., 1875, 1161.

NOTE.—By a close examination of this case the principle is clearly established that, if *at the time the member was taken sick*, he was not in arrears a sufficient amount to place him in bad standing, he would not be debarred from benefits because, *when reported sick*, he was in arrears.

3—Funeral Benefits—(*k*) Full Amount—Payable Though Lodge Fails to Bury.

99. In the matter of Laurel Lodge, No. 4, *vs.* The Grand Lodge, Knights of Pythias, of California, the facts were as follows:

The widow of a deceased member of Laurel Lodge applied for the sum of $60, being balance claimed to be due under a section of the By-Laws of said Lodge, which is as follows:

"Article XII, Section 2. On the death of a brother there shall be appropriated from the funds of the Lodge $100 to defray the funeral expenses."

Of that sum only $40 were expended by Laurel Lodge, $80 additional being contributed by other organizations. The Lodge deny the claim, on the ground that as the sum named in the By-Laws is not now needed for funeral expenses the Lodge is not bound to pay the balance of the $100. An appeal was taken by the widow to the Grand Lodge of California, which appeal was sustained. *Held*, that the decision of the Grand Lodge was correct, and that the widow was entitled to receive the sum of $60 from the funds of Laurel Lodge. No. 4.

Jour., 1872, 551, 588.

100. In 1880, another case, involving the same principle, was decided, and the Supreme Lodge went still further; the state of facts is as follows: George W. Ernest, a member of Clay Lodge, No. 1, Knights of Pythias, of Kentucky, died of yellow fever; his wife died about the same time, and both were buried at the expense of the railroad company, by which Bro. E. was employed. The By-Laws of said Lodge allow a certain amount to be appropriated for the purpose of defraying funeral expenses of a deceased brother, or his wife, to be paid to the nearest competent relative. After all expenses had been paid by the railroad company aforesaid, the mother and sister claiming to be the nearest relatives, demanded the amount prescribed in the By-Laws of said Lodge, which the Lodge refused to pay them, on the ground that they (the mother and sister) having been to no expense, were not entitled thereto.

From this action appeal was taken to the Grand Lodge of Kentucky, who sustained the Lodge in refusing to pay the claim. Appeal was then taken to the Supreme Lodge, which body reversed the action of Clay Lodge, and the Grand Lodge of Kentucky, and ordered the claim paid.

Jour., 1880, 2009, 2010.

NOTE.—The cases presented in the last two Sections are given *in extenso* because of the importance of their bearing; they evidence that the amount provided under the law must be paid irrespective of who bears the expense.

(*l*)—" Widow's Tax "—Payable, if Entitled to Funeral Benefits.

101. Where the law governing a Subordinate Lodge in regard to funeral benefits read:

"In the event of the death of a brother entitled to benefits, etc.," and the Lodge also had a provision for the payment of a "Widow's

Tax," raised by an assessment on each member, the receipts from which were to be paid to the widow "of a brother entitled to benefits"; on an appeal case where the facts evidenced that at the time the brother took sick he was in arrears and not entitled to *weekly* benefits, but having paid up his arrears, while sick, and afterward died, his widow was entitled to and was tendered the funeral benefit, but not the "Widow's Tax," the Lodge claiming that the word "benefits," in the law quoted above, referred to *weekly* benefits, and that as the deceased was not entitled to weekly benefits during his sickness, because of arrears, his widow was not entitled to the "Widow's Tax." The Supreme Lodge, however, held that in such a case the Lodge was liable for funeral benefits, and that that liability rendered it also responsible for the "Widow's Tax.'

Jour., *1884, 3042, 3043.*

(*m*)—Suicide—Payment of, in Case of Suicide, a Matter for Local Legislation.

102. The question whether if a brother, while in good standing in his Subordinate Lodge, commits suicide, it does or not deprive his wife or nearest competent relative from receiving the funeral benefits of such brother, is entirely a matter of Grand Lodge legislation.

Jour., *1873, 684, 734.*

(*n*)—Not in Arrears at Death—Entitled to.

103. A brother in arrears for dues sends in the amount due during his sickness, and becomes square on the books; he afterward dies. His family is entitled to receive his funeral benefits only.

Jour., *1890, 4845, 5319, 5337.*

104. Funeral benefits are payable to dependent relatives in case of the death of a Knight who, *at the time of his death*, is not in arrears to the amount required to place him in bad standing under the law of his Jurisdiction, even though he was in arrears when sick, and paid them up during the sickness which resulted in death.

Jour., *1876, 1318.*
1884, 3043.
1888, 3796, 3992, 4121, 4433,
4575, 4576, 4581, 4663.
1890, 4845, 5319, 5337.

(*o*)—Act of Officer—Lodge Bound by, When Sister Lodge Expends Money on Telegram from Officer.

105. In an appeal case regarding the payment of benefits, the facts appeared as follows :

A brother, away from the vicinity of his own Lodge, was taken sick; the local Lodge took care of him, and expended money in so doing; the latter they did on the strength of a telegram from the Keeper of Records and Seal of his Lodge, viz.:

"Bro. Taylor, non-beneficial. Keep him there. Don't let him suffer. We will stand benefits."

And further, the said brother died, and the Lodge where he died, under authority of the Keeper of Records and Seal of his Lodge, buried him. The Lodge to which the deceased belonged refused to reimburse the Lodge that took care of him.

On appeal, the Supreme Lodge held that the Lodge that buried him should be reimbursed, by the Lodge to which he belonged, the money they had expended for care and for the burial of the deceased, irrespective of any By-Law of his Lodge: and further, that in refusing to make such payments and reimbursements, his Lodge acted in bad faith to the sister Lodge, in a manner unbecoming the Order, and in such a way as to render them liable to charges.

Jour., 1877, 1440, 1441.

NOTE.—The above is the statement as presented to the Supreme Lodge by the committee, and is the record as passed upon. An examination, however, of the original appeal, in the records of the Grand Lodge of Maryland, shows that the defendants set up the plea : *First,*. That "the telegram was not sent by order of the Lodge "; and, *Second,* That they were bound to pay the money to the widow. The action therefore, as above, would evidence that the Supreme Lodge held that the telegram of the Keeper of Records and Seal bound the Lodge.

(*p*)—Intemperance—Lodge cannot Avoid on Plea of, if, during Life, They Failed to Discipline.

106. In an appeal case where funeral benefits were denied simply on the ground that the deceased had been intemperate, though the statement of the case showed that he died of pneumonia, and it did not appear that his death was owing directly or indirectly to intemperance, the Supreme Chancellor decided:

The claim is that he was not entitled to funeral benefits because his sickness was owing to intemperance; this should not avail. There had been no proper finding of the fact; there had been no charge, nor opportunity for him to be heard in his defense. If his habit was the cause of his sickness, the fact that he had the habit for months before his death was well known to the Lodge. The members stood by, took no action, and received his money that kept him in good standing. The deceased member was not three months in arrears at the time of his death, and so was entitled to funeral benefits under the By-Laws of the Lodge.

This ruling was sustained by the Supreme Lodge.

Jour., 1890, 5322, 5323, 5395.

BONDS.

107. It was ordered that, in future, whenever a bond is presented to the Supreme Lodge, there shall be filed with the Supreme Keeper of Records and Seal a sworn statement of the sureties on the bond, showing the pecuniary responsibility of the same.

Jour., 1890, 5391, 5426.

CHANCELLOR COMMANDER.

1. Eligibility—Any Knight eligible to election as (108); if local law permits.
2. Retiring—Resignation—May retire without leave (109); may resign (110).
3. Representative—Eligible for election as, after installation (111); not before (112.)
4. Absence of—In case of, and Vice Chancellor and Past Chancellors, Knight may preside and confer the Ranks (113).
5. Members Retiring—May refuse to allow members to retire (114).

1—Eligibility—Any Knight Eligible to Election, if Local Law Permits.

108. The law requiring rotation in office from lower to higher is local. The Supreme Lodge laws permit any Knight in good standing to be elected to the office of Chancellor Commander.

Jour., 1873, Appendix 37.
1882, 2568.
1884, 2776, 2988.

2—Retiring—Resignation—May Retire without Leave—May Resign.

109. The Chancellor Commander has a perfect right, without leave of the Lodge, to call the Vice Chancellor to the chair, and if he so desires retire from the Lodge for the balance of the session.

Jour., 1888, 4121, 4575, 4581.

110. Though the installation ceremonies require a Chancellor Commander, and that officer only, to obligate himself to perform the duties of his office "for the present term," he can resign at will during the term.

Jour., 1872, 564, 585.

3—Representative—Eligible for Election as Representative, after Installation—Not before.

111. A Chancellor Commander re-elected, would, after his second installation, be eligible to election as Representative to his Grand Lodge, if not disqualified by any local law.

Jour., 1875, 1042, 1114, 1121.

112. A Chancellor Commander is not eligible to be elected Representative to his Grand Lodge on the last night of his term.

Jour., 1886, 3548, 3555.

NOTE.—This ruling, to be in harmony with all legislation in this connection, of course only refers to a retiring Chancellor Commander who is not already a Past Chancellor.

4—Absence of—In Case of, and Vice Chancellor and Past Chancellors, Knight may Preside and Confer the Ranks.

113. In the absence of the Chancellor Commander, the Vice Chancellor and all Past Chancellors, the hour of opening having arrived, where the local law has made such provision, the Knight selected by the members present to preside over the Lodge for the time being becomes "an officer of the Lodge," and may legally conduct the business of the Lodge, and preside while the Ranks are being conferred.

Jour., 1888, 4123, 4409, 4580, 4581, 1659.

5—Members Retiring—May Refuse to Allow Members to Retire.

114. A member of a Lodge sought, in the usual manner, permission to retire, whereupon the Chancellor Commander declined to excuse him and directed him to be seated. Thereupon he appealed to the Lodge; and the Lodge, by vote, sustained the Chancellor Commander in refusing to give him permission to retire, holding that it is optional with the Chancellor Commander whether or not he shall give a member of his Lodge permission to leave the Lodge room.

Thereupon, the brother appealed to the Grand Lodge from the action of the Lodge in sustaining the decision of the Chancellor Commander; the case being decided by the Grand Lodge *against* the action of the Chancellor Commander in so refusing, the matter came before the Supreme Lodge on appeal, the appellants claiming that:

If the Chancellor Commander is powerless to enforce the continued presence in the Lodge room of members who have once entered the inner door, there is no way by which a Lodge can be assured of a quorum, thus retarding the proper transaction of business and eventually imperiling the existence of the Lodge. And the Supreme Lodge, in sustaining the appeal, held:

It is absolutely necessary, for the proper transaction of Lodge business, that the Chancellor Commander should be vested with a sound discretion as to granting or refusing such permission.

Jour., 1886, 3514, 3515, 3687, 3688.

CHARGES.

1. **In a Grand Lodge.**
   - (*a*) Against a Grand Officer—Any one member may bring (115); must try (116).
   - (*b*) In Analogous Case—Rule of Subordinate Lodge may obtain (117).
2. **In Subordinate Lodge.**
   - (*c*) Claim for Money—Cannot be prosecuted under criminal charge (118).
   - (*d*) Chancellor Commander or Vice Chancellor—Preferring, cannot appoint Trial Committee (119).
   - (*e*) Suspension for Non-payment of Dues—Not operative pending charges (120).

1—In a Grand Lodge—(*a*) Against a Grand Officer—Any One Member may Bring—Must Try.

115. It is the right of any member of the Order, who believes that he has just cause, to bring charges against a Grand Officer, and his right cannot be circumscribed by requiring him to obtain other members to join him in the charges.

Jour., *1888, 4003.*

116. A Grand Lodge receiving charges against one of its officers should entertain and act upon the same, giving them a fair and proper consideration.

Jour., *1871, 346, 372, 373, 405, 406, 423.*

(*b*)—In Analogous Case—Rule of Subordinate Lodge may Obtain.

117. Where the General Laws of a Grand Lodge regulating the procedure upon charges and specifications, in their primary meaning refer only to Subordinate Lodges; yet while they are not obligatory upon the Grand Lodge as a rule of action for its own government, there is no impropriety in their being used as a guide for the action of the Grand Lodge when called upon to act in an analogous case.

Jour., *1875, 1128.*

NOTE.—This was adopted before the enactment of the present Code of Procedure in Trial of Grand Officers; but the principle would still hold good wherein the Code fails to sufficiently provide.

(*c*)—In Subordinate Lodge—Claim for Money cannot be Prosecuted under Criminal Charge.

118. When, in an appeal case, it appeared that the complainant in the initial proceedings had brought a charge, in form and substance a criminal charge, looking entirely to the punishment of the Lodge for willfully malicious injury to the complainant, and a willful violation of the Constitution and Laws of the Order, upon which charge the Committee on Appeals of the Grand Lodge reported, acquitting the Lodge in the main, but going further, and rendering a finding in favor of the complainant for a sum of weekly benefits, which report the

Grand Lodge refused to adopt; upon the case coming before the Supreme Lodge, it was held:

That we find the charges against the said Lodge were, in form and substance, criminal charges.

That the claim, in reality, was for money which the complainant held the said Lodge owed him.

That a claim for money owed cannot be prosecuted under a criminal charge.

That upon this ground the Grand Lodge was right in refusing to adopt the report of the Committee on Appeals and Grievances.

Jour., 1882, 2405-2407. 2574.

(*d*)—Chancellor Commander or Vice Chancellor — Preferring, cannot Appoint Trial Committee.

119. When the Chancellor Commander and Vice Chancellor have, in their official capacity, preferred charges against a member, they are thereby rendered incapacitated from, and cannot legally appoint a Committee of Trial.

Jour., 1880, 2062, 2063.

(*e*)—Suspension for Non-Payment of Dues—Not Operative, pending Charges.

120. A member who is under charges cannot be declared suspended for non-payment of dues.

Jour., 1875, 1112, 1156.

CHARTERS.

1. **Of Grand Lodges.**
   (*a*) Exist by Virtue of (121)—May be revoked (122); issuance of, annuls Dispensation (123); issued, in case of loss, only by Supreme Lodge, not Supreme Chancellor (124); must be in Lodge or ante-room 125.
2. **Of Subordinate Lodges.**
   (*b*) Exist by Virtue of (126).
   (*c*) Visiting Knight—May ask to see (127).
   (*d*) Surrender of—Cannot be surrendered, nine members being willing to sustain (128).
   (*e*) Local Legislation—Following subjects governed by—reissuing, to whom (129); what Grand Officers shall sign (130); whose names shall appear on (131).
   (*f*) Revocation and Arrest—Causes for (132, 133, 134).
   (*g*) Suspension of—Cannot be, without trial (135).

1—Of Grand Lodges—(*a*) Exist by Virtue of—May be Revoked—Annuls Dispensation—Issued, in Case of Loss, Only by Supreme Lodge, Not by Supreme Chancellor—Must be in Lodge or Ante-Room.

121. Grand Lodges exist by virtue of a charter or dispensation, issued by authority of the Supreme Lodge, or Supreme Chancellor during its recess.

Const., Art. VII, Sec. 1.

122. Charters of Grand Lodges may be revoked, and Grand Lodges suspended by the Supreme Lodge for nonconformity to the work, ceremonies or ritual adopted by the Supreme Lodge, for disobedience to its legal mandates, and for improper conduct.

Const., Art. VII, Sec. 6.

NOTE.—The Supreme Lodge has at different times recognized the power of a Supreme Chancellor to suspend a Grand Lodge, during recess, for causes arising. See Journals, 1871, 262-281, 291, 386-388, 418-421; 1873, 714, 715. Appendix 44 *et seq.*; 1888, 4014-4088, 4539-4542, 4561-4565, 4568, 4569, 4604, 4605, 4620; 1890, 4831-4834.

123. The issue of a charter to a Grand Lodge rescinds and annuls any dispensation previously issued, whether said dispensation is returned or not, and all acts done thereafter under such dispensation are illegal.

Jour., 1873, 714, Appendix 63.

124. Where the charter of a Grand Lodge had been destroyed by fire, the same happening during recess of the Supreme Lodge; and where the Supreme Chancellor reported that he had ordered the issuance of a new charter, it was ruled that the Supreme Chancellor had no authority to issue a charter, and the same ordered to be issued by the Supreme Lodge. The Supreme Chancellor may, however, in case of loss or destruction of a Charter, issue to such Grand Lodge a Dispensation to serve in lieu of a charter until the next session of the Supreme Lodge.

Jour., 1880, 1822, 2015.
1890, 4837, 5304, 5329, 5452.

125. Neither a Grand nor Subordinate Lodge has a right to work without having its charter or dispensation present in the Lodge or ante-room.

Jour., 1872, 564, 585.
1873, Appendix 36.

2—Of Subordinate Lodges—(*b*) Exist by Virtue of.

126. Subordinate Lodges exist by virtue of dispensations issued by the Supreme Lodge through the Supreme Chancellor, or charters granted in lieu thereof, or directly by the appropriate Grand Lodge; but to each Grand Lodge, when formed, belongs the exclusive right to issue charters to Lodges instituted within its prescribed territorial jurisdiction.

Const., Art. VIII, Sec. 1.

(*c*)—Visiting Knight—May Ask to See.

127. A Knight in good standing, and evidencing the same to a proper officer or party, may or can ask to see the charter or dispensation of the Lodge, but there is no law or usage warranting the demand; therefore, it is optional with the Lodge to exhibit it or not, at its pleasure.

Jour., 1873, Appendix 39.

Charters.

(*d*)—Surrender of—Cannot be Surrendered, Nine Members being Willing to Sustain.

128. No Subordinate Lodge is allowed to dissolve or surrender their charter by their vote so long as nine members remain willing to sustain the Lodge, except by permission of the Grand Lodge, or during the recess of the Grand Lodge by the Grand Chancellor of the Jurisdiction.

Jour., 1872, 563, 594.

(*e*)—Local Legislation—Following Subjects Governed by—Reissuing, to Whom—What Grand Officers shall Sign—Whose Names shall Appear on.

129. As to whether or not a surrendered charter can be given to new petitioners who were not members of the Lodge at its dissolution, is a proper matter for local legislation.

Jour., 1873, 693, 752, 753.

130. The question which set of Grand Lodge Officers shall sign the charters for Subordinate Lodges granted immediately before or after the installation of such Grand Officers, is of a purely local character, to be settled by the Grand Lodge.

Jour., 1870, 209.
1871. 377, 390.

131. The subject of whose names shall appear upon the charters of the Lodges, when a Grand Lodge has been organized, and upon the surrender of the dispensation, is a subject for local action, and not under the control of the Supreme Chancellor.

Jour., 1872, 466, 612.

(*f*)—Revocation and Arrest—Causes for.

132. The Supreme and each Grand Lodge may provide for and order the revocation of any or all dispensations or charters and the suspension of Subordinate Lodges under their jurisdiction for violation of this Constitution, Supreme Lodge orders, enactments, legislation or decisions, or their Grand Lodge constitutional provisions, local laws, or Grand Chancellor's official mandates during recess.

Const., Art. XXVII.

133. Any Subordinate Lodge may be suspended or dissolved and its charter or dispensation forfeited to the Supreme or the proper Grand Lodge :

(*a*) For improper conduct.

(*b*) For neglecting or refusing to conform to the Constitution, laws or enactments of the Supreme or its Grand Lodge, or the General Laws and Regulations of the Order.

(*c*) For neglecting or refusing to make its reports, or for non-payment of dues or taxes to the Supreme or its proper Grand Lodge.

But the charter or dispensation shall not be forfeited in either of the above cases until the Lodge shall have been duly notified of its offense by the Supreme or proper Grand Keeper of Records and Seal, and suitable opportunity given to answer the charges made against it.

(*d*) For neglecting to hold the regular stated meetings as provided by law, without a proper dispensation therefor, or unless prevented from doing so by some unforeseen circumstances.

(*e*) By its membership diminishing, so that less than a constitutional quorum may be left.

Const., Art. VIII, Sec. 3.

134. Article VIII, Section 3, Subdivision *d*, provides that Lodges under the jurisdiction of a Grand Lodge may be suspended, among other causes, for:

Neglecting to hold the regular stated meetings as provided by law, without a proper dispensation therefor, or unless prevented from doing so by some unforeseen circumstances.

But failing to designate how many stated meetings a Lodge must omit, to incur a penalty prescribed in that section, the Supreme Lodge ruled, in that respect:

It is a subject for local Grand Lodge legislation, they having "exclusive original jurisdiction over all Lodges in their limit, and members of the same"; Provided, that some number of meetings must be stated, as the paragraph is an obligatory one in the Constitution.

Jour., 1876, 1285, 1299.
1880, 1827, 1828, 2004.

(*g*)—Suspension of—Cannot be, without Trial.

135. A chartered Lodge cannot be suspended until charges have been brought against it, properly served by the Grand Keeper of Records and Seal, and the Lodge called upon to answer, a trial had, and testimony taken, which shall be made of record, and reported to the next session of the Grand Lodge, which must try the case at *that session*, and then either acquit, reprimand or make permanent the suspension. The Grand Chancellor possesses no *inherent* power of suspension, unless *specifically* conferred on him by constitutional provision. Grand Lodges should provide a proper commission or jury to try charges against a Lodge during a recess, or bear the consequences of reversal.

Jour., 1888, 3796.

CODE OF PROCEDURE IN TRIAL
OF GRAND OFFICERS.

Operative Only Where Grand Lodges Fail to Provide (136, 137).
Sec. 1. Charges must First be Preferred and be in Form 138.
   2. Grand Lodge may Suspend, pending Charges 139.
   3. To Whom Charges Presented during Recess (140).
   4. Charges to be Served (141).
   5. Trial Committee—By whom appointed (142, 143).
   6. Hearing of Charges (144).
   7. Trial Committee—Report testimony and finding to Grand Lodge 145.
   8. During Recess—Report to highest officer, not under charges 146.
   9. Procedure on Findings, by Grand Lodge (147).
  10. List of Legal Penalties (148).
  11. Action, during Recess, on Finding " Not Guilty " (149).

---

136. The Supreme Lodge has provided the following Code of Procedure to be used in all trials where no such form has been provided by the Grand Lodges.

Jour., 1877, 1380, 1428.
1878, 1511, 1573, 1574.

137. This form of procedure shall not apply where a Grand Lodge has prescribed a different mode for the trial of officers under charges.

Trial Code, Sec. 12.

138. Before any officer or officer-elect of a Grand Lodge shall be called upon to answer, a written charge setting forth in general and comprehensive terms the Pythian offense of which he is alleged to be guilty, shall be presented, signed by some member of the Grand Lodge. This charge shall be accompanied by one or more specifications, setting forth in detail with sufficient particularity to enable the accused to prepare his defense, the time, place and circumstances of the alleged offense.

Trial Code, Sec. 1.

139. The charge being presented to the Grand Lodge, that body may, by a two-thirds vote, suspend the officer charged from the exercise of his official functions, until the charge is investigated; and may, by a similar vote, postpone the installation of any officer-elect.

Trial Code, Sec. 2.

140. During the interval between the sessions of the Grand Lodge, charges against an officer thereof may be presented to the Grand Chancellor, or, if that officer is the one charged, to the Grand Vice Chancellor.

Trial Code, Sec. 3.

141. The Grand Keeper of Records and Seal shall at once forward to the officer charged a certified copy of the charges preferred against him. If the Grand Keeper of Records and Seal is himself charged, this duty shall be performed by an officer to be designated by the Grand Chancellor.

Trial Code, Sec. 4.

142. As soon as practicable after the presentation of a charge, a committee of five members of the Grand Lodge shall be appointed to investigate the same, as follows: A majority of said committee shall be appointed by the officer highest in rank of the Grand Lodge, not under charges, and a minority of the same by the officer next in rank, and not under charges.

Trial Code, Sec. 5.

143. A Grand Chancellor being charged with an offense, during the recess of the Grand Lodge, the Grand Vice Chancellor appoints a majority, and the Grand Prelate, being the third officer, and next in rank to the Grand Vice Chancellor, appoints a minority of the committee.

Jour., 1882, 2274, 2275, 2465, 2466.

144. The committee shall meet as soon as practicable after their appointment, and in case of charges preferred at a session of the Grand Lodge, if possible, during that session, and proceed to investigate the charge. The evidence in the case shall be reduced to writing, and the accused shall have due notice of the time and place of meeting, and a full opportunity to be present, by himself and counsel, and to cross-examine witnesses against him and to introduce evidence in his own behalf.

Trial Code, Sec. 6.

145. The committee, or a majority thereof, having heard the testimony, shall report the same to the Grand Lodge, together with their opinion of the guilt or innocence of the accused, on each specification and each charge; and if they report him guilty, shall also recommend what in their judgment would be the proper penalty for the offense charged, as hereinafter provided.

Trial Code, Sec. 7.

146. During an interval between sessions of the Grand Lodge, and in a case in which, in the judgment of the Committee of Investigation, prompt action is necessary, the committee who have found an officer guilty, may make report to the officer highest in rank, not under charges, and that officer may then, with the consent of a majority of all the officers of the Grand Lodge, suspend the officer accused from the exercise of the functions of his office, until the Grand Lodge takes action in the case.

Trial Code, Sec. 8.

147. The Grand Lodge, upon the report of a committee, shall at once proceed to consider the same, and may adopt, change, modify, reverse or disapprove of, the findings of the committee, and also of the penalty recommended, and may itself prescribe a suitable penalty.

Trial Code, Sec. 9.

148. The penalties to be imposed by these proceedings shall be:

Suspension or removal from office.
Suspension or removal from Grand Lodge membership.
Disqualification to hold office in Grand Lodge.
Disqualification to hold membership in Grand Lodge.

Either or all of these penalties may be imposed, but no other than these specifically mentioned. Disqualification may be either indefinitely or for a limited time.

Trial Code, Sec. 10.

149. If the Committee of Investigation find an officer charged with an offense, and who has been suspended from the exercise of the functions of his office, not guilty, they shall, if the Grand Lodge is not in session, report their finding to the acting Grand Chancellor; and thereupon the officer charged shall be entitled to discharge the duties of his office, until the Grand Lodge shall reverse the finding of the committee; Provided, that no officer of the Grand Lodge shall preside therein, pending the consideration of the charges against himself.

Trial Code, Sec. 11.

COMMITTEES
OF THE SUPREME LODGE.

1. Standing Committees—List of (150).
    - (a) Duties of—Constitutional provisions as to; with legislative enactments pertaining to matters within their purview (151, 152, 153, 154, 155, 156, 157, 158, 159, 160, 161, 162, 163, 164, 165, 166, 167, 168, 169, 170, 171, 172).
    - (b) Number and Eligibility—Constitutional provision as to number of members (173) and legislative enactments as to who constitute (174) and for what cause vacate appointment on (175).
2. Special Committees—Permanent in character; on seats (176); on supplies (177); on hotels and transportation (178)
    - (c) Limitation of Powers of (179).
    - (d) Supreme Representative Not Re-elected—Does not vacate position on (180).

1—Standing Committees—List of.

150. The following committees shall be appointed biennially by the Supreme Chancellor :

A Council of Administration.
Committee on Law.
Committee on Finance.
Committee on Appeals and Grievances.
Committee on Credentials and Returns.
Committee on Mileage.
Committee on the State of the Order.
Committee on Written Work.
Committee on Unwritten Work.
Committee on Printing.
Committee on Dispensations and Charters.
Committee on Endowment Rank.
Committee on Uniform Rank.

Const., Art. V, Sec. 1.

(a)—Duties of—Constitutional Provisions as to—With Legislative Enactments Pertaining to Matters within Their Purview.

COUNCIL OF ADMINISTRATION.

151. The Council of Administration shall advise the Supreme Chancellor on any subject when requested by him, and shall examine all constitutions and amendments thereof, which may be submitted to it, as provided by Section 3, Article VII, of the Constitution.

Const., Art. V, Sec. 2.

152. Provided, that such constitutions and amendments, when submitted to the Council of Administration, shall be examined, passed upon and returned by said Council within ninety days after receipt thereof by them, during recess ; and in case of their failure to do so, the same shall go into effect upon the expiration of said period of time. The Council of Administration shall report its action upon constitutions and amendments submitted to it, to the Supreme Lodge at its session next thereafter, for approval or disapproval.

Const., Art. VII, Sec. 3.

COMMITTEE ON LAW.

153. The Committee on Law shall, when such subjects are presented to the Supreme Lodge and duly referred to them, inquire into all cases of infraction of the established laws and regulations of the Order, and recommend such measures as they may deem expedient for correcting the innovation, and further consider and have charge of all matters coming within the purview of that committee.

Const., Art. V, Sec. 3.

154. At the session of 1873 it was enacted, that on and after that session the various Jurisdictions should present their matters of inquiry through the Grand Keepers of Records and Seal, to the Committee on Law, at least three weeks before the session of the Supreme Lodge, and that all matters not presented before the assembling of the Supreme Body should be presented at once to the Chairman of the Committee on Law, and every matter thereafter presented should be subject to pass over to the subsequent session.

Jour., 1873, 768.

The duties of the Committee on Finance, being diverse, they are set forth in separate paragraphs, as follows :

COMMITTEE ON FINANCE.

155. The Committee on Finance shall examine the accounts of the Supreme Master of Exchequer and Supreme Keeper of Records and Seal, before each regular session of the Supreme Lodge, and the Supreme Chancellor shall convene them for that purpose, at such time and place as he may designate. They shall also examine and audit such books whenever required by the Supreme Lodge.

Const., Art. V, Sec. 4.

156. They shall examine and pass upon all bills presented to the Supreme Lodge when in session, and if correct, report, if approving the same for economy, or creating a remedy by legislation for all extravagant expenditures.

Const., Art. V, Sec. 4.

157. They shall make estimates for and recommend appropriations of money for general or specific purposes during the recess of the Supreme Lodge, and bring down an approximate estimate, based on past results, of the probable revenue likely to accrue ; and no expenditures of any character shall be made in excess of the appropriation then made, until the next regular session.

Const., Art. V, Sec. 4.

158. It shall be the duty of the Finance Committee to audit the books and accounts of the Supreme Master of Exchequer and Supreme Keeper of Records and Seal, the fourth week in April of the year in which the Supreme Lodge does not hold a regular session, the committee to meet on such day and place as the chairman shall direct.

Const., Art. V, Sec. 4.

159. The pay of the committee shall be the same as a Supreme Representative, and their report shall be printed, and sent to the Grand Jurisdictions, in sufficient numbers to supply each Lodge with a copy thereof.

Const., Art. V, Sec. 4.

160. It is made part of the duty of the Major General, when called upon by the Supreme Chancellor, to submit his books to the Committee on Finance.

Const., Art. III, Sec. 8.

COMMITTEE ON APPEALS AND GRIEVANCES.

161. The Committee on Appeals and Grievances shall hear all appeals or grievances from Grand Lodges, or members of Lodges, referred to them by the Supreme Lodge, and report thereon with the utmost dispatch.

Const., Art. V, Sec. 5.

COMMITTEE ON CREDENTIALS AND RETURNS.

162. The Committee on Credentials and Returns shall examine and report on the reports of the Grand Lodges, and subordinates under the immediate jurisdiction of the Supreme

Committees of the Supreme Lodge. 43

Lodge, and the credentials of all Past Grand Chancellors and Representatives of the Supreme Lodge.

Const., Art. V, Sec. 6.

163. The Committee on Credentials and Returns, together with the Supreme Keeper of Records and Seal, shall meet one day in advance of the time specified for the meeting of the Supreme Lodge, examine all credentials and certificates in the hands of the Supreme Keeper of Records and Seal, and prepare their report for the opening of the session of the Supreme Lodge.

Jour., 1886. 3760.

COMMITTEE ON MILEAGE.

164. The Committee on Mileage shall compute the mileage and per diem of all Supreme Officers, Representatives and Past Supreme Chancellors by service, at each regular or special called session, making out a proper, complete and accurate roll of the same, and report the amount to which each one on the roll is entitled; and no order shall be drawn for the same until said report is endorsed by a majority of the committee.

Const., Art. V, Sec. 7.

COMMITTEE ON STATE OF THE ORDER.

165. The Committee on the State of the Order shall examine and report upon such portions of reports of the Supreme Officers and Deputy Supreme Chancellors, so far as the same relate to the state of the Order, and upon such other matters as may be referred to them, presenting in their reports and exhibit of the condition and progress of the Order, and recommending such measures for the good and prosperity of the whole Order, as they may think the circumstances require.

Const., Art. V, Sec. 8.

COMMITTEE ON WRITTEN WORK.

166. The Committee on Written Work shall examine and report upon such parts of reports of the Supreme Officers or other matters referred to them pertaining to all written work of the Order of a public nature, covering regalia, jewels, charts, certificates, shields, uniforms, equipments or public ceremonials, forms for and details of matters not properly of a secret nature.

Const., Art. V, Sec. 9.

COMMITTEE ON UNWRITTEN WORK.

167. The Committee on Unwritten Work shall examine and report upon such reports of the Supreme Officers or other matters referred to them of a nature that may be strictly private, or in consonance and keeping with the duties of the name of the committee.

Const., Art. V, Sec. 10.

COMMITTEE ON PRINTING.

168. The Committee on Printing shall have a general supervisory charge of and examine into all matters referred to or coming within the purview of their duties, as suggested by their name; make all contracts not otherwise provided for, compare materials, quality and price, analyze all bills submitted for printing, binding and supplies, establish a standard style, quality and grade of same, and report their findings and recommendations to the Supreme Lodge.

Const., Art. V, Sec. 11.

169. On the recommendation of the Committee on Printing, in 1888 the following rules were adopted for the future government of the printing of the Supreme Lodge, and in 1890 they were reaffirmed:

1. Hereafter all rituals, pamphlets and documents to be printed shall be submitted to the committee for examination and suggestions.

2. Hereafter all bills for printing, except "supplies," must first be audited and approved by this committee before an order be drawn for the payment thereof.

3. The committee shall ask for bids from at least three responsible printing offices for printing the Journal of Proceedings, and when the copy of the Journal has been prepared by the Supreme Keeper of Records and Seal, the committee shall open proposals received, and award the contract for printing.

4. So far as possible, all printing shall be done by the parties to whom the contract for printing the Journal shall have been awarded, subject to approval of this committee as hereinbefore provided. But this shall not prevent officers and committees from procuring printing from other offices for convenience' sake, subject to the approval of this committee.

Jour., 1888, 4637.
1890, 5453.

COMMITTEE ON DISPENSATIONS AND CHARTERS.

170. The Committee on Dispensations and Charters shall examine into all proper matters referred to them from the Supreme Officers' reports; they shall examine and report on all warrants of dispensation issued by the Supreme Chancellor for Subordinate or Grand Lodges, or charters for the same, approving or disapproving of the issuing of the same, and other general dispensations, or Deputy Supreme Chancellors' commissions issued during the recess of the Supreme Lodge.

Const., Art. V, Sec. 12.

COMMITTEE ON ENDOWMENT RANK.

171. The Committee on Endowment Rank shall examine into all matters pertaining to that Rank, and all such matters as may be referred to them by the Supreme Officers, except those pertaining to finances.

Const., Art. V, Sec. 13.

COMMITTEE ON UNIFORM RANK.

172. The Committee on Uniform Rank shall examine and report upon such matters as may be referred to them, and such portions of reports of the Supreme Officers as may relate to the Rank, and recommend such measures for the good of the Rank as they may think the circumstances require.

Const., Art. V, Sec. 14.

(*b*)—Number and Eligibility—Constitutional Provision as to Number of Members, and Legislative Enactments as to Who Constitute and for What Cause Vacate Appointment on.

173. Each of the above committees shall consist of five members, and the Council of Administration of three members, and when serving on general work during a recess, by order of the Supreme Lodge or Supreme Chancellor, shall receive the same mileage and per diem as Supreme Representatives.

Const., Art. V, Sec. 15.

174. Previous to the new Constitution of 1890, before Past Grand Chancellors constituted part of the Supreme Lodge, the following was the rule:

None others than the Past Supreme Chancellors, Officers of and Representatives to this Supreme Lodge, are eligible to appointment, either upon a Standing or Special Committee thereof.

Jour., 1878, 1607.

175. The expiration of the term of a Supreme Representative, who is a member of a Standing Committee, shall, unless he be re-elected, vacate his position on said committee.

Const., Art. V, Sec. 16.

2—Special Committees, Permanent in Character—On Seats—On Supplies—On Hotels and Transportation.

COMMITTEE ON SEATS.

176. The Supreme Chancellor shall appoint a committee on allotment of seats in ample time for the performance of its duties before the opening of the biennial session; they shall draw for seats to be occupied by the Representatives of the several Jurisdictions.

Rule of Order No. 1; Jour., 1871, 428.

COMMITTEE ON SUPPLIES.

177. The Supreme Chancellor, the Supreme Keeper of Records and Seal, and the chairman of the Finance Committee, are *ex officio* a Committee on Supplies, with power to change the selling prices of different articles from time to time, as the cost of such articles varies. In the case of supplies pertaining especially to the Uniform Rank, the matter of prices is left to the decision of the Major General, the Supreme Keeper of Records and Seal and the chairman of the Finance Committee.

Jour., 1888, 4135, 4584, 4654.

COMMITTEE ON HOTELS AND TRANSPORTATION.

178. The Supreme Keeper of Records and Seal and Major General of the Supreme Lodge were constituted by the Supreme Lodge its Committee on Transportation, for the purpose of making, on behalf of that body, such favorable arrangements as may be, looking to securing reduced rates of transportation to and from the Supreme Lodge, and a proper period during which such rates may run, and the Supreme Keeper of Records and Seal, at least sixty days before a session of the Supreme Lodge, shall personally visit the place of the holding of such session, and make such advantageous arrangements as may be, looking to the proper and reasonable hotel accommodations for the members of the Supreme Lodge, and inform the Grand Keepers of Records and Seal of the various Jurisdictions of any arrangements thus effected.

Jour., 1873, 726.
1890, 5316, 5409, 5427.

(c)—Limitation of Powers of.

179. When special committees are appointed to meet during the recess of the sessions, the time and place of their sessions shall be subject to the control of the Supreme Chancellor, and no authority is recognized in any committee to send for persons and papers unless authorized specially by this Supreme Lodge.

Jour., 1884, 3031, 3032.

(d)—Supreme Representative, Not Re-elected, does Not Vacate Position on.

180. Where a committee was, under authority of the Supreme Lodge, appointed for a special purpose, and from among Supreme Representatives, whose term, at that time, had not expired; and where, before the next session of the Supreme Lodge, at which said committee was to report, the term of some of the said appointees, as Supreme Representatives, did expire; and further, where the question was raised as to their legal standing, as members of said committee by reason of their failure to be re-elected Supreme Representatives, it was decided:

They are *legal members* of it and will attend the session and make report upon the special matter placed in their hands for action.

Jour., 1890, 4849, 5330, 5395.

CONSTITUTIONS.

1. **Of Supreme Lodge**—Old, repealed (181).
   (a) Obligatory (182).
2. **Of Grand and Subordinate Lodges.**
   (b) Approval by a Supreme Chancellor—Of no force if in conflict with Supreme Constitution (183).
   (c) Must be Approved—Of no force until approved (184, 185, 186, 187).
   (d) "Obligatory" Provisions—Contained in Supreme Constitution must be incorporated in Subordinate (188).

1—Of Supreme Lodge—Old Constitution Repealed.

181. The Constitution prior to that adopted at the session of 1874, and all previous legislation inconsistent with the Constitution of 1874, is repealed.

Jour., 1874, 947.

(a)—Obligatory.

182. All constitutional provisions contained in all articles, sections or paragraphs of the Constitution and By-Laws are obligatory, in every sense, on all Grand and Subordinate Lodges, Knights of Pythias, and all Grand or Subordinate Lodge Laws in contravention or conflict herewith are rendered void of effect and illegal in enforcement, or, if enforced, are acts of contumacy, liable and subject to proper punishment.

Const., Art. XIII.

2—Of Grand and Subordinate Lodges—(b) Approval by a Supreme Chancellor—Of No Force if in Conflict with Supreme Constitution.

183. The Supreme Lodge Constitution is necessarily and by direct enactment (Article XIII) the paramount authority of the Order. Any provision in a Grand Lodge Constitution conflicting with it is void, and if such Constitution containing such a provision was inadvertently approved by a Supreme Chancellor, it must still be construed in subordination to the Supreme Lodge law.

Jour., 1884, 2776, 2989.

(c)—Must be Approved—Of No Force till Approved.

184. Each Grand Lodge shall adopt a Constitution for its own government, and also a Constitution or General Laws for its subordinates, which shall be in accordance with the Constitution and Laws of the Supreme Lodge.

Const., Art. VII, Sec. 3.

185. All such Constitutions and amendments thereof shall be submitted to the Supreme Chancellor, and be by him referred to the Supreme Lodge, if then in session, or, during the interim between sessions of the Supreme Lodge, to the Council of Administration; and such Constitutions and amendments, when approved by the Supreme Lodge, or by the Council of Administration when the Supreme Lodge is not in session, shall go into effect.

Const., Art. VII, Sec. 3.

186. Provided, That such Constitutions and amendments, when submitted to the Council of Administration, shall be examined, passed upon and returned by said council within ninety days after receipt thereof by them, during recess, and in case of their failure so to do, the same shall go into effect upon the expiration of said period of time.

Const., Art. VII, Sec. 3.

187. Constitutions for the government of Subordinate Lodges, not in conflict with the laws of general application, adopted by the Supreme Lodge, shall be made by the State Grand Lodges for the government of the Subordinates under their jurisdictions.

Jour., 1869, 67, 88, 115.

(*d*)—" Obligatory " Provisions—Contained in Supreme Constitution, must be Incorporated in Subordinate.

188. Grand Lodges shall prescribe a Constitution for the Subordinate Lodges within their jurisdiction; but the following obligatory general rules or principles shall be incorporated into each Subordinate Constitution.

Const., Art. VIII, Sec. 2.

NOTE.—As these general rules are diverse in their character, they have been distributed throughout the work where they respectively belong, and when laying down any rule, are marked "Obligatory," to designate their character as per above clause.

CREDENTIALS.

189. It is the duty of the several Grand Keepers of Records and Seal to forward the certificates of the Supreme Representatives and Past Grand Chancellors to the Supreme Keeper of Records and Seal at least twenty days before the session of the Supreme Lodge.

Jour., 1871, 410.

190. The Credentials of Past Grand Chancellors shall, in the future, set forth the date on which the Grand Chancellor entered upon his duties, and the date on which his duties terminated, and that the Supreme Keeper of Records and Seal prepare and issue the proper forms.

Jour., 1880, 2015.

NOTE.—By some this has been confounded with the "Rank Credential," but this blank is intended only as between the Grand Lodge and the Supreme.

DEPUTY SUPREME CHANCELLORS.

1. Commissioned—By the Supreme Chancellor (191, 192).
2. Removal—Supreme Chancellor may remove (193); appointment of, needs no approval by Supreme Lodge (194).
3. Powers—He may install officers (195); may deputize another to install (195, 196); cannot grant dispensation to organize a Lodge (197); must report all dispensations granted (198).

1—Commissioned—By Supreme Chancellor.

191. All Past Grand Chancellors or Past Chancellors, regularly authorized and commissioned by the Supreme Chancellor to institute Lodges, or to travel under his instructions to exemplify the work, shall be commissioned and styled Deputy Supreme Chancellors; and each Deputy Supreme Chancellor in charge of a Jurisdiction shall be a member of a Subordinate Lodge in such Jurisdiction.

Const., Art. XIX.

192. An official commission to be issued by the Supreme Chancellor, under his Official Seal, to Deputy Supreme Chancellors, was adopted by the Supreme Lodge, and a revised form was adopted in 1878 and 1880.

Jour., 1873, 719, 746,
and Appendix 12, 13.
1878, 1510, 1572.
1880, 1821, 2012.

2—Removal—Supreme Chancellor may Remove—Appointment of, Needs No Approval by Supreme Lodge.

193. The Deputy Supreme Chancellor being the representative of, *in fact*, the Supreme Chancellor, his appointee, created by his selection and authority, necessarily owes his official existence (subject to removal at will or pleasure, and thoroughly under the control of the Supreme Chancellor, who is personally liable for the Deputy Supreme

Chancellor's actions) to no one but the officer vesting him with the rights and prerogatives of that office.

Jour., 1873, 719, 746,
Appendix 13.

194. The appointment of Deputy Supreme Chancellor requires no approval by the Supreme Lodge.

Jour., 1875, 1153.

3—Powers—He may Install Officers—May Deputize Another to Install—Cannot Grant Dispensation to Organize a Lodge—Must Report All Dispensations Granted.

195. All Deputy Supreme Chancellors of Jurisdictions in which there are no Grand Lodges shall install the officers of all Subordinate Lodges within their Jurisdictions, or cause the same to be done, and perform such other duties as the Supreme Chancellor may direct.

Const., Art. III, Sec. 10.

196. A Deputy Supreme Chancellor may appoint a member of a Lodge distant from him, to install the officers and otherwise represent the Deputy Supreme Chancellor in said Lodge. And such appointed member shall be subject to instruction from the Deputy Supreme Chancellor of the Jurisdiction, and is responsible to him for all his acts under the appointment. The Supreme Chancellor will hold the Deputy Supreme Chancellor accountable for all the acts of such members appointed in the several Lodges, and the Lodges must recognize such appointments under the Deputy Supreme Chancellor.

Jour., 1878, 1507, 1607.

197. A Deputy Supreme Chancellor has no authority to grant a dispensation to organize a Lodge.

Jour., 1868, 26, 45, 47.

198. Deputy Supreme Chancellors must report all dispensations they grant, to the Supreme Chancellor.

Jour., 1888, 4121, 4576, 4581.

DEDICATION CEREMONY.

199. In 1871 a new form of dedication ceremony, retaining the former ceremony used, with additional prefatory matter, was adopted for general use by the Supreme, Grand and Subordinate Bodies, which may be given in public when so desired; in 1880 it was ordered reprinted, with changes in names of officers to conform to present laws.

Jour., 1870, 229.
1871, 364, 385.
1880, 2095.

DISPENSATIONS
BY SUPREME CHANCELLOR.

1. To Reduce Minimum Fee.
   (a) Right to Use—Dies with grantor (200).
   (b) How Issued—Only on request of Grand Lodge in session 201.
2. For Special Purposes (202).

1—To Reduce Minimum Fee—(a) Right to Use—Dies with Grantor.

200. All dispensations granted to Grand Jurisdictions or Lodges, previous to the date of the installation of the Supreme Chancellor, whereby the power was given to confer the three Ranks of this Order for a sum less than ten dollars cease at that date, and become absolutely null and void; that right dies with the officer granting it.

Jour., 1888, 3797, 4003.

(b)—How Issued—Only on Request of Grand Lodge in Session.

201. Dispensations granted by a Supreme Chancellor, under Article VIII, Section 2, Paragraph *h*, Supreme Constitution, whereby the total amount of fees for the conferring of the three Ranks is permitted to be reduced below the sum of ten dollars, can only issue on the request made by a Grand Lodge in session. The Grand Chancellor has no power in that connection, unless authorized by the Grand Lodge of which he is presiding officer.

Jour., 1888, 4004, 4123, 4580, 4581.

2—For Special Purposes.

202. The Supreme Chancellor reported having granted dispensations for the following purposes, and the Supreme Lodge approved the issuance:

To a Grand Lodge, to install the Grand Chancellor-elect outside the Grand Lodge, he being sick at the time the session was held.

To a Grand Chancellor to change the time of holding the session of the Grand Lodge on account of the floods prevailing throughout the State.

Jour., 1882, 2275, 2473.

NOTE.—These are given because they were recognized and approved, but nowhere does there appear any law to require either the request for, or the issuance of such dispensations.

DISTRICT DEPUTY GRAND CHANCELLOR.

203. It is within the power of a Grand Lodge to legislate so as to give power to all District Deputies to deputize some Past Chancellor, or some other competent person, with power to install the officers of Subordinate Lodges in case of sickness on his part, or other disabilities, to attend to that duty.

Jour., *1888*, *4508*, *4659*.

204. A District Deputy Grand Chancellor appointed by the Grand Chancellor to institute a new Lodge, cannot deputize another Past Chancellor to perform the duty.

Jour., *1882*, *2274*, *2465*.

DUES.

1. **Local Legislation**—The subject of, a matter for (205); both as to members, and Pages and Esquires (206).
2. **Exemption from**—Cannot make a law exempting Knights from, for a given period (207).
3. **During Suspension**—May not be charged during suspension (208), unless local law so provides (209).
4. **In Advance**—Payment of, required in advance, cannot invalidate member's rights (210); nor does he forfeit advance dues by reason of suspension for cause (211).

1—Local Legislation—The Subject of, a Matter for, both as to Members, and Pages and Esquires.

205. The regulation of dues, as a general proposition, has always been left to each Grand Lodge.

Jour., *1872*, *468*, *612*, *613*, *614*.

206. The charging of and collecting dues from Pages and Esquires rests solely with Subordinate Lodges.

Jour., *1873*, *Appendix 37*.

2—Exemption from—Cannot Make a Law Exempting Knights from, for a Given Period.

207. A Lodge cannot make a law exempting all new members from the payment of dues for six months after being enrolled as Knights, since this would not be consistent with the laws or usages of the Order.

Jour., 1876, 1228, 1296.

3—During Suspension—May Not be Charged during Suspension, unless Local Law So Provides.

208. Since the decision of the Supreme Chancellor in 1870 that "a brother suspended for non-payment of dues ceases to be a member of the Order until reinstated," it is not lawful (unless under the provisions of local constitutional enactments) to charge parties, so suspended, with dues, after the act of suspension, until reinstated.

*Jour., 1870, 225.
1875, 1112, 1156.*

209. In the case of a brother suspended for non-payment of dues, applying for reinstatement, Subordinate Lodges have the right, if provided for by local legislation, and they so desire, to charge that brother the amount charged against him at the time of suspension, and in addition thereto a sum equal to the dues that would have accrued during such suspension.

Jour., 1890, 4846, 5319, 5338.

4—In Advance—Payment of, Required in Advance, cannot Invalidate Member's Rights, Nor does He Forfeit Advance Dues by Reason of Suspension for Cause.

210. A Subordinate Lodge may collect dues in advance; but cannot declare a member in arrears for dues who has paid the same to the first of a term, or allow the advanced payment required to invalidate the member's right to benefits or the S. A. P. W.

Jour., 1875, 1042, 1114, 1121.

Note.—See also Sections 86, 436 of this Digest.

211. A member having charges preferred against him, whose dues are paid in advance, and said charges being sustained, with a verdict of guilty, and he suspended, does not forfeit the dues paid, neither is the Lodge compelled to return them, but will retain them until the expiration of suspension (which is only temporary, and by his own act), at which time full credit of said payment shall be made by the Lodge.

Jour., 1890. 4845. 5319, 5337.

ELECTIONS.

1. **In the Supreme Lodge.**
   - (*a*) **Constitutional Provisions**—When held (212); by ballot (213); electioneering forbidden (214); new election in case of absence at installation (215).
   - (*b*) **One Nominee**—Member may be voted to cast the whole ballot in case only one nominee (216).
2. **In a Grand Lodge**—Absence, *per se*, no bar to nomination (217).
3. **In a Subordinate Lodge**—Void, under certain circumstances, if the Chancellor Commander fails to preside at, and "tellers" are not members of the Lodge (218); not void, because of an excess of votes, when (219)?

1—In the Supreme Lodge—(*a*) Constitutional Provisions—When Held—By Ballot—Electioneering Forbidden—New Election in Case of Absence at Installation.

212. The Supreme Lodge Officers shall be elected biennially by ballot at the forenoon meeting on the third day of the session, except the Major General of the Uniform Rank, who shall be appointed and commissioned by the Supreme Chancellor in the manner and for the term as now provided by the general laws of the Uniform Rank.

Const., Art. XXIV.

213. A majority of all the votes present shall be necessary to constitute a choice. In case of a tie, the balloting shall continue until a choice is made; the name of the brother receiving the lowest number of votes at each balloting shall be withdrawn.

Const., Art. XXIV.

214. Any member seeking directly or indirectly to secure the votes of others for any official position within the gift of the Supreme Lodge, shall thereby be disqualified to fill the position sought.

Jour., 1882, 2438, 2474.

215. If an officer-elect be absent at the time of the installation, unless excused by the Supreme Lodge, his office shall be declared vacant and another and immediate election held to fill the vacancy. But if the absent officer-elect has been excused, then the Supreme Chancellor may be empowered to install during recess, at his convenience.

Const., Art. XXIV.

(b)—One Nominee—Member may be Voted to Cast the Whole Ballot in Case of Only One Nominee.

216. Where there is but one nominee for an office in the Supreme Lodge, it is competent for that body to designate a member to cast the ballot of the Supreme Lodge. But in such a case all members voting against the motion to designate a member to cast the vote of the Supreme Lodge, have an inherent right to vote with such member. And in such case all the ballots being cast for the same person, it is the unanimous vote of the Supreme Lodge, although all of the members do not vote.

Jour., 1870, 195, 196.

2—In a Grand Lodge—Absence, per Se, No Bar to Nomination.

217. Where the Constitution of a Grand Lodge provides for the election of officers by the Past Chancellors in the Lodges, a majority being necessary to a choice, and where it provided for the acceptance, by the nominees, of their nomination; and further where there failed to be an election in the case of one of the officers, and the Grand Lodge proceeded to an election at the next session, the chair excluding from nomination, one of those previously nominated and who had accepted, but was not *then present*, on appeal, the Supreme Lodge held that it was not necessary that the brother should have been present during the election.

Jour., 1884, 3040, 3041.

3—In a Subordinate Lodge—Void, under Certain Circumstances, if the Chancellor Commander Fails to Preside, and "Tellers" are Not Members of the Lodge—Not Void, because of an Excess of Votes, When?

218. Where the Grand Lodge has provided, by a Constitution for its Subordinates, that, at the election of officers in a Lodge, the Chancellor Commander must preside, and that two *members* must be appointed, and act, as tellers, and where at an election the Chancellor Commander, though present, did not preside, but called a Past Chancellor to the chair, and two members, not members of the Lodge, acted as tellers, and the case ultimately coming to the Supreme Lodge, on an appeal involving the legality of the election held in the manner recited, the Supreme Lodge decided the election illegal, holding that the Chancellor Commander should have presided, and that "the word *members*, in that connection, meant members of the Lodge."

Jour., 1880, 2063.

219. An election for officers in a Subordinate Lodge cannot be set aside simply because the ballot box contains more votes than the number of members present and qualified to vote; so long as the ballot box does not develop an excess of votes greater than the majority which the successful candidate receives, the election cannot be disturbed simply in view of the excess of votes.

Jour., 1888, 4005.

EMBLEMS.

220. The display by members of the Order at their places of business of any of the emblems or insignia of the Order, or the use of the same in any manner as a means of advertising, save by those parties who may be engaged in the manufacture or sale thereof, is highly reprehensible, and where made, the Subordinate Lodges should draw the attention of the offender to the matter, and, if persisted in, proceed against him under the law.
Jour., 1875, 1133, 1143.

221. No emblem of the Order should be used, employed or associated by any brother in the advertisement of his business, except he be engaged in the manufacture or sale of Pythian goods and supplies, and it is improper, unlawful and in bad taste for any member of this Order to use its name, device, emblem, or in any manner display the same in any place of business—except by those engaged in the manufacture or sale thereof—and such action is a proper ground of complaint.
Jour., 1888, 1606, 1621.

ENDOWMENT RANK.

1. Adoption of—Now managed, by a Board of Control (222).
2. Suspensions—Notice of, to be sent to Sections (223).
3. Journal of Proceedings—Proportion of cost of to be paid by (224).
4. Board of Control—Jurisdiction co-extensive with Supreme Lodge (225); Grand Chancellor has no power to interfere with circulation of communications from (226); has authority to address Grand and Subordinate Lodges (227).

1—Adoption of—Now Managed, by a Board of Control.

222. This Rank, together with its General Laws and Ritual, was established in 1877, its purpose being the insurance of the lives of members of the Order; its system was changed from time to time, the Ritual being abolished, until, in 1888, the entire management was placed in the hands of a Board of Control composed of the Supreme Chancellor *ex-officio*, and three members of the Supreme Lodge who must be members of the Endowment Rank and be elected by the Supreme Lodge as follows: One for the term of six years, one for the term of four years, and one for the term of two years, and at each biennial session of the Supreme Lodge one member of said Board is elected for a term of six years. The Supreme Secretary is Secretary to the Board.
Jour., 1877, 1378, 1405, 1408, 1410,
1418, 1422, 1433, 1434,
1452, 1453, 1458-1465.
1888, 1598-1602, 1616-1618,
4666, 4667.

2—Suspensions—Notice of, to be Sent to Sections.

223. It shall be the duty of the Master of Finance of every Subordinate Lodge, at the end of every semi-annual term, to report to the Section of the Endowment Rank to which such Lodge may be tributary, a full list of names of all members suspended from membership in such Lodge for any cause.

Jour., 1878, 1675.

3—Journal of Proceedings—Proportion of Cost of, to be Paid by.

224. The proportion of expense of printing of the Journal of Supreme Lodge proceedings, properly chargeable to the Endowment Rank, was ordered to be paid out of appropriate funds of said Endowment Rank.

Jour., 1890, 5335.

4—Board of Control—Jurisdiction Co-extensive with Supreme Lodge—Grand Chancellor Has No Power to Interfere with Circulation of Communications from —Has Authority to Address Grand and Subordinate Lodges.

225. The Board of Control has territorial jurisdiction, co-extensive with the Supreme Lodge, over all matters appertaining to the Endowment Rank, subject to the enactments of the Supreme Lodge.

Jour., 1890, 5129, 5130, 5401, 5420.

226. A Grand Chancellor has no right to forbid the circulating of Endowment matter, emanating from the Board of Control, among Subordinate Lodges.

Jour., 1890, 5129, 5130, 5401, 5420.

227. The Board of Control *has authority* to address Grand and Subordinate Lodges, and to circulate any communication or circular appertaining to or connected with the Endowment Rank or its business.

Jour., 1890, 5129, 5130, 5401, 5420.

EXPULSION.

228. Subordinate Lodges are authorized to impose the penalty of expulsion in cases of trial under the Code of Procedure; Provided, however, that Grand Lodges, on appeal to them shall have full right to review the evidence and proceedings in any case, and approve, modify or annul the penalty imposed.

Jour., 1886, 3521. 3555.

FEES.

1. Minimum — Constitutional provision (229); above that, Grand Lodges control (230).
2. Donating—Cannot evade by donating part of (231, 232).
3. " Charter Books "—Opening of, not allowed (233); the rule applicable to new Lodges (234).
4. Grand Chancellor—Cannot dispense with the rule (235).
5. Division of the Gross Fee—A matter for Grand Lodges (236).

1—Minimum — Constitutional Provision — Above that, Grand Lodges Control.

229. Every application for membership must be accompanied with the initiation fee, the amount of which shall be fixed by each Grand Lodge; Provided, that in no case shall the three Ranks be conferred in North America for a less amount than ten dollars; Provided, further, that the Supreme Chancellor be and he is hereby authorized and empowered, upon the application of a Grand Lodge, through its proper officers, to issue his dispensation, authorizing and permitting such Jurisdiction to confer the three Ranks of the Order for a sum not less than six dollars. (Obligatory.)

Const., Art. VIII, Sec. 2, Sub. h.

230. The provision fixing a minimum as to fees for conferring the Ranks is obligatory, and cannot be changed, except as provided in Article XXIX. While the minimum should be fixed by the Supreme Lodge, below which no Lodge should be permitted to confer the Ranks, yet, with that restriction, the question as to the amount of fees for conferring Rank, subject to the restriction before stated, of right ought to be left in the hands of the several Grand Jurisdictions.

Jour., 1876, 1230, 1286.

NOTE.—The Article referred to, then XXXII, now XXIX, is the provision for amending the Constitution.

2—Donating—Cannot Evade by Donating Part of.

231. The refunding or donating, or promising directly or indirectly to refund or donate, to applicants for membership in this Order, any portion of the initiation fee, is a violation of Article VIII, Section 2, Subdivision *h*, of the Constitution.

Jour., 1875, 1133, 1140.

232. A Subordinate Lodge has no right to refund or donate to the candidate any part of the ten dollars received for conferring the three Ranks.

Jour., 1890, 4844, 5319, 5336.

3—Charter Books—Opening of, Not Allowed—The Rule Applies to New Lodges.

233. There is no constitutional authority for opening "charter books," so-called, so that a Lodge may receive members or applications for a less sum than fixed by the Constitution; and a dispensation for that purpose cannot be issued.

Jour., 1875, 1033, 1113.

NOTE.—This law was passed to prevent the use of a system, prevailing in some Jurisdictions, whereby applicants were accepted, at the organization of a new Lodge, for any fee agreed on, below the full rate provided by law as the minimum, and this privilege extended for some months after by what was called "keeping the charter open."

234. The provisions of Article VIII, Section 2, Subdivision *h*, requiring the payment of at least the minimum fee for the three Ranks, is applicable to persons becoming members at the institution of new Lodges.

Jour., 1884, 2957, 2993, 2994.

4—Grand Chancellor—Cannot Dispense with the Rule.

235. A Grand Chancellor cannot grant dispensations to initiate persons for less than the rates prescribed by law, even though he have directions and authority from his Grand Lodge so to do.

Jour., 1873, 705, 768.

5—Division of Gross Fee—A Matter for Grand Lodges.

236. The Constitution of the Supreme Lodge fails to make a division of the fees, so far as each of the Ranks is concerned. Such division, as the law now stands, leaves the matter to be determined by each Grand Jurisdiction for itself.

Jour., 1888, 4126, 4655, 4656.

FINES.

1. May be Imposed—But only by constitutional provision (237); may be added to dues (237, 238).
2. Derelict Members—May be imposed on, of committees (239); on members for non-attendance at regular meetings (240).

1—May be Imposed—But Only by Constitutional Provision—May be Added to Dues.

237. Fines and assessments levied in accordance with the provisions of the Constitutions of Subordinate Lodges working under the control of the Supreme Lodge and duly approved by the Supreme Chancellor; or Subordinate Lodge Constitutions provided by their Grand Lodges and duly approved by the Grand Lodge or Grand Chancellor, may be charged up and operate as dues, so as to render the delinquent member liable to suspension.

Jour., 1884, 3062, 3063.

238. Fines and assessments aggregating a sum equal to one year's dues, and not paid to a Lodge by a brother, make him liable to suspension, the same as for the non-payment of dues for the period of twelve months.

Jour., *1890, 4845, 5319, 5337.*

NOTE.—So that there may be no misconstruction of this legislation, it should be read in conjunction with the preceding section, whereby it will be seen that this only provides for the *effect* of fines and assessments, *where the Grand Lodge first gives the power to charge them.* No such power can be assumed *direct,* by the Subordinate Lodge, hence this section is only operative where, by Constitutional enactment, duly approved, *the Grand Lodge has so ordained.*

2—Derelict Members—May be Imposed on—Of Committees—On Members for Non-attendance at Regular Meetings.

239. A Grand Lodge has a right to so legislate as to provide for the imposition of a fine or suspension, after charges and trial, as a penalty for failure, on the part of members of a Lodge committee, to obey an order, by their Lodge, to report.

Jour., *1880, 2011.*

240. The matter of fining members for non-attendance at regular meetings is a matter for local legislation, but of very doubtful expediency.

Jour., *1888, 4121, 4122, 4574, 4580, 4581.*

FUNDS.

241. A Grand Lodge may legislate so as to provide that the revenues of a Lodge derived from fees, fines, assessments, dues or donations, or the accumulation thereof, shall not be used except for the business and purposes of the Order.

Jour., *1878, 1565, 1613.*

242. A Subordinate Lodge can make a donation to a distressed brother in destitution and want within its own Jurisdiction.

Jour., *1876, 1308.*

243. Where a Grand Lodge had provided, in its Constitution for Subordinate Lodges, that a two-thirds vote was necessary where the question involved an expenditure of money, the Supreme Lodge ruled, that though the case at issue was upon an appropriation for the payment of nurse hire, out of a fund specifically for that purpose, and to reimburse a sister Lodge, yet that in the face of the above constitutional provision, the expenditure, even for such a purpose, was not one contemplated to be made by a majority vote.

Jour., *1876, 1308.*

FUNERALS.

1. Order of Formation at—By Lodges (244).
2. Rosette—For Members, Officers, Past Officers and Grand Lodges (245); may appear in uniform with or without Jewels (246).
3. Chaplain—Lodge may appoint (247).
4. Kneeling—During ceremony not prescribed (248).
5. When Excluded from Participation In—Lodge excused from attendance if local law provides (249).
6. Ritual—Only that prescribed to be used (250).

1—Order of Formation at, by Lodges.

244. When the Order attends funerals, the line of march shall be taken up in the following order:

First—Outer Guard, bearing a sword, followed by the Pages, Esquires and Knights in the order as laid down.

Second—Inner Guard, bearing a sword.

Third—Keeper of Records and Seal, Master of Finance and Master of Exchequer (three abreast), each bearing the emblems of their respective offices.

Fourth—Master-at-Arms, bearing a staff.

Fifth—Chancellor Commander and Vice Chancellor, each bearing the emblems of their respective offices.

Sixth—Prelate, supported by two Past Chancellors.

Seventh—Past Chancellors and Past Grand Chancellors.

On arriving at the grave the procession halts and opens order, when the coffin and mourners pass through, and the procession follows the corpse in a reversed position.

Jour., 1871, 403, 404, 414.

2—Rosette—For Members, Officers, Past Officers and Grand Lodges—May Appear in Uniform.

245. In 1872 the following was adopted as the new funeral rosette of the Order, which may or shall be worn in lieu of other regalia:

By Knights, Pages and Esquires.—Round rosette, black, flat center, one and a half inches in diameter, with white metal struck up or silver embroidered escutcheon, surrounded by two rows of one-half-inch black satin ribbon, the joint made by the ribbon joining the center of the rosette, to be covered with one-quarter ligne silver braid, the completed rosette to be three inches in diameter. Suspended from the under side of the rosette a white silk ribbon, two and a half inches wide and four and a half inches long, with name and number of Lodge, and the letters "K. P." printed upon it in black, the white ribbon to be covered with black crape.

By Past Chancellors.—Same as for members, but gilt escutcheon.

By Officers.—Same as for members, but substituting the emblem of their respective offices for the escutcheon in center of the rosette.

Jour., 1872, 620, 631.

By Grand Lodges.—A rosette three inches in diameter, with black velvet center of two inches, with gold letters "G. L." and one-half inch red border (ribbon) to be worn as a badge of mourning by Grand Lodges on the occasion of attending funerals.

Jour., 1869, 99, 116.

246. Lodges may appear in public parade, at funerals, wearing the funeral rosette on left breast, with or without Jewels; or in plain citizens' dress; also in uniform, with or without Jewels.

Jour., 1875, 1032, 1124.

NOTE.—This legislation, where it refers to "Uniform," means the old Third Rank uniform, which has never yet been abolished.

3—Chaplain—Lodge may Appoint.

247. Subordinate Lodges have the power to elect, or their presiding officers may appoint, a Chaplain to conduct the devotional exercises at funerals of members of the Order.

Jour., 1872, 563, 598.

4—Kneeling—During Ceremony, Not Prescribed.

248. In 1872 the word "kneel," wherever occurring in the Funeral Services or Ritual, except in the ceremonies of the First Rank, was striken out, and the word "stand" or "standing" inserted in its or their places.

Jour., 1872, 599.

5—When Excluded from Participation in—Lodges Excused from Attendance, if Local Law Provides.

249. A Grand Lodge has the right to so legislate, that at funerals, whenever our Order, as such, shall, either by the direction of the deceased, made during life, or by the surviving relatives or friends of the deceased, be excluded from an equal share and responsibility in the control and direction of such funeral of a deceased brother, the Order shall, by such action, be thereby excused from any further attendance upon such funeral as Knights of Pythias.

Jour., 1878, 1630, 1634.

6—Ritual—Only That Prescribed, to be Used.

250. The Ritual adopted by the Supreme Lodge to be used for funeral services is the only form or Ritual to be used for such services.

Jour., 1886, 3521, 2756.

GRAND CHANCELLOR.

1. **Special Duty**—Must cause names of certain officers to be sent to the Supreme Keeper of Records and Seal (251).
2. **Special Powers**—May deputize a Knight for any purpose (252); may instruct a Chancellor Commander in the Work or the S. A. P. W. outside the Lodge Room (253).

1—Special Duty—Must Cause Names of Certain Officers to be Sent to the Supreme Keeper of Records and Seal.

251. Each Grand Chancellor shall cause the name and address of the Grand Chancellor, the Grand Keeper of Records and Seal and the Supreme Representative-elect to be forwarded to the Supreme Keeper of Records and Seal within twenty-four hours after the election of those officers has occurred.

Jour., 1888, 4134, 4607.

2—Special Powers—May Deputize a Knight for any Purpose—May Instruct a Chancellor Commander, in the Work or the S. A. P. W., Outside the Lodge Room.

252. A Grand Chancellor is justified in appointing a member of the Knights Rank to institute a Lodge, or in commissioning him for any other purpose within the limits of his authority under the laws of the Supreme Lodge and the laws of his Grand Lodge.

Jour., 1888, 4122, 4576, 4577, 4581.

253. The Grand Chancellor or his deputy may give instruction in the secret work outside of the Lodge room, and may also give the S. A. P. W. to a Chancellor Commander.

Jour., 1873, 723, 724.

NOTE.—These three paragraphs cover questions which came before the Supreme Lodge. The general duties and powers are provided for by each Grand Jurisdiction.

GRAND LODGE.

1. Organization—When may be, and how organized (254); officers, and who eligible to office, at organization (255, 256, 257).
2. Powers of—General provisions (258, 259); jurisdiction (260, 261, 262).
3. Composition of—Primarily, of Past Chancellors, but it may restrict its composition (263, 264).
4. Judge of Its Own Members—But Supreme Lodge may correct abuse of privilege (265).
5. Debate in—May not debar its members from right of debate, when (266).
6. Officers of, Terms, Status, Removal—Elected for not less than one year (267, 268); their status while membership is passing from one Lodge to another, a matter for local legislation (269); they may be removed by summary methods (270).
7. Past Chancellor's Rank—Must be conferred in, not in ante-room (271)
8. Constitutional Rights of—Given to, by Supreme Lodge, not operative till legislated for by Grand Jurisdictions (272).
9. Obituary Tablet—Whose name may appear on, matter for local legislation (273).
10. Officers' Reports—May not mutilate reports of officers (274).
11. Right of Action—Grand Lodge cannot legislate to debar a member right of action (275).

1—Organization—When may be, and How Organized—Officers, and Who Eligible to Office, at Organization.

254. When there are five or more Subordinate Lodges established and in working order in any Jurisdiction, they, through the Deputy Supreme Chancellor thereof, may petition the Supreme Chancellor, who, if he approve the application for a Grand Lodge, shall cause the Supreme Keeper of Records and Seal to direct each of the Lodges of that Jurisdiction to notify each of its Past Chancellors thereof.

Const., Art. VI, Sec. 2.

255. The Past Chancellors of the five or more Lodges shall meet at such place as may be specified by the Supreme

Chancellor, and procede to organize a Grand Lodge by electing a

    Sitting Past Grand Chancellor,
    Grand Chancellor,
    Grand Vice Chancellor,
    Grand Prelate,
    Grand Master of Exchequer,
    Grand Keeper of Records and Seal,
    Grand Master-at-Arms,
    Grand Inner Guard,
    Grand Outer Guard, and
    Two Supreme Representatives,

all of whom must be Past Chancellors, and thereupon the Supreme Chancellor shall install, or cause to be installed by a Deputy Supreme Chancellor, the officers-elect of said Grand Lodge, after which it shall proceed to adopt a Constitution and By-Laws for its own government, not inconsistent with Laws of the Supreme Lodge.

Const., Art. VI, Sec. 3.

256. Any Past Chancellor of the Jurisdiction in good standing is eligible to any Grand Lodge office, including that of Supreme Representative, at the formation of a Grand Lodge.

Jour., 1884. 2776. 2988.

257. A notice of their organization. together with a list of the officers, shall be forwarded to the Supreme Keeper of Records and Seal as soon as practicable.

Const., Art. VI, Sec. 5.

2—Powers of—General Provisions—Jurisdiction.

258. Grand Lodges exist by virtue of a Charter or Dispensation, issued by authority of the Supreme Lodge, or Supreme Chancellor during its recess.

Const., Art. VII, Sec. 1.

259. They shall conform to the Ritual, forms, ceremonies, work, regalia, Jewels, uniform, charts, shields and certificates, and regulations prescribed by the Supreme Lodge, in accordance with this Constitution.

Const., Art. VII, Sec. 1.

260. They shall (subject to the provisions hereof and right of appeal) have exclusive original jurisdiction over all

Subordinate Lodges within their territorial limit, and over the members attached to the same.

Const., Art. VII, Sec. 1.

261. The Grand Lodge holds jurisdiction over its own members, and when charges are preferred against them as such, all laws operative there or below are applicable until the matter is fully determined.

Jour., 1873, Appendix 37.

262. All power and authority not herein reserved to the Supreme Lodge is hereby delegated to the Grand Lodges, the Supreme Lodge, however, reserving to itself the right, at any time, by proper amendments, duly adopted, to this Constitution, to resume any additional power necessary to promote the well being and harmony of the Order.

Const., Art. VII, Sec. 2.

3—Composition of—Primarily, of Past Chancellors, but It may Restrict Its Composition.

263. Grand Lodges shall be composed only of Past Chancellors; but said Grand Lodges may provide for a representative system, and may limit the rights and privileges of Past Chancellors on the floor of the Grand Lodge.

Const., Art. VII, Sec. 4.

264. Any amendment to a Grand Lodge Constitution, making the Grand Lodge a representative body is entirely within the legitimate authority of the Grand Lodge; and when properly made and adopted, should receive the approval of the Supreme Lodge or the Supreme Chancellor.

Jour., 1870, 197, 207.
1877, 1412, 1444.

4—Judge of Its Own Members, but Supreme Lodge may Correct Abuse of Privilege.

265. While Grand Lodges are the judges of the qualifications of their own members, as a general proposition, yet the Supreme Lodge has the power to correct any abuse of discretion or violation of law or principle by a Grand Lodge.

Jour., 1886, 3685, 3686.

NOTE.—This decision was made in a case coming from the Grand Lodge of Wisconsin, wherein it was alleged that the Grand Lodge overstepped its own Constitution in seating a Representative who was out on Card.

5—Debate in—May Not Debar Its Members from Right of Debate—When?

266. Where a Grand Lodge Constitution declared that the Grand Lodge should be composed of all Past Chancellors in good standing in

Subordinate Lodges in the State, and who should be admitted as *members;* and in the same Article declared that all elective officers and representatives should be entitled to one vote each, and nowhere debarred *members* from debate, but in its rules of order provided for the right of debate by *members*. On an appeal from the action of the Grand Lodge refusing to one who, though a *member*, was neither a Grand Officer nor Representative, the right of debate, the Supreme Lodge sustained the appeal on the above statement of facts.

Jour., *1888*, *4474-4482*, *4530*, *4531*.

6—Officers of, Terms, Status, Removal—Elected for Not Less than One Year—Their Status while Membership is Passing from One Lodge to Another, a Matter for Local Legislation—They may be Removed by Summary Methods.

267. The officers of a Grand Lodge shall be as prescribed in Section 3, of Article VI, of this Constitution, who shall be elected or appointed as the Supreme Lodge and the Constitutions of the respective Grand Lodges may prescribe, and who shall hold office for a term of not less than one year.

Const., Art. VII, Sec. 5.

268. All questions of organization and government of Grand Lodges, the determining when and how often they will hold their sessions, and when officers shall be nominated and elected, so far as the same do not interfere with obligatory law, are left to local legislation.

Jour., *1870*, *176*, *200*.
1871, *342*, *394*.
1872, *564*, *594*.
1876, *1236*, *1274*.

269. It is within the jurisdiction of a Grand Lodge to legislate for itself as to what is the status of a Grand Lodge Officer, while his membership is passing from one Lodge to another.

Jour., *1878*, *1567*, *1606*.

270. In the occasional cases which arise, calling for the application of the principle of self-preservation, circumstances are presented which *ex necessitate*, are above and beyond all written rules; in such cases Grand Lodges have the right to deprive an officer of the exercise of official powers, by such summary methods as may be deemed necessary.

Jour., *1874*, *861-868*, *945*.
1875, *1127-1129*.

NOTE.—This legislation grew out of the troubles in Pennsylvania and the misconduct, at that time, of the Grand Chancellor.

7—Past Chancellor's Rank—Must be Conferred in, Not in Ante-room.

271. The Past Chancellor's Rank, being a ritualistic Rank, and fully provided for in the Grand Lodge Rituals, can only be conferred in the Grand Lodge, with its attendant ceremonies. It is, therefore, not proper or competent for a Grand Lodge or the Grand Chancellor to direct that, after the admission and instruction of new Past Chancellors at the opening of the session, all Past Chancellors who may afterward present themselves for instruction be obligated and instructed in the ante-room by the Grand Prelate.

Jour., 1874, 913, 935.

8—Constitutional Rights of—Given to by Supreme Lodge, not Operative till Legislated for by Grand Jurisdiction.

272. Where the Supreme Lodge, by constitutional provision or legislative enactments, gives certain rights to the Grand Lodges, the Grand Lodge shall take advantage of those rights, and by statutory enactments provide for the use of the privilege which the Supreme Lodge extends to them, but, failing to do so, they cannot attempt by indirection to make the privilege operative unless they take some advantage of the right given them.

Jour., 1888, 3996.

9—Obituary Tablet—Whose Name may Appear on, a Matter for Local Legislation.

273. The question as to entering upon the Obituary Tablet of a Grand Lodge the name of one who had been, but at the time of his death was not, a member of the Order, is one purely of local concern and regulation.

Jour., 1878, 1628, 1640, 1669, 1677.

10—Officers' Reports—May Not Mutilate Reports of Officers.

274. For a Grand Lodge to mutilate the report of its Grand Chancellor when it contains no objectionable language, nor any matter connected with the private work of the Order, is a wrong and injustice.

Jour., 1870, 199.

11—Right of Action—Grand Lodge cannot Legislate to Debar a Member Right of Action.

275. Grand Lodges cannot, by constitutional provision, debar a member from bringing an action at law, in connection with differences in the Order until he has exhausted all his remedy within the Order.

Jour., 1888, 3995, 4025.

GRAND VICE CHANCELLOR.

276. Only when representing the Grand Chancellor is the Grand Vice Chancellor, *per se*, clothed with any more authority than any other member.

Jour., *1888, 4122, 4579, 4581.*

HAWAIIAN ISLANDS.

1. **Membership**—Natives, or descendants of, ineligible (278).
2. **Past Chancellors**—Rank of, conferred by Deputy Supreme Chancellor (279).

1—Membership—Natives, or Descendants of, Ineligible.

277. The Constitution of the Order does not permit the initiation of natives of the Hawaiian Islands and their descendants.

Jour., *1875, 1037-1039, 1129, 1130.*
1878, 1515, 1624.
1886, 3306, 3702.
1888, 4423-4426, 4550, 4551.

2—Past Chancellors — Rank of, Conferred by Deputy Supreme Chancellor.

278. Acting on the recommendation of the Supreme Chancellor, in 1884, the Supreme Lodge ordered:

That in the Hawaiian Islands, until the organization of a Grand Lodge, the Deputy Supreme Chancellor be vested with authority to confer the Rank of Past Chancellor upon those brothers of Subordinate Lodges, in such islands, who have served a full term as Chancellor Commander; and the Deputy Supreme Chancellor shall transmit certificates of such Past Chancellors to the Supreme Keeper of Records and Seal, who shall keep a correct roster of such Past Chancellors.

And, in 1888, these same parties petitioning that the further power be granted the Deputy Supreme Chancellor to confer the Rank of Past Chancellor on those brothers who are entitled to receive it, by virtue of their having served a full term as the first elective officers of a new Lodge, the Supreme Lodge further enlarged his powers by enacting the following:

The Deputy Supreme Chancellor for the Hawaiian Islands shall have the power to confer the Rank of Past Chancellor on all officers entitled to receive it under the statements contained in the legislation of 1875, 1043, 1114, 1121; 1884, 2775, 2988.

Jour., 1884, 2771, 3062.
1888, 4425, 4426, 4550, 4551.

NOTE.—The legislation of 1875 and 1884, above referred to, is as follows:

At the institution of a Subordinate Lodge, working under the immediate supervision of the Supreme Lodge, the Past Chancellor, Chancellor Commander, Vice Chancellor, Prelate, Keeper of Records and Seal, Master of Finance and Master of Exchequer, take the rank of Past Chancellor, provided they serve till the end of their official term. After this the rank is obtained only by service as Chancellor Commander.

Jour., 1875, 1043, 1114, 1121.

If, during the first official term of a Lodge (under immediate supervision of the Supreme Lodge) the Prelate, Vice Chancellor, Keeper of Records and Seal and Master of Finance resign, and others are elected to fill the unexpired term, these last elected are entitled to the Rank of Past Chancellor, provided they serve to the end of the term.

Jour., 1884, 2775, 2988.

HONORS.

279. The honors of the same office cannot be given to but one person for the same term.

Jour., 1872, 564, 585.

280. Where a Grand Lodge, by constitutional amendment changed the time of holding its annual session, thereby shortening the tenure of office of its Grand Officers; and where the question was presented as to the effect said change would have upon "honors" of office, the Supreme Lodge held:

The Grand Lodge Constitution must not provide for terms of less than one year, though it is perfectly competent for a Grand Lodge, by constitutional amendment, to change the time of the year in which to meet, in which event, the officers serving until the changed time of meeting, and election and installation of their successors, are entitled to the honors of a full term of service.

Jour., 1880, 1969, 1988, 2004, 2005.

HYPOTHETICAL QUESTIONS.

281. Neither the Supreme Chancellor nor the Supreme Lodge will hereafter receive or answer any hypothetical propositions or questions submitted to them either in recess or during the session of the Supreme Lodge, except the same come from a Grand Lodge or a Subordinate Lodge under the jurisdiction of this Supreme Lodge, and under the seal thereof.

Jour., 1876, 1311. •

282. While by the decisions made at different times, the Supreme Chancellor was inhibited from ruling on hypothetical questions, it was decided that where they came to the Supreme Chancellor from the Grand Chancellor of a Jurisdiction, notwithstanding they did not emanate from the Grand Lodge itself, they were properly before him for his answer.

Jour., *1888, 4122, 4578, 4581.*

283. The Supreme Lodge refused to act on questions presented by Supreme Representatives, the same being reported by the committees, to whom referred, as not evidencing that they came over a request from a Grand Lodge.

Jour., *1877, 1426, 1433, 1445.*
1878, 1559, 1561, 1605.
1880, 2023, 2024, 2037.
1882, 2568.
1884, 3064.

IMPOSTORS.

284. It would be perfectly proper for Grand Officers to give such notification as to impostors, as would protect their Lodges and membership.

Jour., *1880, 1827, 2003.*

INCORPORATION.

1. **Of the Supreme Lodge**—Act of incorporation, as it now stands, inclusive of all amendments (285).
2. **Grand Lodges**—Legislation regarding the effect of their incorporation (286, 287).

1—Of the Supreme Lodge—Act of Incorporation, as it Now Stands, Inclusive of All Amendments.

285. WHEREAS, It is deemed advisable to have the Supreme Lodge Knights of Pythias an incorporated body, under the laws of the Congress of the United States, for the more perfect working of the beneficent intentions of the said Order;

AND WHEREAS, With a view to promote this object, and as Grand and Subordinate Lodges of the said Order have been formed or organized in various States and Territories, and will be hereafter formed in various other States and Territories of the United States, as well as other foreign countries:

1. *Now, therefore, be it known*, That in accordance with the Act of Congress entitled "An Act to Provide for the Creation of Corporations in the District of Columbia by General Law," approved May 5, 1870, the undersigned have associated themselves for the purpose and with the design of establishing and creating the corporation to be known and named the Supreme Lodge Knights of Pythias, do hereby make and authorize to be filed in the office of the Register of Deeds in the District of Columbia, this Certificate and these Articles of Association for the government of themselves, their associates, assigns and successors.

2. *And be it further known*, That the beneficial association of which this is the Certificate, shall be known as the Supreme Lodge of the Knights of Pythias, the seal of which has been copyrighted by the Supreme Recording and Corresponding Scribe in the Clerk's Office of the Supreme Court of the District of Columbia, and has also been recorded in the Office of the Librarian of Congress in the Capitol of the United States, at Washington, D. C.

3. The Supreme Lodge shall consist of all Past Grand Chancellors; the Supreme Officers and two Representatives from each Grand Lodge, under the jurisdiction of said Supreme Lodge, until there are 20,000 members under the jurisdiction of a Grand Lodge, and one Supreme Representative for each additional 10,000 members. Provided, that no Grand Lodge shall be entitled to more than four (4) Supreme Representatives.

4. The Board of Trustees shall consist of Supreme Chancellor S. S. Davis, of New Hampshire; Supreme Keeper of Records and Seal Joseph Dowdall, of Ohio; Supreme Master of Exchequer John B. Stumph, of Indiana, and Supreme Vice Chancellor D. B. Woodruff, of Georgia, who shall serve until the election of their successors, it being understood that the four principal officers of the Supreme Lodge shall compose the Board of Trustees.

5. *And be it further known*, that the officers of the said Supreme Lodge Knight of Pythias of the World shall consist of Past Supreme Chancellor, Supreme Chancellor, Supreme Vice Chancellor, Supreme Prelate, Supreme Master of Exchequer, Supreme Keeper of Records and Seal, Supreme

Secretary of the Endowment Rank, Major General of the Uniform Rank, Supreme Master-at-Arms, Supreme Inner Guard, Supreme Outer Guard, all of whom shall be elected by ballot, every alternate year, and the said Supreme Keeper of Records and Seal and Supreme Master of Exchequer shall give such security for the faithful performance of their duty as may be ordered by said Supreme Lodge.

6. That sessions of the Supreme Lodge shall be held at such times and in such places as the Supreme Lodge may, in accordance with Constitution and laws, determine, for the transaction of all business for the benefit and welfare of the Order, and the Supreme Chancellor shall convene extra sessions of the Supreme Lodge in the manner prescribed in the Constitution of the said Supreme Lodge.

7. *And be it further known*, That a Representative from a majority of the Grand Lodges working under the jurisdiction of the Supreme Lodge shall constitute a quorum for the transaction of business.

8. *And be it further known*, That the said Supreme Lodge shall have power to alter and amend its Constitution and By-Laws at will, and that it shall have power to prescribe modes of initiation, etc., for the working of said Order, and no Grand or Subordinate Lodges purporting to be Knights of Pythias shall have legal standing unless chartered by or through the regularly elected officers of this Supreme Lodge in regular or called session, or by the Supreme Chancellor during the recess of said Supreme Lodge.

9. That the said Supreme Lodge shall have power to establish the Uniform Rank and the Endowment Rank upon such terms and conditions, and governed by such rules and regulations as to the said Supreme Lodge may seem proper.

2—Grand Lodges—Legislation regarding the Effect of Their Incorporation.

286. Since a Grand Lodge exists only and solely by and through a charter issued by the Supreme Lodge, the act and articles of incorporation of any Grand or Subordinate Lodge of the Order have no bearing, weight, influence or relation, save as relates to such matters as exist, or may exist, between them and extraneous individuals or corporations.

Jour., 1874, 934.

287. Unless the State Laws under which a Grand Body is incorporated give to it a proprietary right in the goods, chattels and money of a Subordinate Lodge, the power and authority of a Grand Lodge to seize and possess itself of such goods, chattels and money would not extend, except so far as by virtue of the compact made between it and the Subordinate Lodge in that behalf. The obligation which binds the membership to their Grand Lodge is the only tie which controls; but a refusal to deliver such goods, chattels and money would constitute an offense should the charter of the Lodge be vacated either by their own act or by suspension.

Jour., 1888, 4123, 4580, 4581.

INSTALLATION.

1. In a Grand Lodge (288)—Cannot be done by proxy (289).
2. In a Subordinate Lodge—Constitutional provision (290).
3. General Ruling as to the Effect of (291).

1—In a Grand Lodge.

288. While according to the Ritual the Supreme Chancellor or the retiring Past Grand Chancellor should install the newly elected Grand Officers, and make the official proclamation of their installation, if neither the Supreme Chancellor or Past Grand Chancellor be present, it is perfectly regular to have the ceremony performed by a Past Grand Chancellor.

Jour., 1872, 626.
1884, 3046.

NOTE.—By a typographical error the word "Past" was omitted in the Ritual before "Grand Chancellor," but subsequently corrected. (See 1884, 3046.)

289. It is contrary to the established customs and ritualistic ceremonies of the Order that, in the absence of an elective Grand Officer at the time of installation, he may be installed by proxy.

Jour., 1875, 1139.

2—In a Subordinate Lodge—Constitutional Provision.

290. Officers shall be installed at the first regular meeting in the new term, if unforeseen circumstances do not prevent; but no officer shall be installed unless he has fully paid to his Lodge the amount of all dues and claims of whatsoever nature then accrued. (Obligatory.)

Const., Art. VIII, Sec. 2, Sub. f.

3—General Ruling as to the Effect of.

291. The *installation* and not the *election* of his successor is what determines the status of the outgoing presiding officer and establishes his claim to the past official Rank.

Jour., 1886, 3681, 3682, 3704.

INSTITUTING LODGES.

The Following "Directions for Instituting a Subordinate Lodge of Knights of Pythias" was adopted, and all other legislation on the subject repealed. Jour., 1886, 3297, 3316, 3689, 3691, 3756.

292. Having received from the Supreme Chancellor (or the Grand Chancellor, as the case may be) a commission to institute a Lodge of Knights of Pythias, the instituting officer will proceed, as soon as practicable, to make the necessary preliminary arrangements. He will:

(1). Agree with the applicants on a date for the institution of the Lodge.

(2). Make provisions for having the necessary working paraphernalia in readiness at the time appointed.

(3). Secure the services of a sufficient number of members of the Order (in no case less than three) to assist him in conferring the Ranks.

Having arrived at the locality at which the Lodge is to be instituted, the instituting officer will:

(1). Examine the hall which it is proposed to use, and satisfy himself that it is adapted to the purpose.

(2). Examine the paraphernalia and see that every necessary article is in place.

(3). Notify his assistants of the part which each is expected to perform in conferring the Ranks, if he has not already done so.

(4). The charter applicants having assembled, the instituting officer having read to them his commission, will call the list of names as they appear on the application, and satisfy himself of the identity of each individual.

(5). He will then collect from each applicant who is not already a member of the Order, the fees for the three Ranks (in no case less than ten dollars), at the same time notifying them that no one can be considered a charter member whose fees are not then paid. Provided, however, that in Grand

Jurisdictions to which the Supreme Chancellor has granted a dispensation to confer the three Ranks for six dollars, that sum shall be collected from each applicant.

(6). He will then require the applicants to vote by secret ball ballot on each name on the list, beginning with the last. He may, however, at his discretion allow a single ballot to be taken for the entire list, having previously notified the applicants that if one black ball (or two black balls if the local law requires that number to reject) shall appear on the general ballot, a separate ballot will be required on each name. If the general ballot be "fair" he shall declare all the applicants elected. If one black ball (or two, as above) appear, he will then require a separate ballot as above directed.

(7). If the number of applicants be large, the items of business embraced in paragraphs four, five and six, above, may be transacted at a preliminary meeting held during the day. If such meeting be held, all of the applicants should have due notice thereof. At this meeting officers for the new Lodge may be selected, subject, of course, to formal ratification by ballot after the Lodge shall have been instituted, and a name may be chosen for the Lodge, subject to subsequent approval.

(8). The instituting officer will then exclude from the hall all who are not in possession of the S. A. P. W., and proceed to fill as far as practicable the stations of a Subordinate Lodge. It is desirable that all the stations be filled, but in any event those of the Chancellor Commander, Master at Arms, Inner Guard and Outer Guard must be occupied, the Chancellor Commander acting when necessary as Prelate and the Inner Guard as Vice Chancellor. (The instituting officer may himself occupy the station of Chancellor Commander, or appoint another brother to do so.) The Lodge having been duly opened—

(9). The Ranks of Page, Esquire and Knight shall be conferred in full, according to the Ritual, on the applicants. If officers have been previously agreed upon, they should have precedence in receiving the Ranks, to be followed by the other applicants in the order in which their names appear on the list. The instituting officer will exercise his judgment in deciding whether or not the Ranks shall be conferred at that meeting on all the applicants ; but under no circumstances shall any one on whom the three Ranks have not been conferred in full, according to the ritualistic form, be considered a member of the Lodge, or be allowed to remain in the Lodge room during the transaction of any business or work, except to receive a Rank or to witness the conferring of one which he has already received.

(10). The election of officers will then be held under the immediate supervision of the instituting officer, or the previous election will be formally ratified by ballot.

(11). The bonds of the bonded officers having been approved by vote of the Lodge, the instituting officer will proceed to install the officers-elect.

(12). He will then turn over to the Master of Exchequer of the Lodge the entire amount received from applicants, taking a receipt therefor, which he will transmit with his report. At the same time he will cause to be drawn an order for the payment of the amount of his expenses in instituting the Lodge.

(13). He will then cause a name for the Lodge to be selected, or the former selection to be ratified by vote.

(14). He will then officially declare the Lodge duly instituted, as "——— Lodge No. ——, of the Grand Jurisdiction of ———" (or "under the jurisdiction of the Supreme Lodge," as the case may be), and deliver to the Chancellor Commander the Dispensation under which the Lodge is to work.

REPORT.

As soon as practicable after the institution, the instituting officer must forward to the Grand Chancellor (or to the Supreme Chancellor if commissioned by him), a report, showing:

(*a*) The name, number and location of the Lodge, together with the date of its institution.

(*b*) The number of charter applicants and the number on whom each Rank was conferred.

(*c*) A list of the names of the applicants rejected on ballot.

(*d*) An itemized statement of the expenses incurred by him in instituting the Lodge.

Together with any other information which he may consider of interest.

JEWELS.

1. Adoption of—For Supreme, Grand and Subordinate Lodges and Knights (293); sale of, under control of Supreme Lodge (294).
2. **Of Supreme Officers**—New, size reduced (295); each officer retains, during recess (296).
3. Reduction of Size of—Of Grand, Subordinate and Members'; rule governing procurement of special Jewels of past Rank, for members (297, 298).
4. Pythian Public Occasions—Permitted to be worn on (299).
5. Special Badges—To distinguish Representatives, cannot be required by Grand Lodges, in addition to (300).
6. Presentation Jewels—Obtainable, after expiration of present contract, by payment of stated royalty (301).

1—Adoption of—For Supreme, Grand and Subordinate Lodges, and Knights—Sale of, under Control of Supreme Lodge.

293. At the session of 1874 the Supreme Lodge adopted the designs of Jewels for the officers of the Supreme, Grand and Subordinate Lodges, and also a Jewel for Knights, all of which, except those for "Attendants," are still in use, unchanged, except as to size; the following legislation was then adopted and stands unrepealed:

Any and *all* Jewels of the Order of Knights of Pythias, when used, if *not* coming from or through the Supreme Keeper of Records and Seal of the Supreme Body, and according to and in keeping with the legislation of 1874, are illegal, and prohibited from use by any person or persons, Lodge or Lodges; and the Grand Officers and Deputy Grand Officers are solicited to aid and assist in causing the legal Jewels now adopted being used, and *ordered* to see that *all* others, of whatsoever nature, character, make or kind, unless as set forth in said legislation of 1874, are, if used, *ordered discontinued at once*, under penalty, and that none be permitted used in any way, shape or manner, except those made and procured under said legislation, and from the proper officers as therein named and set forth.

In 1880 a design for Jewel for Past Supreme Representative and for Representatives to Grand Lodges was presented, the former only being adopted. In 1886, Jewels for Past District Deputy Grand Chancellors, and Representatives to Grand Lodges, were adopted. In 1884, a Jewel for Supreme Secretary of the Endowment Rank was proposed and in 1886 adopted, but the description being left out of the new Constitution, its adoption was reaffirmed in 1890. (See 1884, 3064; 1886,

3559; 1890, 5467.) These comprise the whole list of Jewels now furnished.
Jour., *1874, 973, 975, 979.*
1880, 1860, 2057.
1884, 3064.
1886, 3553, 3559.
1890, 5467.

294. The sale of all Official Jewels is under the control of the Supreme Lodge.
Jour., *1880, 2065.*

2—Of Supreme Officers—New, Size Reduced—Each Officer Retains, During Recess.

295. New Jewels, two and one-half inches in diameter, of sixteen-karat gold, and platinum, were ordered, and Jewels of same size were to be placed on sale to Past Supreme Chancellors.

Jour., *1886, 3553, 3556, 3557.*

296. Each Supreme Officer was authorized to retain in his possession, during recess, the Jewel of his office.

Jour., *1890, 4861, 5320, 5338.*

3—Reduction of Size of—Of Grand, Subordinate and Members'—Rule governing Procurement of Special Jewels, of Past Rank, for Members.

297. The Supreme Keeper of Records and Seal was authorized to issue a permit to any member of the Order to procure and use a Jewel of the Rank attained, made of the legal and approved form, but of smaller size, upon the receipt of two dollars therefor, and the Supreme Keeper of Records and Seal was directed to have the Seal of the Supreme Lodge impressed thereon, whereupon the said Jewel should be legal, and in 1886 this was construed so as to require that such Jewels must be manufactured by the manufacturer having the Supreme Lodge contract for Jewels.
Jour., *1882, 2561.*
1886, 3323, 3324, 3553.

298. In addition to the legislation of 1882, page 2561, permitting the manufacture of Jewels for *members*, half size, similar permission to manufacture Jewels for Grand and Subordinate Lodges was granted.

Jour., *1886, 3553.*

4—Pythian Public Occasions—Permitted to be Worn on.

299. The Jewels of the Order now in use for Subordinate Lodges and members, are hereby declared legal to be worn on funeral or Pythian public occasions only.
Jour., *1888, 4559, 4597.*
1890, 4845, 5319, 5337.

5—**Special Badges—To Distinguish Representatives, cannot be Required by Grand Lodges, in Addition to.**

300. Grand Lodges cannot require Representatives attending their sessions to wear special badges designating the Lodge to which they belong, in addition to their Jewel.

Jour., *1888, 4004, 4005, 4025.*

6—**Presentation Jewels—Obtainable, after Expiration of Present Contract, by Payment of Stated Royalty.**

301. Future contracts for Official Jewels shall provide that any Grand or Subordinate Lodge of the Order desiring to present to any member of the Order an Official Jewel of Rank, of a quality or value different from those kept in stock by the Supreme Keeper of Records and Seal, be permitted to procure the same from any manufacturer, paying to the Supreme Keeper of Records and Seal ten per cent of the cost of such Jewel, and upon such payment the seal of the Supreme Lodge will be impressed upon such Jewel.

Jour., *1890, 5395, 5453, 5454.*

NOTE.—That there may be no misunderstanding as to the effect of the foregoing, it is proper to state that it was first proposed to make it operative *at once;* but the first eight words were affixed after the Supreme Keeper of Records and Seal stated (see Journal, page 5454,) that "it could not if adopted, take effect until the expiration of the present contract for the manufacture of Jewels, May 1, 1891."

JOURNALS OF PROCEEDINGS.

302. All Grand Lodges are required to forward to the office of the Supreme Keeper of Records and Seal two complete sets of their Journals of Proceedings, and each year, or so soon thereafter as printed, two copies of the same.

The Supreme Keeper of Records and Seal is required to have the same bound in suitable-sized volumes in legal style, one set to be retained in the office of the Supreme Keeper of Records and Seal, the other to be retained in the office of the Supreme Chancellor.

Jour., *1875, 1106, 1124.*

LADIES,
DIPLOMA AND JEWEL FOR.

303. The Supreme Keeper of Records and Seal was directed to prepare a "Ladies' Diploma" and Jewel, which shall be sold as other supplies, and which Subordinate Lodges shall be empowered to issue to the wives, daughters, mothers, sisters and widows of their members in good standing—the purpose of this Diploma and Jewel being to provide the female members of Knights' families with a means of manifesting their claim to protection and assistance whenever and wherever needed.

Jour., 1888, 4608, 4652.

LADIES' RANK.

304. The Supreme Lodge has, with persistent regularity, refused to establish or recognize a Rank of the Order for ladies, as will be seen by reference to the Journals.

Jour., 1868, 16.
1870, 190, 191.
1871, 396.
1872, 564, 599.
1877, 1455.
1878, 1565, 1615.
1880, 1993, 2012, 2013.
1882, 2394, 2473.
1886, 3501, 3543, 3544.
1888, 4402, 4419, 4428, 4429, 4430, 4431, 4506, 4509, 4513, 4558, 4559, 4651.
1890, 5268, 5269, 5332, 5396, 5397, 5414.

LAWS AND LEGISLATION.

305. All laws, enactments or legislation of the Supreme Lodge become of force from date of the publication of the official Journal of the Supreme Lodge, unless otherwise provided by the Supreme Lodge.

Const., Art. XIV.

306. The legislative acts of the Supreme Lodge, when they accord with the Supreme Lodge Constitution, are binding and obligatory upon Grand and Subordinate Lodges and members.

Jour., 1876, 1232, 1302.

NOTE.—The foregoing declaration would at first seem unnecessary, but it appears by the Record to have grown out of the following statement made by the then Supreme Chancellor, as follows:

My attention has been called to the force and meaning of Section 2, Article VII of the Constitution of this Supreme Lodge, viz.: "All power and authority not *herein* reserved to the Supreme Lodge, is hereby delegated to the Grand Lodges, the Supreme Lodge, however, reserving to itself the right at any time, by proper amendments, duly adopted, to this Constitution, to resume any additional power necessary to promote the well being and harmony of the Order." It is contended by some that no legislation outside of the Constitution, or amendments to it, is binding upon Grand Lodges. Although this may *seem* to be the literal construction of this law, I do not agree that it should be so construed. It would be most unfortunate in the administration of your laws if this is the fact. I therefore ask you to give this provision careful consideration, and a construction which shall have the force of law.

LODGES SUBORDINATE TO
SUPREME LODGE.

These bodies are variously denominated throughout the legislation of the Supreme Lodge, and are spoken of as: Lodges under the "immediate jurisdiction" of the Supreme Lodge; the "immediate control," "immediate supervision," "direct control," "Lodges where no Grand Lodge exists"—all these forms of description refer to Lodges subordinate to the Supreme Lodge, and reporting direct to the Supreme Keeper of Records and Seal and taking orders and instructions from the Supreme Chancellor.

All legislation specifically referring to these bodies is given under this head.

1. Organization—Under control of the Supreme Lodge (307); shall pay per capita tax and make semi-annual reports to the Supreme Keeper of Records and Seal (307); tax payable on Pages, Esquires and Knights (308); S. A. P. W. withheld till tax paid and reports made (309).

2. Application to Organize—Must be approved by Deputy (310); objections by existing Lodge must be filed with it (310).
    (a) Objections filed with Deputy—After application, estops institution till passed on by Supreme Chancellor (311); rejected material cannot be accepted by Deputy (312).

3. Past Chancellors—Certain first officers, serving their term, entitled to Rank (313); failing to serve, those who fill out that term are entitled to the Rank (314); Deputy, or any Grand Lodge, on authority of Supreme Chancellor, may confer the Rank (315, 316).

4. Membership—
    (b) Minimum Fee—Shall not be less than ten dollars (317).
    (c) Special Dispensations—"Maimed persons" admitted under dispensation by Supreme Chancellor (318); and persons over fifty, under dispensation by Deputy (319), who may also permit conferring of Page Rank on same night as applicant elected (319).
    (d) An Elected Applicant—May, for certain reasons, be refused admission (320).
    (e) A Rejected Page or Esquire—May reapply in one month (321).
    (f) Rejected Material—Sister Lodge cannot accept, without consent of rejecting Lodge (322).
    (g) Reinstatement—How reinstated after suspension for non-payment of dues (323).
    (h) Withdrawal Cards—Provisions for granting, to members of defunct Lodges (324, 325).

5. Appeals—How taken (326).

6. Name—Cannot be changed without authority (327).

7. Constitution—Uniform one prescribed (328).

8. Meetings—Must hold regular (329).

9. Consolidation—May be done (330).

1—Organization—Under Control of the Supreme Lodge—
Shall Pay Per Capita Tax, and make Semi-Annual
Reports to Supreme Keeper of Records and Seal—
Tax Payable on Pages, Esquires and Knights—S.
A. P. W. Withheld till Tax Paid and Reports
Made.

307. All Subordinate Lodges, in Jurisdictions in which no Grand Lodge exists, shall be under the immediate control of the Supreme Lodge until the institution of a Grand Lodge for that Jurisdiction. Each of such Lodges shall pay to the Supreme Lodge, while under its immediate control, twenty-five cents per capita of its membership, payable semi-annually, and shall make out and forward to the Supreme Keeper of Records and Seal, on the blank furnished by him for that purpose, on or before the first day of March and the first day of September, respectively, of each year, semi-annual reports of its work and business.

Const., Art. VI, Sec. 1.

308. Per capita tax is due and payable to the Supreme Lodge on every member of each Subordinate Lodge working under the immediate jurisdiction thereof, and Pages and Esquires are to be considered members for this purpose.

Jour., 1884, 2776, 2988.

309. The Supreme Chancellor was authorized by the Supreme Lodge to withhold the S. A. P. W. from Subordinate Lodges under the jurisdiction of the Supreme Lodge, until a full account is given of their condition, and reports and tax forwarded to the Supreme Keeper of Records and Seal.

Jour., 1878, 1516, 1622.

2—Application to Organize—Must be Approved by Deputy
—Objections by Existing Lodge must be Filed
with It.

310. Persons, not necessarily members of the Order, have the right to petition for the establishment of a Lodge of the Knights of Pythias in a place where no Grand Lodge has been organized. but where the Order is already established, provided the application has the approval and sanction of the Deputy Supreme Chancellor or officer having charge of the territory where occurring, indorsed thereon. Should this be done in opposition to the wishes of the Lodge or Lodges in active working order, or at least without the recommendation of an established Lodge, it is held : That it is the duty of the Deputy Supreme Chancellor to receive and forward all applications made to him for the institution of new Lodges, and he must approve or disapprove thereof, in writing, of the same, he, the Deputy Supreme Chancellor, having no right or authority to arrange with or agree to any side stipulations in the premises, and any Lodge or Lodges objecting thereto must file their objections in writing over their seal with the Deputy Supreme Chancellor, which authenticated objection, alleging reasons therefor, must be forwarded by the Deputy Supreme Chancellor to the Supreme Chancellor for final passing on the issue raised.

Jour., 1873, Appendix 37, 39.
1880, 1827, 2003.

(a)—Objections Filed with Deputy—After Application, Estops Institution till Passed on by Supreme Chancellor—Rejected Material cannot be Accepted by Deputy.

311. The Deputy Supreme Chancellor cannot proceed to initiate the charter members of a new Lodge, upon the receipt of a Dispensation, over the protest or of another Lodge already in existence. The protest or objection being filed in regular form, and on valid grounds, must be heard and passed upon, and orders issued from the office of the Supreme Chancellor to proceed before it can be done.

Jour., 1873, Appendix 39.

312. Rejected material cannot be accepted by the Deputy Supreme Chancellor on a roll of charter members for a new Lodge, where such fact is existing and known to him; if done innocently or negligently it is censurable, but not criminal; further, it ought always to be made a preliminary interrogatory, "Have you ever applied to any Lodge of this Order and been rejected?" If the answer is negative, then proceed; if afterward found to be a falsehood, the penal law should be applied in its most stringent shape.

Jour., 1873, Appendix 39.

3—Past Chancellors—Certain First Officers, Serving Their Term, Entitled to Rank—Failing to Serve, Those Who Fill out That Term are Entitled to the Rank—Deputy, or Any Grand Lodge, on Authority of Supreme Chancellor, may Confer the Rank.

313. At the institution of a Subordinate Lodge, working under the immediate supervision of the Supreme Lodge, the Past Chancellor, Chancellor Commander, Vice Chancellor, Prelate, Keeper of Records and Seal, Master of Finance, and Master of Exchequer take the rank of Past Chancellor, provided they serve till the end of their official term. After this the rank is obtained only by service as Chancellor Commander.

Jour., 1875, 1043, 1114, 1121.

314. When, during the first official term of a Lodge under the immediate jurisdiction of the Supreme Lodge, the Master of Finance, Vice Chancellor, Keeper of Records and Seal, and Prelate, resigned,

and officers were elected to fill the unexpired term, those brothers last elected were entitled to the rank of Past Chancellor, provided they served to the end of the term.

Jour., 1884, 2775, 2988.

315. The Supreme Chancellor is clothed with power to authorize Deputy Supreme Chancellors to confer the rank of Past Chancellor upon such as shall be entitled to said rank by *actual service*, in portions of the Supreme Jurisdiction where Grand Lodges do not exist.

Jour., 1888, 4596.

NOTE.—It will here be noticed that the powers are not as wide as those now given to the Deputy for the Hawaiian Islands, and only extend to Past Chancellors *by service*, and not to those who gain the rank by being among the first officers, other than the Chancellor Commander. The meaning of the words "by service" was construed by the Supreme Lodge in its action regarding Past Supreme Chancellors (Jour., 1878, 1577-1579), and can only refer to service in the chair of presiding officer.

316. If requested by the Supreme Chancellor, any Grand Lodge shall confer the rank of Past Chancellor on any member of a Subordinate Lodge under the immediate jurisdiction of the Supreme Lodge, who presents the proper credentials that he has become entitled to the rank.

Jour., 1884, 2935, 2959.

4.—Membership—(*b*) Minimum Fee—Shall Not be Less than Ten Dollars.

317. Where, under a constitutional provision similar to that at present existing, the Supreme Chancellor granted dispensations to Lodges under the immediate jurisdiction of the Supreme Lodge, to confer the three Ranks for six dollars, the Supreme Lodge held:

The minimum fee is fixed by Section 2, Article VIII, of the Constitution of the Supreme Lodge, at ten dollars, and no power is anywhere vested in the Supreme Chancellor to dispense with this provision, as to Lodges under jurisdiction of the Supreme Lodge.

Jour., 1880, 1822, 2004.

(*c*)—Special Dispensations—"Maimed Persons" Admitted under Dispensation by Supreme Chancellor, and Persons over Fifty, under Dispensation by Deputy Who may Also Permit Conferring of Page Rank on Same Night as Applicant Elected.

318. Applications coming from Subordinate Lodges under the immediate jurisdiction of the Supreme Lodge, for dispensations to admit maimed persons, must be made to the Supreme Chancellor by vote, and under the seal of the Subordinate Lodge, approved by the Deputy Supreme Chancellor of the Jurisdiction; and the Supreme Chancellor may grant a dispensation for the admission of a maimed person, if in his judgment it appears proper, subject to the same restrictions made to Grand Lodges, viz.: The applicant must be capable of earning a livelihood for himself and family.

Jour., 1875, 1040, 1114, 1121.

319. A Deputy Supreme Chancellor has the power to grant a dispensation to a Lodge to confer the Ranks on a person over fifty years of age, and also to confer the Rank of Page upon a candidate on the same night upon which his petition has been reported on favorably.

Jour., 1888, 4120, 4574, 4580, 4581.

(*d*)—An Elected Applicant—May, for Certain Reasons, be Refused Admission.

320. In Lodges under the immediate jurisdiction of the Supreme Lodge an applicant for membership who, having been elected for the Page Rank, and before being instructed in it, is found to be unworthy, from facts not made known when his case was before the Lodge, may be refused admission by a majority vote of the Lodge present; and if rejected the fee must be returned to him.

Jour., 1875, 1042, 1114, 1115, 1121.

(*e*)—A Rejected Page or Esquire—May Reapply in One Month.

321. In Lodges under the immediate jurisdiction of the Supreme Lodge, if a Page is rejected on a ballot for the Rank of Esquire, or an Esquire is rejected on a ballot for the Rank of Knight, another ballot may be had in either case in one month thereafter.

Jour., 1875, 1043, 1114, 1121.

(*f*)—Rejected Material—Sister Lodge cannot Accept, without Consent of Rejecting Lodge.

322. A Lodge of the Knights of Pythias, under the immediate jurisdiction of the Supreme Lodge, cannot accept of rejected material from another Lodge in the same locality, even after the expiration of the six months' probation required by the Lodge to which the first application was made, without the consent of the Lodge rejecting in the first place.

Jour., 1873, Appendix 39.

(*g*)—Reinstatement—How Reinstated after Suspension for Non-payment of Dues.

323. A member of a Lodge, under the immediate jurisdiction of the Supreme Lodge, who has been suspended for non-payment of dues, wishing to be reinstated, should pay the amount of one year's dues and all assessments charged during that year. Beyond this, it is discretionary with the Lodge.

Jour., 1875, 1043, 1114, 1121.

Lodges Subordinate to Supreme Lodge. 87

(h)—Withdrawal Cards—Provisions for Granting, to Members of Defunct Lodges.

324. For the purpose of making some provision for the rehabilitation of members of defunct Lodges, in cases where the records of such Lodges have been lost or destroyed, hereafter, in all such cases occurring in States or Territories where no Grand Lodge has been organized, the Supreme Chancellor is authorized and empowered, upon satisfactory evidence to him that the persons so applying therefor have been members of the Order, to issue to them a certificate to that effect, upon the presentation of which, if otherwise worthy, they will be entitled to admission to membership in the Lodge to which the same is presented, upon the payment of the same, as is charged by said Lodge for admission by deposit of Withdrawal Card.

Jour., *1876, 1231.*
1882, 2279, 2473.

NOTE.—The word "certificate," used in this Section, no doubt means Withdrawal Card; this is evidenced by reading Section 325. There are no such things as certificates, for the transfer of membership.

325. The Supreme Officers can only grant Withdrawal Cards to members of defunct Lodges who were clear on the books when the Lodge became defunct; or, who (not being suspended) will pay a fee sufficient to make them "clear on the books." If the books are not in the hands of the Supreme Keeper of Records and Seal, satisfactory evidence must be adduced to show former membership and standing of applicant, before Card can be granted.

Jour., *1884, 2776, 2777, 2988.*

5—Appeals—How Taken.

326. An appeal may be taken from the action or decision of any Subordinate Lodge under the immediate jurisdiction of the Supreme Lodge of the World to said Supreme Lodge by any member of such Subordinate Lodge or by any other person whose rights have been denied by such action or decision upon giving written notice to said Subordinate Lodge, of said appeal within two weeks from and after such action or decision; Provided, that appeals to this Supreme Lodge shall be accompanied by one hundred and fifty printed copies in each case. The expense of printing shall be borne by the party taking the appeal, and the pages to be of the same size as the Journal of the Supreme Lodge.

Const., Art. XVII, Sec. 2.

6—Name—Cannot be Changed without Authority.

327. The proper name of a Lodge in a Territory under the immediate jurisdiction of the Supreme Lodge, is the one designated in the warrant. The brothers cannot change this name without authority.

Jour., 1884, 2776, 2988.

7—Constitution—Uniform One Prescribed.

328. A uniform Constitution for the government of Subordinate Lodges under the immediate jurisdiction of the Supreme Lodge, by the selection of various sections and paragraphs of the Constitution of the Supreme Lodge and arranging them appropriately, was adopted and ordered promulgated.

Jour., 1884, 3062.

8—Meetings—Must Hold Regular.

329. Lodges under the immediate jurisdiction of the Supreme Lodge neglecting for three months to hold the regular stated meetings provided by law, without a proper Dispensation therefor, or unless prevented from doing so by some unforeseen circumstances, may be suspended or dissolved, or their Charters or Dispensations forfeited to the Supreme Lodge.

Jour., 1880, 1828, 2004.

9—Consolidation—May be Done.

330. Lodges in the same locality, under the jurisdiction of the Supreme Lodge, allowed to consolidate, upon such equitable terms as might be agreed upon at union meetings held for that purpose.

Jour., 1877, 1405, 1407.

NOTE.—The specifically defined rights and duties of Lodges and members, where the organizations are under the direct control of the Supreme Lodge, are contained in the Constitutions provided for them, and the foregoing only covers such matters as arose out of decisions of Supreme Chancellors, or questions brought to the Supreme Lodge through Deputies, Lodges or individual members.

LOTTERIES, GIFT ENTERPRISES, ETC.

331. No Grand Lodge, nor Subordinate Lodge of this Order, nor any individual member of any Lodge, shall, in the name of the Order, resort to, institute or promote any scheme of raffle, lotteries, gift enterprises, or schemes of chance of any kind. Any Grand Lodge violating this rule shall forfeit its charter to the Supreme Lodge. Any Subordinate Lodge violating this rule shall forfeit its Charter to its Grand Lodge. Any individual member of any Lodge who shall violate this rule shall be suspended from the Order.

Jour., 1876, 1231, 1232, 1264, 1299.

MAIMED PERSONS.

1. Initiation of—Permitted, by dispensation (332).
2. As Officers—Eligible (333).

1—Initiation of—Permitted, by Dispensation.

332. The discretion in regard to the initiation of maimed persons, which, by resolution at top of page 745, Journal of 1873, is allowed to Grand Lodges when in session, is now extended to Grand Chancellors during the recess.

Jour., 1876, 1235, 1285, 1286, 1294.

The resolution itself, which is as follows—

"*Resolved*, That the Laws of this Order do not require the suspension of a member who, after his initiation, has been maimed.

"*Resolved*, That this Supreme Lodge hereby authorize any Grand Lodge, in open session, to grant a Dispensation to any of its Subordinates to initiate a maimed person into the Order; Provided, that in no instance shall a Dispensation be granted to a person incapable of making an honest livelihood for himself and family"—

does not appear from the Journal to have been acted upon, till it was adopted (at least the last one) by reference in 1876, in the terms above stated.

2—As Officers—Eligible.

333. A member that is maimed by the loss of an arm or otherwise, is eligible to office in a Grand or Subordinate Lodge. All members in good standing of like rank and service, are entitled to the same privileges, benefits and emoluments, when received in full membership, and if elected to office, cannot be debarred from filling such office, because of being maimed.

Jour., 1877, 1372, 1427, 1428.

(7)

MAJOR GENERAL.

Qualifications Required, Appointment, Term, Prerogatives and Duties.

334. The Major General, at the time of his appointment, shall be a Past Grand Chancellor and a member of the Supreme Lodge and of the Uniform Rank, in good standing. He shall be appointed by the Supreme Chancellor, and shall hold his office for a term of four years from the date of appointment and until his successor shall have been duly appointed and installed.

Const., Art. III, Sec. 8.

335. It is the prerogative and duty of the Major General to have command and a watchful supervision over all the Brigades and Divisions, regimental and subordinate, within the jurisdiction of the Supreme Lodge Knights of Pythias of the World, and see that all the constitutional enactments, laws and edicts of the Supreme Lodge are duly and promptly observed, and that the work and discipline of the Uniform Rank everywhere are uniform throughout the Jurisdiction of the Supreme Lodge, and that the dress is uniform, unless otherwise ordered by the Supreme Lodge.

Const., Art. III, Sec. 8.

336. Among his special duties and prerogatives are the following:

To appoint the members of his individual staff. To visit and preside in and over Brigades or Divisions, regimental or subordinate, and give such instructions or directions as the good of the Order may require, always adhering to the Constitution, statutes and edicts of the Supreme Lodge; and upon the general assembling of the Uniform Rank Knights of Pythias, he shall, when present, take command.

Const., Art. III, Sec. 8.

337. To examine, in conjunction with the Supreme Chancellor, all laws enacted by any Brigade, regimental or subordinate Division, which, upon being confirmed by the Supreme Chancellor and Major General, shall be the laws governing the respective Grand Jurisdictions.

Const., Art. III, Sec 8.

338. He shall keep a register, which shall contain a full and complete list of all warrants issued and Divisions instituted, giving numbers and dates of each, and at each session of the Supreme Lodge shall present a full and complete report of all the transactions of his office, and of the general condition of the Uniform Rank.

Const., Art. III, Sec. 8.

339. He shall have power to provide himself, at the expense of the Supreme Lodge, with such books, paper and stationery as are necessary for the proper discharge and fulfillment of his duties.

Const., Art. III, Sec. 8.

340. He shall submit his books and accounts for inspection by the Supreme Chancellor, the Trustees or Finance Committee of the Supreme Lodge, whenever required so to do.

Const., Art. III, Sec. 8.

341. He shall prepare the forms for all blanks to be furnished by the Supreme Keeper of Records and Seal.

Const., Art. III, Sec. 8.

342. He shall decide all tactical questions, and all questions connected with the general government and management of the Uniform Rank, subject, however, to appeal to the Supreme Chancellor and the Supreme Lodge.

Const., Art. III, Sec. 8.

343. He shall review all court martial proceedings in which the penalty is suspension or dishonorable discharge.

Const., Art. III, Sec. 8.

344. The countersign of the Uniform Rank shall be promulgated by the Supreme Chancellor to the Major General, and by him furnished to the Divisions.

Const., Art. III, Sec. 8.

345. He shall receive, for his services to the Uniform Rank, such compensation as the Supreme Lodge shall from time to time determine.

Const., Art. III, Sec. 8.

MEMBERSHIP.

1. **By Initiation**—Constitutional provisions (346, 347).
    - (a) **Investigating Committee**—Report of, local as to time (348); may not be questioned (349).
    - (b) **Ineligible Material**—Colored Persons (350, 351, 352, 353); Ladies (353); Minors (353); Chinamen (354); Indians (355); Persons unable to write (356); Person already a member of a Lodge (358).
    - (c) **Medical Certificate**—May be required (359); a matter for Subordinate Lodge (359).
    - (d) **Saloon Keepers**—Their admissibility (360).
    - (e) **In New Lodges**—Grand Lodges regulate as to all or any applicants being already members (361); but those who are members must present Withdrawal Cards (362).
    - (f) **Withdrawing Proposition**—May be done, by consent, before (363), but not after report (364, 365).
    - (g) **Fees**—Must be paid before admission (366).
    - (h) **Soliciting Candidates**—Disapproved (367).
    - (i) **Rejected Candidates**—After six months may reapply to same or other Lodge (368); but applying before, and concealing the facts, and being admitted, are members, subject to trial (369).
2. **By Withdrawal Card**—Constitutional provisions (370).
    - (j) **Membership Begins**—Grand Lodges regulate, on election or signing roster (371); not so providing, it begins on election (372).
    - (k) **Non-resident**—Must have permission of his Grand Chancellor (373).
    - (l) **Irregular Admission**—On documents other than of legal form (374, 375); without proper delay (376); both being error by the Lodge, not the member, membership not disturbed.
    - (m) **Readmission**—Lodge may refuse (377).
    - (n) **Reapplication**—May be made immediately, if local law does not preclude (378).
    - (o) **Pages and Esquires**—Membership of, transferred by Card (379, 380).
3. **Suspension for Non-payment of Dues**—Brothers under, cease to be members of the Order (381); the action suspending them may be revoked for purpose of trial (382); their status and application for reinstatement, matters for local legislation (383, 384).
4. **Pages and Esquires**—Not advancing, may be dropped, under local law: the manner of their reinstatement is also subject to local law (385, 386).
5. **Change of Name**—Member may change name and have it recorded (387).
6. **In Revived Lodge**—Status of membership in, same as when Lodge surrendered (388, 389).
7. **In Defunct Grand Lodge**—Under control of recognized new Grand Lodge (390).

1—By Initiation—Constitutional Provisions.

346. Applications for initiation must be signed by the petitioner, stating his age, residence and occupation, and indorsed by two Knights in good standing, who are members of the Lodge, which must be entered on the records, and the petition referred to a committee of three for investigation (neither of whom shall have recommended him), whose duty

Membership. 93

it shall be to report on the character and qualifications of the petitioner at a subsequent regular meeting, except a Dispensation has been granted permitting it at the same meeting. The applicant shall then be balloted for by secret ball ballot, and if approved, he may be admitted. (Obligatory.)

Const., Art. VIII, Sec. 2, Sub. i.

347. No person shall be initiated into a Lodge of this Order who has not reached the legal age of majority in the country where the Lodge is located, nor unless he be a white male, of good moral character, sound in health and a believer in a Supreme Being, nor unless he has been a resident of the Grand Jurisdiction in which he makes application for at least six months next preceding. (Obligatory.)

Const., Art. VIII, Sec. 2, Sub. h.

(*a*)—Investigating Committees—Report of, Local, as to Time—May Not be Questioned.

348. The question as to whether or not, upon an application for initiation being received by a Lodge, one week must elapse between the appointing of the investigating committee and the acceptance of the report of said committee by the Lodge, was declared to be a matter for local legislation.

Jour., 1890, 4844, 5319, 5336.

349. The members of an investigating committee are not required to state their reasons for a favorable or unfavorable report, on an application. Their functions are *quasi* judicial, and they cannot be questioned as to their conclusions as to the character of an applicant.

Jour., 1886, 3286, 3525, Errata, page i.

(*b*)—Ineligible Material—Colored Persons—Ladies—Minors—Chinamen—Indians—Persons Unable to Write—Person Already a Member of a Lodge.

350. This Supreme Lodge has never recognized any body of colored persons as a Lodge, or as members of the Order of Knights of Pythias; but on the contrary has repeatedly and persistently refused to recognize any such persons as having any connection whatever with this Order.

Jour., 1869, 86, 96.
1871, 379, 382, 383.
1878, 1628.
1888, 4109, 4110, 4534.

351. The so-called Lodges styling themselves "Knights of Pythias," composed of colored persons, or of which colored persons are members, exist without any authority or recognition from this Supreme Lodge or from any Grand Lodge.

Jour., *1888*, *4109*, *4110*, *4534*.

352. The Constitution of our Order provides that, to become a member of the Order, the applicant *must* be a *white* person. It is made mandatory by the Supreme Lodge Constitution that this provision be contained in every Subordinate Lodge Constitution, and no Subordinate Lodge exists without the same being therein incorporated. Any Lodge violating this provision of law subjects itself to suspension; and if any colored person has ever obtained membership in this Order, he obtained it under the false representation of being a *white* person, and, upon being discovered to be a colored person, must be expelled from the Order.

Jour., *1888*, *4109*, *4110*, *4534*.

353. The Supreme Lodge does not recognize Lodges of the Order composed of ladies, persons under age, or colored persons; and the Supreme Chancellor is authorized to make such public declaration or publication of this fact as may in his judgment be necessary to prevent deception or imposition.

Jour., *1871*, *382*.

354. A Chinaman, though a naturalized citizen, a member of a church, and a believer in a Supreme Being, is not eligible to membership in the Order—he is not a Caucasian.

Jour., *1886*, *3285*, *3525*, *Errata*, *page i*.

355. The applicant herewith described was declared ineligible to membership in the Order. His grandmother was an Indian, her husband was a white man, their son married a white woman, their son is the present applicant for membership.

Jour., *1890*, *4845*, *5319*, *5337*.

356. Persons who cannot write are ineligible for membership in the Order.

Jour., *1870*, *177*, *204*, *229*.
1873, *Appendix 35*.

357. If a candidate can write his name he is entitled to advance.

Jour., *1873*, *687*, *768*.

358. A person cannot be a member of two Lodges at one time.

Jour., *1873*, *Appendix 37*.

(c)—Medical Certificate—May be Required—A Matter for Subordinate Lodge.

359. A Subordinate Lodge can require from an applicant (for membership) a physician's certificate as to the state of his health at the time of his application.

Jour., *1886, 3286, 3521, 3525, 3527, 3555.*

(d)—Saloon Keepers—Their Admissibility.

360. In 1888 (Journal, Document 61, pages 4507, 4508) the following resolutions were offered, and referred to the Committee on State of the Order:

Resolved, That all persons engaged in the business of retailing intoxicating liquors, and generally known as saloon keepers, and their employes, generally known as bar tenders, etc., are hereby declared to be not of "good moral character," as contemplated by the Constitution, by reason of such occupation; and be it further

Resolved, That persons so occupied are hereby declared ineligible to membership in the Order while engaged in such business, and it shall be unlawful for any Subordinate Lodge to admit any such person to membership therein; and be it further

Resolved, That all Subordinate Lodges shall suspend or expel from membership therein all who shall engage in the pursuit herein defined, who shall, upon reasonable notice from the Lodge, refuse to abandon such business.

On pages 4531, 4532 the Committee on the State of the Order made a report, which was adopted, and of which the following is a part:

The Committee on the State of the Order, to whom was referred Document 61, report that it is the judgment of the committee that the law as it now exists, which, in our opinion, leaves the question of the qualifications of applicants for admission to our Order to the Subordinate Lodges, is upon the whole the best and possibly the only practicable course to be maintained by an Order like ours.

In the opinion of your committee, it is far better to leave the question of the fitness of an applicant for admission to our Order to the best judgment and determination of the Subordinate Lodges, subject to the provisions and limitations of existing law, as they are satisfied that there can be no better arbitrators of the qualifications of one applying for membership than those among whom he lives and moves; and it is the judgment of the committee that it is ill-advised to add any absolute and positive prohibition of any class of our fellow-citizens, except as now provided.

Subsequent to this action, the Grand Lodge of Indiana adopted an amendment to their Constitution, excluding persons engaged in the liquor traffic, which, it appears, on presentation to the Committee on Law, was by them disapproved.

At the session of the Supreme Lodge, in 1890, it appears from the record, page 5334, Document 118, that Supreme Representative Shiveley, of Indiana, offered the following, which was adopted:

Resolved, That the Committee on Law and Supervision be required to report to this session of the Supreme Lodge its decision in which it disapproved an amendment made and submitted to that committee by the Grand Jurisdiction of Indiana to her Constitution, in which that

Jurisdiction prohibited any person from becoming a member of the Order who is engaged in the sale or traffic of intoxicating liquors.

On the above resolution, the Committee on Law reported, Document 247, page 5448, that not having kept any record of their action, none being required by law, it was impossible for them to comply with the requirements thereof.

Pending action on their report, Supreme Representative Shiveley offered the following resolutions:

1. *Resolved*, That the decision of the Committee on Law and Supervision, in which it decides that an amendment of the Constitution of the Grand Jurisdiction of Indiana, prohibiting any person engaged in the sale and traffic of intoxicating liquor from joining the Order in that Jurisdiction, is unconstitutional and void, be not concurred in by this Supreme Lodge; and be it further

2. *Resolved*, That said subject is a matter of local legislation for the several Grand Lodges.

And it appears, by the record, that "the Acting Supreme Chancellor ruled that *the first resolution was not in order.*"

A vote was then taken *on the second resolution*, and it was defeated, by a vote of: Yeas 42, nays 44. (See pages 5448, 5449.)

The Supreme Chancellor having ruled out the *first resolution* and the Body having defeated the *second resolution*, the record then shows that (page 5449):

The question then recurred on the adoption of the report of the Committee (Document 247), which was rejected by a vote of 32 to 34.

Subsequently, a motion to reconsider the action rejecting the *second resolution*, was adopted, by a vote of: Yeas 50, nays 40, and on a motion to adopt the *second resolution*, the same was adopted: Yeas 56, nays 34. (See pages 5449, 5450, 5451.)

NOTE.--The compiler is, in view of the peculiar status of the question, compelled to give the entire legislation had, and has given the exact record. That in 1888 the Supreme Lodge refused to adopt a general law proscribing the admission of persons engaged in the liquor traffic, and gave the absolute right of judgment, in this connection, to Subordinate Lodges, goes without question, but whether, taking the record as it stands, the legislation of 1890 disturbed this right and gave it over to Grand Jurisdictions, is at best doubtful. The introduction of the last two resolutions by Supreme Representative Shiveley, and their admission *at that stage of the proceedings*, made the "first resolution" the substantive proposition; this "the Acting Supreme Chancellor ruled out of order," and it then ceased to exist. The Supreme Lodge then proceeded to and rejected the "second resolution" which, by the decision of the Chair, had no premises, and as if to add to this, after the rejection of the "second resolution," the Supreme Lodge, instead of "recommitting with instructions," rejected the report of the Committee on Law, thereby carrying with it the whole proposition originally offered by Supreme Representative Shiveley, on page 5334. After thus completely destroying every vestige of the documents which described the subject under consideration, to wit: The liquor traffic, *without reviving either of the substantive propositions*, the Supreme Lodge reconsidered the action rejecting the "*second resolution*," and adopted it, and it alone. Under these conditions the compiler was forced to give the entire record and leave its construction to the reader.

Jour., *1888, 4507, 4508, 4531, 4532.*
1890, 5334, 5448, 5451.

(*e*)—In New Lodges—Grand Lodges Regulate as to Any or All being Already Members, but Those Who Are Members must Present Withdrawal Cards.

361. Grand Lodges have a right to legislate whether or not, at the institution of new Lodges, all or any of the applicants shall be members of the Order.

Jour., 1873, Appendix 37.

362. Any member of the Order desiring to assist in the formation of a new Lodge, and signing an application for such purpose, must, upon the institution of such Lodge, present his Withdrawal Card from his Lodge.

Jour., 1870, 225.

(*f*)—Withdrawing Proposition—May be Done before, but Not after Reference.

363. No proposition for membership shall be withdrawn unless by consent of the Lodge, after it has been referred to a committee, and all cases so referred shall be balloted for upon the report of the committee, whether it be favorable or unfavorable. (Obligatory.)

Const., Art. VIII, Sec. 2, Sub. n.

364. An application for membership cannot be withdrawn at any time or stage after the report of the investigating committee.

Jour., 1886, 3521, 3554.

365. An application for membership cannot be withdrawn by unanimous consent after report of committee is read. A petition once submitted, read to the Lodge, referred to a committee, and reported upon by said committee, becomes Lodge property, cannot be withdrawn under any circumstances, but must go to ballot and take its chances.

Jour., 1873, Appendix 38.

(*g*)—Fees—Must be Paid before Admission.

366. No Rank shall be conferred under any pretense whatever, unless the same shall have been previously paid for. (Obligatory.)

Const., Art. VIII, Sec. 2, Sub. q.

(*h*)—Soliciting Candidates—Disapproved.

367. While in 1871 it was decided that great caution and discrimination should be exercised in the matter of soliciting candidates for membership in the Order, at a subsequent date the Supreme Chancellor, on the authority of the preceding action, ruled that members of the Order are not permitted to solicit citizens to join.

Jour., 1871, 401, 413;
1873, Appendix 39.

(*i*)—Rejected Candidates—After Six Months, may Reapply, to Same or Other Lodge, but Applying before, and Concealing the Facts, and being Admitted, are Members, Subject to Trial.

368. Under a proper construction of the law, as it now stands, a person, whose application for initiation has been rejected, and after the expiration of six months desires to again apply for initiation, is not restricted to the Lodge which rejected him, but may apply to any Lodge he desires; Provided, that if he makes application to a Lodge other than the one nearest his residence, he must comply with local laws permitting such application.

Jour., *1888*, *4126*, *4655*, *4656*.

369. A person who makes application for membership in a Lodge and is rejected, and who subsequently applies to another Lodge, concealing the fact of his former rejection, and is admitted to membership, must be regarded as a member of the Order until he is regularly tried and the proper penalty imposed.

Jour., *1884*, *2777*, *2988*.

NOTE.—This rule was made before the law of 1888 (Section 368), and at a time when general custom and usage gave the rejecting Lodge exclusive jurisdiction, hence the gravity of the offense under Section 369 would be somewhat mitigated in view of the provisions of Section 368.

2—By Withdrawal Card—Constitutional Provisions.

370. Any brother of the Order, in good standing, desirous of becoming a member of a Lodge, shall make application as in the case of an unitiated person, and accompany same with his Withdrawal Card from the Lodge of which he was last a member, or the Card granted by the Supreme or Grand Lodge in lieu thereof, which shall be referred to a committee of three, whose duty it shall be to report as to the standing and qualifications of the applicant at a regular meeting. The brother shall then be balloted for by a secret ball ballot, as in the case of an initiate. (Obligatory).

Const., Art. VIII, Sec. 2, Sub. m.

(*j*)—Membership Begins—Grand Lodges Regulate—On Election, or Signing Roster—Not So Providing, It Begins on Election.

371. It is the prerogative of each Grand Lodge, by legislation, to define when a brother, who deposits his *Card* in a Lodge, becomes a *member* of the same; upon his *election*, or upon his *signing* the *roster*.

Jour., *1878*, *1611*, *1650*.

372. When a person makes application for membership by Card and is elected, the Card passes into the possession of the Lodge receiving the application, and cannot either be withdrawn by him or returned by them; the membership under such circumstances cannot be undone;

the simple act of appearing in the Lodge room within the specified time cannot operate as against his right at any time to complete his membership by signing the roster, if the local laws of the Jurisdiction so require; if no provision of that character exists, then upon his election to membership he at once become a member, and it is not necessary for him to appear in person in order to complete it.

Jour., 1888, 3994.

(k)—Non-Resident—Must have Permission of His Grand Chancellor.

373. In 1878, the Supreme Chancellor asked the following question:

Can a brother holding a Withdrawal Card, and residing in one State or Jurisdiction, deposit his Card in a Lodge of another State or Jurisdiction, especially if there are Lodges in the immediate vicinity of his residence?

And the subject being referred to a committee, the Supreme Lodge decided:

As the Constitution of the Supreme Lodge (Article VIII. Section 2, Subdivision *m*) requires an application for membership by deposit of card, to be made "as in the case of an initiated person," under said clause, and Subdivision *o* of the same Section and Article, said question should be answered; that the deposit of Card could not be made in the case cited "without the written consent of the Grand Chancellor of such Grand Jurisdiction."

Jour., 1878, 1508, 1608.

NOTE.—The above was rendered when the "consent of the Lodge nearest his residence" was required, but as the application of the latter subdivision was predicated upon the former, in which no change has been made in the feature stated, and as the character of "consent" is only changed, this ruling applies now with equal force.

(l)—Irregular Admission—On Documents Other than of Legal Form—Without Proper Delay—Both Being an Error by the Lodge, Not the Member, Membership Not Disturbed.

374. On an appeal the following facts appeared:

The appellant applied for a Withdrawal Card, which was granted—the Lodge had no Cards on hand, and in place of a regular Withdrawal Card issued a certificate over seal; the Grand Chancellor accepted this certificate in connection with the application for the organization of a new Lodge—the new Lodge was formed—the appellant became first Chancellor Commander, and during a lengthened period occupied various offices. Three years after, the question was raised in his Lodge as to his good standing, it being urged that he was not then, and, indeed, had not been, a member of the Lodge, which position was sustained by the Grand Lodge of New Jersey. Upon the appeal to the Supreme Lodge, it was, in view of the facts in the case—that he not having a Card in regular form was no fault of his; that, from testimony, he originated the new Lodge, and acted with it, bearing his portion of all its burdens until quite recently; that no charges had been preferred against him; that all concerned were, at the time, and have ever since been, acting in good faith: *Resolved*, that the appellant was a Past Chancellor and a member in good standing of said Lodge.

Jour., *1876*, *1305*, *1306*.

NOTE.—While this would establish the general principle that a Lodge has no right to take advantage of its own error to the detriment of an innocent party, yet it should not be accepted as in any way countenancing, directly or indirectly, the right on the part of a Lodge to the issuance of any other than the prescribed card. If they have none on hand, that is their own fault—they should always be provided with them.

375. A Lodge accepted a proposition of a brother to become a member on Card, which Card, from some cause, he did not have in his possession. The brother in lieu thereof, deposited an official receipt that contained an acknowledgment of the payment of the Card. Upon the above showing, the Lodge accepted the proposition, and the candidate was balloted for and elected.

Two weeks after this the District Deputy Grand Chancellor annulled the whole procedure, declaring the brother was not a member. The Lodge accepted the annulling, received a second application, professing to come from the brother, which went through the regular course, and the candidate was rejected.

Appeal was taken to the Grand Lodge, which sustained the action of the District Deputy Grand Chancellor, from which action of the Grand Lodge, appeal was taken to the Supreme Lodge.

On this statement of facts the Supreme Lodge decided:

First—A Grand Lodge has not the power to annul the action of a Subordinate Lodge without trial.

Second—A brother should not be held responsible for the illegal action of a Lodge.

Third—A brother admitted to membership in good faith cannot be expelled or suspended, unless by due process of law, according to the Constitution and By-Laws.

Fourth—The District Deputy Grand Chancellor transcended his power in annulling the action of the Lodge, and the error was not made right by the action of the Grand Lodge.

Jour., *1878*, *1558*, *1625*, *1626*.

376. A Lodge received a Card from a brother, and at the same meeting when the Card was deposited immediately acted upon the same without the legal delay of one week; it was decided that though said action was illegal and erroneous, a member so admitted is in good standing in the Lodge thus accepting his membership, and entitled to all its privileges and benefits; that he is not responsible for the erroneous action of the Lodge in admitting him. The Lodge cannot take advantage of its own wrong. Once admitted to membership a brother cannot be deprived of the rights thereof except by suspension or expulsion by trial according to the Constitution and Laws of the Order.

Jour., *1890*, *5410*, *5464*.

(*m*)—Readmission—Lodge may Refuse.

377. A Lodge may refuse to readmit to membership one to whom it had granted a Withdrawal Card, and in such case the Grand Lodge cannot compel the Lodge to do so.

Jour., 1886, 3517, 3525, Errata, page i.

(*n*)—Reapplication—May be Made Immediately, if Local Law does Not Preclude.

378. A brother holding a Withdrawal Card in force, who applies to a Lodge for membership by said Card, and is rejected, may apply to any other Lodge, or in the absence of any local law, to the same Lodge at any time, but this is a subject for local legislation, and clearly within the province of Grand Lodges to so legislate as to determine the probationary period of such applicants within their respective Jurisdictions, not to exceed six months after rejection.

Jour., 1876, 1228, 1296.
1888, 3993, 3994, 4544, 4573.

(*o*)—Pages and Esquires—Membership of, Transferred by Card.

379. A Page initiated, and made such in a Subordinate Lodge, changing his residence and desiring to become a member of a Lodge in a distant part of the same Jurisdiction, must obtain a Withdrawal Card from the Lodge that conferred the Rank of Page upon him, with his Ranks stated upon it, and present it for the consideration of the Lodge which he desires to become a member of.

Jour., 1890, 4844, 5319, 5336.

380. The transfer of membership of Pages and Esquires from one Lodge to another is only by Withdrawal Card, the same as with Knights, their Rank being stated in the Card.

Jour., 1878, 1508, 1607.

3—Suspension for Non-payment of Dues—Brothers under, Cease to be Members of the Order—The Action Suspending Them may be Revoked for Purpose of Trial—Their Status and Application for Reinstatement, Matters for Local Legislation.

381. A brother suspended for non-payment of dues ceases to be a member of the Order until reinstated.

Jour., 1870, 225.

382. In the case of a Deputy Supreme Chancellor for Dakota, a Past Grand Chancellor in Nebraska, who was a defaulter to the

Supreme Lodge, but who had been suspended by his Lodge for non-payment of dues, the Supreme Lodge requested the Grand Lodge holding jurisdiction over the Lodge of which he had been a member, to require said Lodge to rescind their action suspending him for non-payment of dues, and that the said Lodge be requested to prefer charges against the said Past Grand Chancellor, for conduct unbecoming a true Knight.

Jour., 1877, 1362, 1425.

NOTE.—By this action the Supreme Lodge made the precedent that, for cause appearing, a Lodge could revoke the action suspending a member for non-payment of dues, and bring him within the jurisdiction of the Lodge for trial.

383. The Supreme Lodge refused to define by specific law or laws, the exact status of suspended brothers who had been suspended for more than twelve months for non-payment of dues, and others who might be suspended for any cause whatsoever; or the mode and manner by which they can again be admitted to the Order, and it was held that the entire question was "a matter of Grand Lodge legislation."

Jour., 1873, 690, 734.

NOTE.—Since this decision, the Supreme Lodge has modified it by providing for the manner of reinstatement after definite and indefinite suspension, for cause. See Sections 525, 526 of this Digest.

384. The question of the manner of application for reinstatement by one suspended for non-payment of dues, and the vote thereon, is a subject for local legislation.

Jour., 1874, 902, 909.
1888, 4126, 4655, 4656, 4665, 4666.

4—Pages and Esquires—Not Advancing, may be Dropped, under Local Law—The Manner of Their Reinstatement Is Also Subject to Local Law.

385. The question of how Pages and Esquires who, for failure to advance, have been dropped from the roster, may regain membership, was declared to be a matter for local legislation.

Jour., 1890, 5446.

386. Grand Lodges may so legislate as to permit their Subordinates to drop from the roster the names of those members who have been Pages or Esquires for more than one year without applying for advancement.

Jour., 1886, 3711, 3725.
1888, 4125, 4655, 4656.

5—Change of Name—Member may Change Name and Have It Recorded.

387. A person who in good faith joins a Lodge under a name which he had been bearing for years, but which, for cause, had been an assumed one, may resume his real name, and have the same entered upon the roster in place of the name under which he joined—always provided that he comply with the local, State and Territorial laws made and provided in such cases. A person desiring to change his name, and doing so in the way made and provided by the laws of the State and Territory in which he resides, may ask and have the change made and recorded in his Lodge; and this being so done, he shall henceforth be entitled to be so known in his Lodge or Grand Lodge.

Jour., *1888, 4124, 4580, 4581.*

6—In Revived Lodge—Status of Membership in, Same as When Lodge Surrendered.

388. In the case of the reorganization of a Lodge all members are revived with it, and their standing in that Lodge is the same as existed at the time of its having been suspended or become defunct: Provided, however, that this would apply only to those who had not received Withdrawal Cards.

Jour., *1878, 1618.*
1888, 4121, 4574, 4576.

NOTE.—This ruling of Supreme Chancellor Douglass was approved by the committee. and action, for some cause not stated, deferred till later in the session, but was not called up. It stands unreversed.

389. The face of the record showing that a brother had applied for and been granted a Withdrawal Card previous to the suspension of his Lodge, the brother was declared not to be a member of that Lodge upon its revival, notwithstanding that he denied having applied for a Card, as stated, and in reviewing the case, the Supreme Lodge held, in referring to the record:

There is nothing to show that he took any steps to correct it, or gave the Lodge an opportunity to correct it. He has not appealed from any action of the Lodge, that until he does so, and thus lays a foundation for an appeal, he has no grievances entitled to consideration.

Jour., *1886, 3509, 3683, 3684.*

7—In Defunct Grand Lodge—Under Control of Recognized New Grand Lodge.

390. Where a Grand Lodge had been suspended and a new Grand Lodge formed and recognized by the Supreme Lodge, it was decided that the status of the members of the suspended Grand Lodge and the manner of their reinstatement was under the control of the Grand Lodge that had been so recognized.

Jour., *1871, 428.*

MEMORIAL DAY.

391. It is hereby enacted that the Tuesday following the second Sunday in June of each year be and is hereby set apart as the Memorial Day of the Order of Knights of Pythias; and that the Subordinate Lodges of the Order are hereby authorized and earnestly requested to meet in their respective localities upon said day in each year, whenever the same is practicable and convenient, for the purpose of decorating the graves of our departed brethren, and for the purpose of engaging in such services and exercises as may be in harmony and appropriate to the day and the occasion.

And be it further enacted, that whenever a Subordinate Lodge shall elect to perform such services upon a different day, they may select any day of each year that the climate and circumstances make most desirable.

Jour., *1888*, *4532*, *4533*, *4598*.
1890, *5251*, *5303*, *5329*, *5372*,
5424, *5425*, *5465*.

NOTE.—By the action taken in 1886, pages 3757, 3758, in making selection of a "Memorial Day," Lodges were precluded from naming Sunday.

392. A service for use on Memorial Day, presented by the Grand Lodge of Iowa, was adopted, and the Supreme Keeper of Records and Seal directed to have the same printed, to be furnished to Grand Jurisdictions for use in Subordinate Lodges.

Jour., *1890*, *4862*, *5245*, *5323*, *5395*.

MEMORIAL SERVICE.

393. A memorial service for use in Subordinate Lodges was adopted in 1884, and five copies of same ordered distributed to each Subordinate Lodge then in existence. It is now on the list of supplies sold by the Supreme Lodge.

Jour., *1884*, *2947*, *3021*, *3027*.
1886, *3557*.

NOTE.—This "Service" must not be confounded with that for Memorial Day, this being for services in the Lodge.

MILEAGE AND PER DIEM.

394. The Supreme Lodge shall pay the mileage and ecessary expenses of its Officers, Representatives and Past upreme Chancellors by service, and the necessary time conmed in traveling to and from the sessions, unless otherwise provided for. The mileage shall be at the rate of four cents per mile, by the nearest practicable route, and the per diem four dollars.

Const., Art. XI.

395. No Supreme Lodge Officer or Representative is entitled to receive mileage and expenses unless he is present at the close of the session, or is excused by the Supreme Chancellor.

Jour., 1869, 94.

396. No Supreme Lodge Representative, elected to office therein, shall receive mileage, etc., for both offices.

Jour., 1870, 221.

NAME.

1. Of the Order—Use of forbidden, for business (397, 398, 399, 400, 401, 402).
2. Of Living Persons—Use of by Lodges, forbidden (403).

1—Of the Order—Use of Forbidden, for Business.

397. No member of the Order has the right to make use of the name of the Order publicly in any manner for pecuniary benefit, except in advertising periodicals, supplies or regalia for the Order.

Jour., 1870, 229.

398. The Committee on Law and Supervision being directed to inquire "by what authority parties are using the name of the Order of Knights of Pythias, without the permission of this Supreme Lodge," reported, that if any one has been guilty of such a practice, he has acted wholly without authority, and should be brought to justice by the Supreme Chancellor, in the name of the Supreme Lodge.

Jour., 1884, 2989.

399. Benefit or Insurance Associations of members of the Order, other than the regularly established Endowment Rank of the Order, will work injuriously to the Endowment Rank, and the organization of any such association is prohibited.

Jour., 1886, 3730.

(8)

400. Under the action of the Supreme Lodge (Document 320, page 3730, 1886), any organizations claiming to be acting under the name of the Order of Knights of Pythias, and which provide for a death benefit, are illegal if organized since the legislation referred to.

Jour., *1888*, *4121*, *4503-4506*, *4550*, *4556*, *4574*, *4575*, *4653*, *4654*.

NOTE.—This decision was made in regard to a Maryland Association, which organization then presented their case to the Supreme Lodge. The committee reported sustaining this decision, but action was deferred, pending action on the claim of the Association. The Supreme Lodge decided against the Association, but failed to pass on the decision. It stands unreversed.

401. A document was presented in 1888 which, by those presenting it, was stated to be:

By-Laws of a proposed plan to increase the death benefits in the Lodges of that State, which they desire to submit, in order to ascertain if any of the sections are in conflict with Supreme Lodge Law.

The first Article of this document specifically set forth the objects, as follows:

This organization shall be known as the "Knights of Pythias of Maryland Death Benefit Fund," its purpose being to provide, at a moderate rate, for the widows, orphans or legal heirs of deceased members an additional or larger amount than now paid by the Lodges. And the qualifications for membership in this organization are, that he shall be a member of some Subordinate Lodge, in good normal health; and shall, of his own volition, make the application as hereafter provided. This organization shall be under the control of the Grand Lodge Knights of Pythias of Maryland.

The Supreme Lodge received and considered this document, and the following ruling was made thereon:

The papers and By-Laws submitted provide for the establishment of such an association as is prohibited by legislation of the session of 1886, Document No. 320.

Jour., *1888*, *4503-4506*, *4550*, *4653*, *4654*.

402. This Supreme Lodge does hereby again declare that any use by members of this Order of the words "Knights of Pythias" or "Pythian," or of words, names, language, emblem or device, germane thereto, in connection with any life insurance or endowment association or society other than by the Endowment Rank, is contrary to the jurisprudence established by this Supreme Lodge and to the laws governing the Order of Knights of Pythias; that it having come to the knowledge of this body, that members of the Order in some of the Grand Jurisdictions are connected with such organizations, this Supreme Lodge, having entire confidence and faith in the loyalty of such Knights to the Supreme law of the Order, and not believing that any true and worthy Knight of Pythias will knowingly and willingly evade the laws of this Order or the judgment and decision of this Supreme Lodge, or refuse to comply therewith, this Supreme Lodge only considers it necessary at this time to call to the attention of the members of the Order, belonging to, or connected with such associations or societies, the jurisprudence and law governing this Order as above recited, and to declare that every member of the Order in any way connected with such associations or societies should sever connection therewith without delay, unless such associations or societies shall, within a reasonable time, not to exceed one year, conform their charters, constitution and laws to the letter and spirit of the laws and jurisprudence of the Order, as enacted and interpreted by this Supreme Lodge, and all Grand and Subordinate Lodges are hereby prohibited from assisting, encouraging, approving, endorsing, supervising or managing any such organizations.

Jour., 1890, 4838, 4839, 5386, 5416, 5417, 5418, 5421, 5422, 5447, 5461, 5462, 5463.

NOTE.--The existence of unauthorized societies using the name of the Order in the furtherance of their business in opposition to the Endowment Rank, being brought to the notice of the Supreme Lodge, and the matter being referred to a committee, they recited previous legislation, and reported:

In view of the above legislation, the committee recommend that the Supreme Lodge at this session so legislate as to *prohibit* any and all insurance organizations from doing business under the name of the Order of Knights of Pythias, or any derivative of that term, except the duly organized Endowment Rank of the Order as adopted by the Supreme Lodge;

Which was adopted, and in consonance with that action at a subsequent period in the session the foregoing was enacted.

2.—Of Living Persons—Use of, by Lodges, Forbidden.

403. State Jurisdictions are prohibited from naming Lodges after living persons.

Jour., 1869, 85, 95.

NOMINATIONS.

404. Nominations for the elective officers may be made on the night preceding and on the night of election. (Obligatory.)

Const., Art. VIII, Sec. 2, Sub. e.

405. Section 2, Subdivision *e*, of Article VIII of the Supreme Lodge Constitution, which provides:
"Nominations for the elective officers of a Subordinate Lodge may be made on thè night preceding and on the night of election," authorizes independent nominations on the night of election, and not merely the confirmation of those previously made.

Jour., 1875, 1131, 1139, 1140.

OFFENSES.

1. **What Constitute**—Blasphemy (406); giving untrue answers preceding initiation, except where there was no criminal intent (407); drawing benefits illegally, except where no fraud existed (408).
2. **Not Offenses**—Private debt (409); refusing to advance (410); professional advice during convalescence (411).
3. **Disclosing Vote for Membership**—Local law determines if it is an offense (412).

1—What Constitute—Blasphemy—Giving Untrue Answers preceding Initiation, except Where There Was No Criminal Intent—Drawing Benefits Illegally, except Where No Fraud Existed.

406. In reply to the question, "Is cursing God an offense against the Order," the answer was, Yes. It is not only an offense against the Order, but against society.

Jour., 1888, 4120, 4575, 4581.

407. On an appeal from the action of the Grand Lodge of New Jersey, it appeared that the plaintiff was suspended for a period of five years by his Lodge, on the grounds of not giving true answers to the questions propounded at the time of initiation, and which finding was approved by the Grand Lodge. The evidence in this case was of a conflicting character, and the committee being unable to detect any criminal intent on the part of the appellant, the appeal was sustained.

Jour., 1874, 938.

408. A brother is not guilty of any Pythian offense by merely claiming benefits to which he may not be entitled, except it be shown that he knew he was not entitled to them, and made the claim with intent to defraud the Lodge.

Jour., 1886, 3524, 3684.

2—Not Offenses—Private Debt—Refusing to Advance—Professional Advice during Convalescence.

409. It is not an offense against the Order for a brother of the organization to obtain credit from any other brother and then fail to pay his debt; Lodges cannot be made collection agencies; matters of account are subjects for consideration of courts and not Lodges; if there is attached to this any positive evidence of fraud, the party aggrieved could proceed on the ground of fraud, but cannot bring charges simply for the failure to discharge a debt.

Jour., 1888, 4005.

410. Charges cannot be preferred against a member who, having received the ranks of Page and Esquire, proceeds through a portion of the Knight's Rank, and refuses to proceed any farther with that rank. The Esquire is, however, not entitled to any benefits, privileges or honors of the Knight's Rank.

Jour., 1875, 1133, 1140.

411. In a case of appeal it appeared that the charges against accused were to the effect that while receiving sick benefits from his Lodge, he professionally examined and prescribed for two patients and received from them a fee, all of which he concealed from his Lodge, and thereby defrauded the same. The Subordinate Lodge found him guilty, and suspended him. On appeal to the Grand Lodge this judgment of the Subordinate Lodge was reversed, and on appeal to the Supreme Lodge it approved the action of the Grand Lodge and the language of its Appeals Committee, as follows:

There is no statement in the charges that the accused was able to practice or did practice his profession while receiving sick benefits, except in so far as he made the two examinations above referred to. It does not follow because the accused was able to examine and prescribe for the two persons mentioned, that he was not disabled from practicing his profession or following some other business. Hence the charges do not state any offense against Pythian Law.

Jour., 1882, 2574.

3—Disclosing Vote for Membership—Local Law Determines if It Is an Offense.

412. The question whether or not it is lawful for one member of a Lodge to be allowed to disclose to another member of the Lodge or Order the name of a brother who may speak or vote against a candidate for membership, presents a matter for local legislation not proper for determination by the Supreme Lodge.

Jour., 1876, 1284, 1300.

OFFICIAL CHARTS.

1. Promulgation of (413); none others to be used (414); name changed (415).
2. Supplies—On the list of (416).
3. Signatures to—The officers of the respective bodies (417).

1—Promulgation of—None Others to be Used—Name Changed.

413. At its session in 1874 the Supreme Lodge adopted and provided for the issue of an Official Memorial Membership Chart and

Patent of the Order; prescribed the design, forms, specifications, regulations, distinctions, colors, arrangement of placing same, and also officially recommended its purchase by every member of the Order.

Jour., 1874, 980.

414. By this legislation the Supreme Lodge also withdrew, rescinded and annulled any and all official recognition theretofore given, any chart issued by individuals or concerns, and requested the different Grand Lodges to *order* their Subordinate Lodges to thereafter only use or attach their seals, either in impress or imprint, to none other than the Official Memorial Chart of the Order, as issued by the Supreme Chancellor.

Jour., 1874, 980.

415. At the session of 1886 the name was changed to "Official Chart."

Jour., 1886, 3689, 3690, 3691.

2—Supplies—On the List of.

416. The Official Memorial Chart and Patent of Membership is now furnished by the Supreme Keeper of Records and Seal to the Grand Keepers of Records and Seal, and through them to the several Subordinate Lodges in the same manner as all other supplies.

Jour., 1875, 1155.

3—Signatures to—The Officers of the Respective Bodies.

417. The "Official Charts" so changed as to have the Knights' Chart signed by the Subordinate Lodge Officers; the Past Chancellor's Chart, by the Grand Lodge Officers; and the Past Grand Chancellor's Chart, by the Supreme Lodge Officers.

Jour., 1886, 3321, 3322, 3689, 3691.

OFFICIAL DIGEST.

418. The Official Digest is a mere compilation of laws and decisions governing the Order, and it would be improper to repeal any part of the Official Digest. If a Representative desires to accomplish the end proposed, he should seek out the legislation, and decisions referred to in the Official Digest, and propose a resolution repealing such legislation.

Jour., 1880, 2034, 2037, 2038.

OFFICIAL ORDERS.

419. An official order from the Supreme Lodge or Grand Lodge to any Subordinate Lodge of the Order, and in the order as here given, takes precedence over *all* other business, and when notified of its being there—unless while working one of the sections of a rank, and should such be the case the Lodge must be brought to its proper working rank—the contents should be made known and acted upon *at once* prior to proceeding with any other business. Should the order be irregular, exceptional or even arbitrary the after course will be to obey it until remedied through the proper channels.

Jour., 1873, Appendix 35.

OFFICIAL ORGAN.

420. While the Supreme Lodge is pleased to encourage all reputable publications in the interest of the Order, it does not recognize any publication of whatever name, as its official organ.

Jour., 1870, 221.
1873. 721.
1888, 4494, 4636.

OFFICIAL RECEIPT.

1. Promulgation of (421); only legal evidence of payment (421, 422); its use obligatory (423).
2. Conclusive—As evidence of payment, in a general sense (424); not, as between Lodge and member (425).
3. Endorsement on—Changed to an order for S. A. P. W. (426).
4. Uniform Issue—Only authorized issue, by Supreme Keeper of Records and Seal (427).
5. Holder's Property—Lodge cannot retain after communicating password (428).

1—Promulgation of—Only Legal Evidence of Payment—Its Use Obligatory.

421. Much trouble and difficulty having from time to time occurred from the want of an authoritative receipt, which shall, upon its face, not only show the payment of all claims of the Lodge against a brother, but also be authoritative evidence to the Order throughout the World, not only of membership, but good standing in the Order, it was, in

1875, enacted by the Supreme Lodge that the Supreme Chancellor and the Supreme Keeper of Records and Seal issue receipts, which shall be furnished to all Grand and Subordinate Lodges; and that no receipt shall be authoritative or evidence of payment of dues, assessments or other claims of the Lodge against a member of a Subordinate Lodge, unless written upon such receipt, and bearing the seal of the Supreme Lodge; and that such receipt go into effect on and after July 1, 1875.

Jour., 1875, 1165.

422. Only the Official Receipt can be recognized as legal.

Jour., 1876, 1227, 1296.

423. The legislation by which the Official Receipt makes it obligatory on Lodges to issue the same upon the payment of dues is positive, and Lodges must not evade the law by giving to a member any other evidence of payment.

Jour., 1888, 4121, 4575, 4581.

2—Conclusive—As Evidence of Payment, in a General Sense—Not, as between Lodge and Member.

424. The Official Receipt is not only the "usual evidence of good standing," but conclusive evidence thereof.

Jour., 1876, 1227, 1296.

425. An Official Receipt, properly signed and under the seal of the Lodge, is *prima facie* evidence that the member has paid all the demands acknowledged in said receipt to have been paid by him; but as between the Lodge and the member, such receipt is not conclusive upon the Lodge, if, in point of fact, such demands, so acknowledged, have not been paid.

Jour., 1882, 2536, 2567.

3—Endorsement on—Changed to an Order for S. A. P. W.

426. The original endorsement, containing the legislative promulgation, on the Official Receipt, was changed, and in its place was put a blank order for the S. A. P. W.

Jour., 1886, 3680, 3690, 3691.

4—Uniform Issue—Only Authorized Issue by Supreme Keeper of Records and Seal.

427. The Supreme Keeper of Records and Seal has no right to issue Official Receipt, "with the Supreme Lodge seal and the order for the S. A. P. W. on the back, but with the face blank, that the Grand Keeper of Records and Seal might from time to time have the latter printed in such style as to conform to the local regulations of his Grand Jurisdiction." The "Official Receipt" is an official document of the Supreme Lodge, the form of which has been definitely fixed by that body, and it should be precisely the same in every Grand Jurisdiction.

Jour., 1888, 4136, 4584, 4653.

5—Holders' Property—Lodge cannot Retain after Communicating Password.

428. The Official Receipt is the property of the holder, and the fact that it bears an endorsement in the form of an order for the S. A. P. W. does not entitle the Lodge to which it is presented, for the purpose of obtaining the password, to retain it.

Jour., 1888, 4121, 4575, 4581.

PARAPHERNALIA.

1. Sale of, by Dealers—Regulated; certification of Grand Keeper of Records and Seal required (429, 430).
2. Exposure of—By members of the Order, an offense (431).

1—Sale of, by Dealers, Regulated—Certification of Grand Keeper of Records and Seal Required.

429. Subordinate Lodges are required to purchase all working paraphernalia used in conferring ranks through the Grand Keeper of Records and Seal of their Grand Jurisdiction; dealers in said paraphernalia receiving orders for the same through any other source are hereby requested to send the same to the Grand Keeper of Records and Seal of the Jurisdiction from which it came for endorsement before shipping the goods.

Jour., 1888, 4543, 4596. 4597.

NOTE.—The well understood purpose of this legislation was for the protection of the Order. It was not intended that a Grand Keeper of Records and Seal should in any respect control the sales of paraphernalia in his Jurisdiction, or interfere with dealers except to the extent of preventing the sale of paraphernalia to any but legally authorized parties. This legislation only covers the secret paraphernalia, and has no reference to anything else.

430. When it shall come to the knowledge of the Supreme Chancellor that any dealer in society goods, or other person, is disregarding the request of this body as to sales of paraphernalia, that officer is authorized to advertise the fact in such manner as he may deem proper, that said person is dealing clandestinely in Knights of Pythias paraphernalia, and also to forbid all members and Lodges of the Order to deal with said person.

Jour., 1890, 4861. 5405, 5426.

2—Exposure of, by Members of the Order, an Offense.

431. The exposure or sale of any part of the secret working properties of this Order by any person or persons members of this Order to any person or persons not members of the Order, is hereby declared an offense against the Order. The various Grand Chancellors and Deputy Supreme Chancellors are hereby ordered to take such action as will carry out the purpose of the resolution.

Jour., 1886, 3760.

PASSWORD.

1. **S. A. P. W.**—Issued (432, 434), and rescinded (432, 433), by Supreme Chancellor.

   (a) Use of—By whom and to whom given (435, 436, 438, 439); where used (437).
   (b) Arrears—How long in, disqualifies for, local legislation (440).
   (c) Possession of, Essential—None can remain in Lodge or ante-room without it (441, 442, 443, 444, 445).
   (d) Order for—Member, qualified, entitled to (446); limited to six months (447, 448); must be on back of Official Receipt (450,); exception (449).

2. Rank Password—Separate order must be presented for (451, 452); taken, from Lodge, visiting in a body, by Master-at-Arms, in ante-room (453).

3. Grand Lodge Password—Universal (454); changed annually (454); visiting Past Chancellors must have current word (455).

1—S. A. P. W.—Issued and Rescinded by Supreme Chancellor.

432. The Supreme Chancellor shall have exclusive right of creation and promulgation of all passwords—to rescind, call in and change the same, if circumstances require, or the exigencies of the case warrant.

Const., Art. XV.

433. The Supreme Chancellor can rescind the S. A. P. W. of a Grand Jurisdiction if the exigencies of the case demand it.

Jour., 1875, 1115, 1116.

434. The Supreme Chancellor is authorized to issue a universal S. A. P. W., which, in connection with the usual evidence of good standing, is sufficient to admit any brother into any Lodge of the Order.

Jour., 1868, 18, 55.
1869, 67, 101.
1875, 1103, 1106, 1144-1146.
1876, 1197.

(a)—**Use of—By Whom and to Whom Given—Where Used.**

435. The term password is communicated to Knights only.

Jour., 1870, 229.

436. Upon election to the Rank of Knight, the person receiving that rank is at once entitled to the semi-annual password, and cannot be compelled to pay his dues in advance before receiving the S. A. P.W.

Jour., 1888, 4120, 4121, 4575, 4581.

437. The S. A. P. W. cannot be used, given or taken in any rank but that of Knight, except it be in opening at the outer door, or in examining the Lodge preparatory to passing from the Page or Esquire Rank to that of Knight; yet the Lodge has—or its official head, the Chancellor Commander—the right to exact the S. A. P. W. whenever and wherever it deems the safety of the work requires, or any doubt exists as to propriety of proceeding without it, as an evidence of good standing in the Order, and privilege of attending, etc.; but it cannot exact from the Page or Esquire that which they are not in possession of, they not having been invested with it.

Jour., 1873, Appendix 38.

438. The Chancellor Commander is empowered to instruct the members of his Lodge in the S. A. P. W.; also, all members in or out of his Jurisdiction presenting an order for it, under seal of his Lodge, signed by the Chancellor Commander and attested by the Keeper of Records and Seal, and presenting the usual evidence of his good standing.

Jour., 1876, 1227, 1228, 1296.

439. A Chancellor Commander must require a visiting member presenting an order for the S. A. P. W. to show a receipt for dues before instructing him in the word. A receipt should always accompany an order for the S. A. P. W. Both the order and the Official Receipt must be signed and sealed. Only the Official Receipt can be recognized as legal. Care should be taken that the word is not given on a receipt that is out of date.

Jour., 1876, 1227, 1296.
1877, 1373, 1427, 1428.

(*b*)—Arrears—How Long in, Disqualifies for—Local Legislation.

440. The length of time a member may be arrears for dues before he can be deprived of the S. A. P. W., is a question subject to the legislation of State Grand Bodies so long as said Jurisdictions comply with the requirement of this Supreme Body by suspending members who are twelve months in arrears for dues.

Jour., 1872, 466, 468, 613, 614.
1875, 1121.

(*c*)—Possession of, Essential—None can Remain in Lodge or Ante-room without It.

441. The Lodge, or its officers, has the right, and it is their duty, to refuse admission to any one unless in possession of the S. A. P. W., as also the ante-rooms must be cleared of all who are without it, be they members or candidates, so that the Outer Guard has complete control of who enters, unless otherwise ordered by the Chancellor Commander.

Jour., 1873, Appendix 38.

442. A member cannot remain in the Lodge when opening, or when in session, if not in possession of the S. A. P. W., if not entitled to it by the payment of dues under the local laws; this decision has no reference to the time *when* they shall not be entitled to the S. A. P. W., as that is determined by local law. But *when* by such laws they are not entitled to it, and are not in possession of it, they cannot remain in a Lodge when opening or in session.

Jour., 1877, 1372, 1427, 1428.

443. No member or person can remain in the Lodge room without the S. A. P. W. If entitled to it under local law, he will receive it from the Chancellor Commander; and if he refuses to receive the word, he must retire, without regard to the advance payment of his account.

Jour., 1880, 1827, 2003.

444. It is the positive duty of the Outer Guard and Chancellor Commander to see that no visiting Knight can pass the outer door or remain in a Lodge room at any time during the conference of any rank without being in possession of the S. A. P. W.

Jour., 1888, 4558, 4635.

445. It is neither proper, legal nor ritualistic for the Outer Guard to admit through the outer door, or the Chancellor Commander to permit to remain in a Subordinate Lodge room during the conference of the Ranks of Page and Esquire, any visiting Knight who is not in possession of the S. A. P. W.

Jour., 1888, 4558, 4635.

(*d*)—Order for—Member, Qualified, Entitled to—Limited to Six Months—Must be on Back of Official Receipt—Exception.

446. Any member, whether resident or otherwise, has a right to ask for and receive an order for the S. A. P. W., providing he complies with the law in this connection.

Jour., 1888, 4122, 4578, 4579, 4581.

447. No officer of a Subordinate Lodge is authorized to give an order for the S. A. P. W. covering a longer period than six months.

Jour., 1888, 4558, 4574.

448. An order for the S. A. P. W. can be given for a period of six months from the date of the order, and no longer. Said order has full force and effect during the said six months.

Jour., 1890, 4844, 4845.

NOTE.—The Supreme Lodge failed to act on this decision of the Supreme Chancellor. It stands unreversed. It was to be considered in connection with Document 113 (see page 5337), but it never was called up.

449. While the Official Receipt provides on its back for an order for the S. A. P. W., a member in possession of the receipt without an order endorsed thereon would be entitled (should he call for it) to claim a properly certified order for the password; and a document of that character in conjunction with the Official Receipt, though not upon the back of it, would entitle him to receive the S. A. P. W. from the Lodge to which he presents it.

Jour., 1888, 4121, 4575, 4581.

450. No order for the S. A. P. W. shall be recognized unless it be upon the back of the Official Receipt; and Chancellor Commanders, before communicating the word, shall, in every instance, satisfy themselves by a thorough examination that the person presenting the order is the one whose name appears therein.

Jour., 1890, 5468.

NOTE.—Read separately, these last two sections would appear to conflict, but read together, they can be made to harmonize, as the separate order is only good in *conjunction with the receipt.*

2—Rank Password—Separate Order must be Presented for—Taken from Lodge, Visiting in a Body, by Master-at-Arms, in Ante-room.

451. It is not proper for a Chancellor Commander to instruct a visiting brother in the passwords of the several ranks, he being in possession of the S. A. P. W., unless such visiting brother should present a proper order therefor.

Jour., 1878, 1508, 1607.

452. If a brother presents a properly signed and sealed order for the S. A. P. W. to a Chancellor Commander and requests the Chancellor Commander to instruct him in the rank password also, it is not lawful for him to do so unless a properly signed order for the same is presented.

Jour., 1890, 4844, 5319, 5336.

453. It is competent for the Chancellor Commander to instruct the Master-at-Arms to receive the password in the ante-room after each of the visiting Knights have worked their way through the outer door; and a Lodge, as a body, can thus be admitted to the Castle Hall of a Lodge in session without the password being given by each individual member at the inner door.

Jour., 1874, 913, 935.

3—Grand Lodge Password—Universal—Changed Annually—Visiting Past Chancellors must have Current Word.

454. The password of the Grand Lodge is changed annually, and is uniform throughout the Order, and to emanate from the Supreme Lodge through the Supreme Chancellor.

Jour., 1869, 67, 101.
1878, 1564, 1566, 1616.
1880, 1986, 2061.

NOTE.—Nowhere does there appear to be any provision for the manner of the issuance of the Grand Lodge password, nor its communication to the members.

455. Past Chancellors visiting a Grand Lodge other than their own must be in possession of the Grand Lodge password for the current term, or a proper order for the same, in order to gain admission.

Jour., *1884, 3049, 3050.*

PAST CHANCELLOR.

1. Meritorious Services—Grand Lodges fully empowered to confer the rank for (456, 457, 458).
2. Sitting Past Chancellor—General definition of status of, a matter for local legislation (459).
   - (*a*) Officer of Lodge—So ruled, subject to fines, if imposed (460).
   - (*b*) Withdrawal of—Honors not lost by taking Card (461).
   - (*c*) Of New Lodge—Any member eligible (462, 464); serving, entitled to honors (462, 463).
   - (*d*) Of Lodge Already Organized—Only Past Chancellor eligible (465, 466).
3. Re-election as Chancellor Commander—Becomes, on second installation (467).
4. "In Full"—Not, until obligated and instructed (468).
5. Indebtedness—No bar to obtaining certificate as (469).
6. Lodge Record—Failure of, to evidence installation as Chancellor Commander, does not vacate right to rank, if service proved (470).
7. Surrender of Charter—Occurring prior to end of service, vacates honors (471).

1—Meritorious Services—Grand Lodges Fully Empowered to Confer the Rank for.

456. Whether or not the rank of Past Chancellor shall be conferred upon certain officers of a Subordinate Lodge, who have served a specified time, or upon any Knights who may be recommended to the Grand Lodge to receive the rank, or who may, in accordance with provisions of Subordinate Lodge Constitutions, be elected by Subordinate Lodges to receive from their Grand Lodge the rank of Past Chancellor, is a matter for local legislation.

Jour., *1870, 185, 199.*
1873, 699, 704, 710, 721, 734, 735.
1874, 927, 940, 944.
1875, 1132, 1140, 1146, 1156.
1880, 2037.
1888, 4431-4461, 4593-4595, 4662-4664.

457. The contingencies under which the Subordinate Lodge may select one of its Past Chancellors to act, or provide which one may fill the chair of Past Chancellor when vacant, or when the same may be deemed vacant, is a matter entirely within the control and under the jurisdiction of the Grand Lodge, or the Subordinate Lodges when the

Grand Lodge may choose to delegate that authority to them, and the Supreme Lodge has not abridged the right of Grand Lodges to determine how Past Chancellors shall be created in their respective Jurisdictions.

Jour., 1888, 4431-4461, 4593-4595, 4662-4664.

458. The question as to whether or not in the case of a new Lodge, any of the officers elected, with the exception of the Past Chancellor-elect and Chancellor Commander-elect, take the rank of Past Chancellor at the expiration of their first term of office, was declared to be a matter for local legislation.

Jour., 1890, 4846, 5319, 5338.

2—Sitting Past Chancellor—General Definition of Status of, a Matter for Local Legislation.

459. The status of officiating Past Chancellors and questions as to whether a sitting Past Chancellor can decline serving in his official position while a member of the Lodge, and so situated that he could serve if he would; whether he can be suspended from serving in that office for inefficiency or neglect to attend to the duties of the office; whether he can resign as sitting Past Chancellor; how in case of a vacancy from any cause, the office shall be filled, are proper subjects for local legislation.

Jour., 1876, 1234, 1302.

(*a*)—Officer of Lodge—So Ruled, Subject to Fines, if Imposed.

460. On an appeal of a Sitting Past Chancellor against the decision of the Grand Lodge of Tennessee, in 1875, it appeared that he was assessed a fine for non-attendance at a regular meeting of a Subordinate Lodge, which fine he refused to pay, on the ground that he was neither an elected nor appointed officer. This decision was affirmed by the Grand Lodge, which held that by a strict construction of the Constitution, a Chancellor Commander, by virtue of his election, necessarily becomes the acting Past Chancellor, and by this is a sitting officer of the Lodge, and liable to fines for non-attendance, the same as other officers, and on appeal to the Supreme Lodge this decision was affirmed.

Jour., 1876, 1306.
1878, 1617.

(*b*)—Withdrawal of—Honors Not Lost by Taking Card.

461. If a sitting Past Chancellor take a Withdrawal Card from his Lodge, his rank when he deposits his Card, would be the rank of Past Chancellor, and he must receive with his Card a rank credential as Past Chancellor, and will be entitled to the Grand Lodge rank.

Jour., 1875, 1043, 1114, 1121.

(*c*)—Of New Lodge—Any Member Eligible—Serving, Entitled to Honors.

462. In the formation of a Subordinate Lodge, the office of Past Chancellor thereof should be filled by selection of the Charter members at the institution of the Lodge, and the person serving in that capacity until the end of the term, would have the honors of the office.

Jour., 1872, 620, 630.

463. The member elected to fill the position of Past Chancellor at the institution of a Lodge is entitled to all the honors, rights and privileges as though he had filled the chair of Chancellor Commander.

Jour., *1888, 4120, 4574, 4580, 4581.*

464. At the organization of a new Lodge, any Knight in good standing may be elected Past Chancellor. Afterward, the outgoing Chancellor Commander takes the position of Past Chancellor, and at the installation of his successor as Chancellor Commander, is entitled to the rank and title of Past Chancellor.

Jour., *1884, 2776, 2988.*

(*d*)—**Of Lodge Already Organized—Only Past Chancellors Eligible.**

465. No one but a Past Chancellor can be directly elected to fill the position of Sitting Past Chancellor, in case of a vacancy for any cause occurring in said position.

Jour., *1876, 1234, 1302.*

466. Under no circumstances can the chair of Sitting Past Chancellor be filled by a Knight, either by election or appointment.

Jour., *1888, 3993, 3997.*

3 - Re-election as Chancellor Commander—Becomes, on Second Installation.

467. A Chancellor Commander who is elected for another term is entitled to the Past Chancellor's rank in his Grand Lodge; Provided, that said Chancellor Commander-elect shall be installed for his second term.

Jour., *1875, 1042, 1114, 1121.*

4—"In Full"—Not until Obligated and Instructed.

468. A brother having served a term as Chancellor Commander, at the installation of his successor is *entitled* to the rank, but is not a Past Chancellor in full until he has been obligated and instructed; though it seems there is no good reason why he may not wear a Past Chancellor's Jewel in his own Lodge during the interim between the time of service and the Grand Lodge session.

Jour., *1872, 468, 613.*
1874, 845.

NOTE.—The word " regalia," after the words " Past Chancellor's," is changed to " Jewel," to comport with the present regulations.

5—Indebtedness—No Bar to Obtaining Certificate as.

469. A member who shall serve one term as Chancellor Commander, though indebted to the Lodge, shall be entitled to a certificate as Past Chancellor; while indebtedness to the Lodge might affect his membership, it cannot possibly affect his claim to the Past Official Rank.

Jour., *1888, 3997.*

6—Lodge Record—Failure of, to Evidence Installation as Chancellor Commander does Not Vacate Right to Rank, if Service Proved.

470. A member elected and installed into the office of Chancellor Commander, and serving therein for the regular term, is entitled, upon the installation of his successor, to take rank thereafter as a Past Chancellor, even though the minutes of the Lodge should fail to show the fact that he had been duly installed as Chancellor Commander of the Lodge.

Jour., 1877, 1406, 1447.

7—Surrender of Charter—Occurring prior to End of Service, Vacates Honors.

471. A Chancellor Commander, serving but two months, the Charter of his Lodge being surrendered prior to the expiration of his term of office, is not entitled to the honors of a Past Chancellor.

Jour., 1877, 1406, 1439.

PAST GRAND CHANCELLORS.

1. **Rank of, How Attained**—By service (472, 473, 474, 475); by Vice Grand Chancellor filling balance of term (472); by election as Sitting Past Grand Chancellor of new Grand Lodge (476); by election as first Supreme Representatives (477).
2. **Passing**—No ceremony in (478).
3. **Admission**—Entitled to, when duly recognized (479); admitted without certificates (480).
4. **Rights of**—Will not be disturbed after credentials approved (481, 482); may be, before (483).
5. **Sitting Past Grand Chancellor**—No election of, Grand Chancellor being re-elected (484, 485).
6. **German Deputy Grand Chancellors**—Legislation covering cases of those whose terms had not expired at the time the law was changed (486).

1—Rank of, How Attained—By Service—By Vice Grand Chancellor Filling Balance of Term—By Election as Sitting Past Grand Chancellor of New Grand Lodge—By Election as First Supreme Representatives.

472. Except as otherwise provided in this Constitution, the grade or rank of Past Grand Chancellor shall not be conferred upon any Past Chancellor who has not served as Grand

Chancellor, or a Grand Vice Chancellor who, under the law, serves out the unexpired term of a Grand Chancellor in case of a vacancy in the office of Grand Chancellor.

Const., Art. XVIII.

NOTE.—The only other ways, "provided in this Constitution," are found by referring to Sections 255, 477 of this Digest.

473. Any Grand Chancellor, who has served a full term in that office, and against whom no charges are pending, shall be entitled to the rank and title of Past Grand Chancellor as soon as his successor is installed.

Jour., 1875, 1035, 1113, 1121.

474. A Grand Chancellor, on being re-elected, shall be entitled to the rank and title of Past Grand Chancellor immediately after his second installation.

Jour., 1875, 1035, 1113, 1121.

475. The retiring Grand Chancellor of each Grand Lodge shall become a Past Grand Chancellor without any regard to the length of time he has served in that office.

Jour., 1868, 55.
1873, 710, 735.

476. Under Section 3, Article VI, of the Supreme Lodge Constitution, upon the organization of a Grand Lodge in a new Jurisdiction, a Past Grand Chancellor is required to be elected to fill that office in the Grand Lodge; and upon such election, and after service in said office until the election and installation of a successor at the regular election and installation of officers in such Grand Lodge, the Past Grand Chancellor would be entitled to take rank thereafter as a Past Grand Chancellor.

Jour., 1877, 1365, 1423.

477. The Supreme Representatives, elected as provided in Section 3, are hereby declared Past Grand Chancellors.

Const., Art. VI, Sec. 4.

2—Passing—No Ceremony.

478. There is no ceremony provided for or necessary, in passing from the office of Grand Chancellor to the office and rank of Past Grand Chancellor.

Jour., 1873, 710, 735.

3—Admission—Entitled to, when Duly Recognized—Admitted without Certificates.

479. All Past Grand Chancellors, duly recognized by the Supreme Lodge. shall be admitted to its session and shall be entitled to seats therein, but shall not be entitled to speak, unless by permission of the Supreme Lodge, and shall not be entitled to vote.

Const., Art. II, Sec. 3.

480. Past Grand Chancellors, whose certificates had not been forwarded by the Grand Keeper of Records and Seal of their Jurisdiction, were admitted to the Supreme Lodge on the evidence of the Grand Lodge Journal and statements of Representatives and also on the simple statement of their Supreme Representative that "he knew them to be Past Grand Chancellors in good standing."

Jour., 1882, 2268, 2269.
1890, 5238, 5255.

4—Rights of—Will Not be Disturbed after Credentials Approved—May be, before.

481. It was resolved by the Supreme Lodge that any Brother who has heretofore been acknowledged as a Past Grand Chancellor and received as such by the Supreme Lodge, is entitled to that rank.

Jour., 1878, 1554.

NOTE.—This arose out of a report of a committee on that subject, and was intended to dispose of the question of the right possessed by those on whose credentials the body had already passed.

482. When the credentials of a Past Grand Chancellor have been passed upon by the Supreme Lodge, a Grand Lodge cannot vacate the rank, nor, under similar circumstances, can they, without sufficient charges, vacate the office of Supreme Representative, and elect another for the remainder of his term.

Jour., 1874, 906, 932.
1882, 2265.

483. In a case where a Grand Chancellor was duly elected, installed, served his term, and credential as Past Grand Chancellor issued; subsequently, charges having been preferred against him, and he, by resolution in his Grand Lodge deprived of his certificate and suspended for three years; on a question arising as to the validity of the credentials, his status and rights as Past Grand Chancellor and as an applicant for admission as a member of the Supreme Lodge; *Held*, that although service is the base of honor in this Order, and although he having served the full term, as expressed in the law at the time of his election, would be, and *prima facie* was, entitled to admission, yet this did not hinder or prevent the Supreme Lodge from barring its portals against the entrance of an improper person, or from excluding from admission such an one for matters arising after the issuing of the certificate; and that, without passing upon the guilt or innocence of the party, his certificate having been withdrawn by the Grand Lodge,

and he never having been introduced to the Supreme Lodge, and instructed in the Supreme Lodge rank, he was not entitled to admission as a member of the Supreme Lodge.

Jour., 1874, 945.
1875, 1127-1129.

5—Sitting Past Grand Chancellor—No Election of, Grand Chancellor being Re-elected.

484. In case of the re-election of the Sitting Grand Chancellor it is not proper to elect a Past Grand Chancellor in the same manner as the other officers.

Jour., 1886, 3682, 3704.

NOTE.—In this case the Constitution of a Grand Lodge contained a proviso giving the right to so elect, but it was disapproved by the Supreme Lodge.

485. In cases where the Grand Chancellor is re-elected, the Junior Past Grand Chancellor, when present, should fill the station of Sitting Past Grand Chancellor; no election to that position, under the circumstances stated, is either necessary or legal.

Jour., 1871, 380, 392.
1872, 469, 613.
1877, 1351, 1352.
1888, 3993.

6—German Deputy Grand Chancellor—Legislation governing Cases of Those Whose Terms had Not Expired at the Time the Law was Changed.

486. Under the provisions of Article XXI, Supreme Constitution, prior to the Supreme Lodge session of 1888, in order to be entitled to the rank of Past Grand Chancellor, among other requirements, German District Deputy Grand Chancellors were required to serve as such for *three* successive years; in 1888, the term was changed to *five* years, and claims being made for the rank of Past Grand Chancellor by certain deputies who, at the time the law was changed to *five* years, were serving a *three* years' term, and completed their *three* years' term *after* the change in the law, the matter being referred to a committee, the Supreme Lodge, acting on their report, decided:

The constitutional law, until the session of 1888, required a service of three consecutive years to be entitled to the rank of Past Grand Chancellor. In 1888, the law was changed so as to require five years' service; any one who had not served three full years at the time the law as changed was in force had not acquired any vested right so that he would become entitled to the rank at the expiration of three years, nor before the expiration of five years.

Jour., 1890, 4840, 5233, 5251, 5252,
5265, 5330, 5395, 5396.

PAST OFFICIAL CHAIR.

487. The laws governing Subordinate, Grand and Supreme Lodges provide that the retiring Executive Officer *shall* fill the office and chair of the Past Officer, and in case of their absence the Junior Past Officer should occupy that official position.

Jour., 1877, 1351, 1352.

PAST SUPREME CHANCELLORS.

There are two classes under this head, viz.:
First—Past Supreme Chancellors, "by service."
Second—" Honorary " Past Supreme Chancellors.
The following are the names of those comprising the first class, with the dates of service:

*Samuel Read, of Mt. Holly, New Jersey, 1868-1872.
Henry Clay Berry, of Chicago, Illinois, 1872-1874.
*Stillman S. Davis, of Nashua, New Hampshire, 1874-1878.
David B. Woodruff, of Macon, Georgia, 1878-1880.
George W. Lindsay, of Baltimore, Maryland, 1880-1882.
John P. Linton, of Johnstown, Pennsylvania, 1882-1884.
*John Van Valkenburg, of Fort Madison, Iowa, 1884-1886.
Howard Douglass, of Cincinnati, Ohio, 1886-1888.
William Ward, of Newark, New Jersey, 1888-1890.

*Deceased.

The second class attained the honor, in the manner indicated by their title: a list of them, six in number, appears in the Journal of Proceedings, 1878, 1578—some are dead—none of them have attended the Supreme Lodge for over fifteen years. The first class have now a voice and vote and entitled to mileage and per diem if present.

488. The Sitting Past Supreme Chancellor shall have charge of and supervise the arrangement of the altar or any other necessary floor work.

Const., Art. III, Sec. 1.

PER CAPITA TAX.

1. For What Purpose—Grand Lodge may set aside portion of, for building hall (489).
2. On Pages and Esquires—Grand Lodge may levy (490).

1—For What Purpose—Grand Lodge may Set Aside Portion of, for Building Hall.

489. On appeal against the action of the Grand Lodge of Maryland, in passing the following resolution — " That the levy of per capita tax for the year 1875 shall be at the rate of 25 cents per member, semi-annually ; one-fifth of the amount to be made a sinking fund to aid in the purpose of building a Pythian Castle, and in the event of the building not being commenced in five years, the amount paid in by each Lodge, and the interest which has accrued thereon, shall be returned to it"—which resolution was objected to on the ground of the proviso that one-fifth of the amount be retained for the purpose of building a Hall for the Order: *Held*, that the resolution was in accordance with the Constitution of the Grand Lodge of Maryland, and the appeal was dismissed.

Jour., *1875, 1148, 1149.*

2—On Pages and Esquires—Grand Lodge may Levy.

490. The charging of per capita tax on Pages and Esquires, by a Grand Lodge, is a subject for local legislation.

Jour., *1880, 2002, 2039.*

PROTEST.

1. In the Supreme Lodge—Member may submit (491).
2. In a Grand Lodge—Must receive (492).
3. In a Subordinate Lodge—Against admission of an applicant, of no force as a black ball (493, 494).

1—In the Supreme Lodge—Member may Submit.

491. A Supreme Representative desiring to protest against any action of the Supreme Lodge must present the same in writing, or it will not be entertained.

Jour., *1888, 4497.*

2—In a Grand Lodge—Must Receive.

492. It is the duty of a Grand Lodge to receive a protest from its Grand Chancellor, when no misstatements, disrespect or unfairness are contained therein.

Jour., *1870, 199.*

3—In a Subordinate Lodge—Against Admission of an Applicant, of No Force, as a Black Ball.

493. A protest against admission to membership emanating from a sister Lodge has not the force of an adverse ballot. Each Lodge has jurisdiction over whom it may admit, but at the same time should pay respectful recognition to a protest of the character named.

Jour., *1888, 4120, 4575, 4581.*

494. A sister Lodge cannot file an objection or protest and prevent the election of a petitioner in the Lodge to which application was made. In such instances, while any Lodge has a right to counsel with reference to an application in any other Lodge, the same should only be considered in an advisory capacity, and cannot act as an estoppel or operate as a black ball.

Jour., *1888, 4001, 4002.*

PYTHIAN COLLEGE.

495. The Supreme Lodge "recommended to the favorable consideration of the Order universal" the proposition of Rowena Lodge, of Gallatin, Tennessee, to establish a "Pythian College," and ruled that they "be permitted to call on Subordinate Lodges and Grand Lodges of the Order, wherever situated, for financial aid in the endowment and building up of said school."

Jour., 1890, 5273, 5408, 5427.

496. The whole subject of the establishment of schools, etc., for the education of the children of Knights, should be left to each Jurisdiction for such action as may be deemed proper in the premises.

Jour., 1877, 1413, 1418.

PYTHIAN PERIOD.
(See Anniversary.)

497. The Order having been inaugurated and established in the year A. D. 1864, it was enacted at the session of 1871 that thereafter the term "Pythian Period" should be used immediately after any date given of day, year or month of the vulgar era, as follows: "This the —— day of ——, A. D. 18—, and of Pythian Period the ——," in all official documents, dispensations or charters emanating from or issued by the Supreme Lodge or Grand Lodges under its jurisdiction; and that the date of the Pythian Period should date back and commence on the 19th of February, 1864, and that each and every year thereafter and to come should succeed in regular numerical order, commencing on the 19th day of February of each year.

Jour., 1871, 364, 385.

PYTHIAN SISTERHOOD.

1. Permission to Organize—Supreme Lodge assumes no responsibility for (498).
2. Not Recognized—As part of the Order (499).

1—Permission to Organize—Supreme Lodge Assumes no Responsibility for.

498. The mothers, wives, widows, sisters and daughters of the Knights of Pythias in good standing in the various Jurisdictions were allowed to establish an order, to be known as "The Order of Pythian Sisterhood"; but if an order of Pythian Sisters is established, the

Supreme Lodge assumes no legal or financial responsibility in connection with the establishment or maintenance of the order. It was deemed advisable that the various chief officers of the Sisterhood report their numerical and financial strength to the Supreme Keeper of Records and Seal every two years, at least thirty days previous to the session of the Supreme Lodge.

Jour., 1888, 4402, 4651.

2—Not Recognized—As a Part of the Order.

499. On the question of a recognition of a Ladies' Rank, as presented by Representative Morrison, of Nebraska, by which an endorsement was sought for the "Sisterhood," as organized by one of two claimants to priority of right, it was ruled:

Two distinct organizations, conducted by the ladies, are asking or claiming recognition by this Supreme Lodge, and it would be unwise to express a preference in any way. The Constitution expressly fixes the qualifications of membership in the Order of Knights of Pythias, and the Supreme Lodge will not recognize any bodies outside of those now under the control of the Supreme Lodge, as members of the Order.

Jour., 1890, 5268, 5269, 5332, 5396, 5397, 5414.

NOTE.—Previous to the legislation of 1888 (Section 498 of this Digest) there existed an organization of ladies known as "Pythian Sisterhood." After the legislation referred to, the "Pythian Sisters" was organized. Between these two the Supreme Lodge was asked to decide. The compiler simply gives these facts for the information of the reader.

RANKS.

1. "Degrees"—This title changed to "Ranks" (500).
2. "Sir Knight"—Not to be used to designate Third Rank members (501).
3. "Prove and Charge"—Adopted in place of "Passed and Raised" (502).
4. When Conferred—One week must elapse between (503, 504); exceptions (503, 504).
5. Ballot on—Separate on each (505, 506).
6. Pages and Esquires—Admitted in, how? (507); may be conferred on, on request of sister Lodge (508).
7. Rank Teams—Permitted to confer, under restrictions (509).
8. Outer Guard—Must acquaint members as to what rank Lodge is working (510).

1—"Degrees"—This Title Changed to "Ranks."

500. At the session of the Supreme Lodge in 1872 the word "degree" and "degrees" was ordered to be struck out wherever appearing in the Ritual, Laws, Installations or Odes, or when used in connection with the Order of Knights of Pythias, or its legislation and workings, and the word "rank" inserted in its or their place.

Jour., 1872, 561, 598.

2—"Sir Knight"—Not to be Used to Designate Third Rank Members.

501. The title "Sir Knight" should not be used in designating members of the Third Rank of the Order of Knights of Pythias.

Jour., 1872, 564, 598.

3—"Prove and Charge"—Adopted in Place of "Passed and Raised."

502. The use of the words "passed" and "raised" being inapplicable to this Order, was in 1871 abjured by the Supreme Lodge, and all Grand and Subordinate Lodges of the Order were recommended to abjure and drop the use of said words, and substitute therefor the words "prove" and "charge" in all official documents, dispensations or charters thereafter issued, as also recommend said rectification to those already issued, wherever possible or practicable so to do.

Jour., 1871, 365, 385.

4—When Conferred—One Week must Elapse between Exceptions.

503. One week must elapse between the conferring of the ranks in all cases, except the first four meetings of a new Lodge; but in every instance, one week must elapse between the application and the conferring of the initiatory rank of Page.

(The above paragraph shall not apply to cases where Dispensations are granted by a proper Grand Officer or through his Deputy.) (Obligatory.)

Const., Art. VIII, Sec. 2, Sub. l.

504. The Supreme Lodge Constitution is necessarily and by direct enactment (Article XIII, Supreme Lodge Constitution), the paramount authority of the Order, hence, *in all cases* (except the first four meetings of a Lodge, or when a Lodge is working under a Dispensation), one week must elapse between the conferring of Ranks. Any provision in a Grand Lodge Constitution conflicting with this is void.

Jour., 1884, 2776, 2989.

5—Ballot on—Separate on Each.

505. A ballot should be taken upon each application for Ranks, and the same number of black balls shall reject as in case of an application for membership; the ballot in the first instance is for initiation only.

Jour., 1877, 1379, 1428.
1880, 1828, 2003.

506. A ballot is required for advancement in the ranks. The ballot in the first instance is for initiation only, and a ballot is requisite for further advancement in the ranks, each rank requiring a separate and distinct ballot.

Jour., 1890, 4844, 5319, 5336.

6—Pages and Esquires—Admitted in, How ; may be Conferred on, on Request of Sister Lodge.

507. Pages and Esquires are entitled to and can be admitted in a Lodge when opened and working in that rank. They can pass the outer door, if having to do so by the order of the Chancellor Commander.

Jour., 1873, Appendix 38.

508. A Subordinate Lodge may confer the ranks of Esquire and Knight on a Page who has received that rank in another Lodge, in the same or another Jurisdiction, by a written official request of his Lodge, certifying that he has received the rank of Page, and has paid for the other ranks, and been elected thereto. The Lodge conferring those ranks should, when the rank or ranks are conferred, send to the Lodge making the request an official notice of the ranks having been conferred, with date, and he should be entered on their books holding rank accordingly.

Jour., 1875, 1043, 1114, 1121.

7—Rank Teams—Permitted to Confer, under Restrictions.

509. A Subordinate Lodge or its officers has the right to transfer the work of conferring the various ranks to a team drilled or organized for that purpose outside of the regular officers of the lodge, provided that the lodge remain under the control of an officer qualified under the local law to preside.

Jour., 1888, 4605, 4634.

8—Outer Guard—Must Acquaint Members as to What Rank Lodge is Working.

510. The Outer Guard has no right to refuse to inform a brother (applying for admission) what Rank his Lodge is at labor in, if such information be asked for at the outer door. It is his duty to state what Rank the Lodge is working in, that no errors may occur in giving the signs, etc.

Jour., 1873, Appendix 38.

RANK CREDENTIAL.

1. Constitutional Requirement—Only evidence of Past Rank (511, 512, 516).
2. Withdrawal Cards—Rank on, of no force, as credential (513, 514, 515, 516).

1—Constitutional Requirement—Only Evidence of Rank.

511. Any member having past rank, removing from one Grand Jurisdiction to another, and desiring to affiliate on a

Withdrawal Card, must also present a rank credential to entitle him to the same.

Const., Art. XXI.

2—Withdrawal Cards—Rank on, of No Force, as Credential.

512. The Past Official rank of Past Chancellor or Past Grand Chancellor must be evidenced by a certificate signed by the proper Grand Officers, duly attested with the Grand Lodge seal, prior to said official rank being recognized when affiliating by Card in any other Lodge than the one in which being a member where said rank was attained.

Jour., 1873, Appendix 36.

513. Withdrawal Cards evidence no rank in the Order of higher grade than that of Knight, and any prefix or affix thereto, setting forth that the bearer was a Past Chancellor or Past Grand Chancellor is void, and of no value whatever as a credential of those two higher grades of rank.

Jour., 1873, Appendix 35.

514. A withdrawal card, with the prefix of "Past Chancellor" thereto, and the printed proceedings of the Grand Lodge, with a name the same as that appearing on the Withdrawal Card, as having been admitted and enrolled *as a* "Past Chancellor" in that Grand Lodge are not sufficient evidence of the rank of Past Chancellor. The Withdrawal Card, although in regular form, carries no evidence of rank under the law higher than that of a Knight ; and it cannot be claimed or admitted in any sense as a credential of rank or visiting card beyond the purposes as intended on its face. The printed proceedings are of weight so far as being unquestionably true, but in the absence of evidencing connection as between the claimant and the party therein set forth by an authenticated certificate are insufficient.

Jour., 1873, Appendix 10.

515. On appeal of a Subordinate Lodge of the State of Kansas against the action of the Grand Lodge of that State in ordering said Subordinate Lodge to place "Past Chancellor" on a Withdrawal Card, the law of the Grand Lodge Constitution reading as follows: "That a Past Chancellor, previous to being admitted as a member of the Grand Lodge, *must* present a certificate from his Lodge certifying that he had passed the chair of his Lodge"; it was resolved that the Grand Lodge of Kansas transcended the power of the Grand Lodge Constitution, and its action was reversed.

Jour., 1876, 1306.

516. Lodges can only recognize a credential emanating from the Grand Lodge office certifying to the fact of the past official rank of the member removing from one Jurisdiction to another, notwithstanding the fact that his Withdrawal Card states his rank.

Jour., 1888, 4004.

REGALIA.

1. Constitutional Provisions (517, 518).
2. Collars—Not to be worn in public (519, 520).

1—Constitutional Provisions.

517. The regalia of the Supreme, Grand and Subordinate Lodges shall be such as is prescribed by the Supreme Lodge, or adopted and approved from time to time at the regular sessions of the Supreme Lodge.

Const., Art. XII.

518. Pages shall wear a blue collar, Esquires a yellow collar, Knights a red collar or a Knight's Jewel in Subordinate Lodges, and Past Chancellors, Past Grand Chancellors and Past Supreme Chancellors the respective Jewels of their rank, and Past Supreme Representatives may wear their appropriate Jewels at all meetings of Subordinate, Grand or Supreme Lodges, unless when acting in an official capacity, when the Jewels of office shall be worn; Provided, that in Lodges now provided with the red collar, Knights may wear such collars; and nothing herein shall be construed as requiring Lodges provided with red collars to replace the same with Knight's Jewels, except in case of purchase of new regalia, nor to warrant or authorize the further purchase of such red collars.

Const., Art. XXVI.

2—Collars—Not to be Worn in Public.

519. The collar cannot be worn in a street parade of any character.

Jour., 1875, 1032, 1124.

520. Subordinate Lodges may not use the collar of the Knight's rank in attending the funeral of a member of the Order.

Jour., 1886, 3682, 3704.

RELIEF AND RELIEF BUREAUS.

1. Relief—Lodge not responsible for, if unauthorized (521, 522).
2. Relief Bureaus—A matter for local legislation (523).

1—Relief—Lodge Not Responsible for if Unauthorized.

521. A Lodge is not responsible for money advanced to one of its members, on his individual request, by another Lodge, without the authority of the Lodge to which he belonged, duly authenticated.

Jour., *1880*, *2009*.

NOTE.—It should be noted that this in no respect refers to money paid in connection with benefits. It was purely financial aid.

522. Where a member of the Order died, away from home, and the Lodge in the place where he died buried him, first having telegraphed to his Lodge, but received no reply; and, further, where it was admitted that among the effects of the dead brother was a notice from his Lodge of the brother's arrearage for dues, the Supreme Lodge, on a complaint being made, held that the Lodge burying the brother had no legal claim upon the Lodge to which the deceased had belonged.

Jour., *1888*, *4547*, *4591*, *4592*.

2—Relief Bureaus—A Matter for Local Legislation.

523. The organizing and maintaining of Relief Bureaus for the care of sojourning sick members of the Order, is a matter for local legislation.

Jour., *1872*, *535*, *536*, *578*.
1873, *688-690*, *722*.
1875, *1134*, *1142*.

RENOUNCING THE ORDER.

524. A member who shall, from any cause whatsoever, renounce the Order, the Lodge to which said member belonged may, upon proof of renunciation, withhold all pecuniary benefits, but the Supreme Lodge refused to adopt a proposition requiring such renunciation to be in writing and signed in presence of two Knights.

Jour., *1884*, *2949*, *2990*, *2991*, *3020*.
1886, *3681*, *3725*.

REINSTATEMENT.

1. After Definite Suspension—Requires no action by the Lodge (525).
2. After Indefinite Suspension—By application and regular ballot (526).
3. After Suspension for Non-payment of Dues—Governed by local law (527, 528).
4. With Revival of Suspended Lodge—Part of membership may be reinstated, part, for cause, refused (529).

1—After Definite Suspension—Requires No Action by the Lodge.

525. On the termination of a definite suspension for cause a member is reinstated without any action on the part of the Lodge.

Jour., *1888*, *4003*.

2—After Indefinite Suspension—By Application and Regular Ballot.

526. A member of a Lodge indefinitely suspended for cause, may be reinstated in his Lodge on the presentation of a written application, said application being referred to a committee and receiving a favorable report, and by passing a regular ball ballot.

Jour., 1884, 2776, 2988.

NOTE.—While this decision does not state the fact, yet it is no doubt intended to mean, that when a member is suspended for a period beyond the usual term of life, he may apply for a termination of the suspension, and that doing so the Lodge acts as above indicated.

3—After Suspension for Non-payment of Dues—Governed by Local Law.

527. The manner of regaining membership after suspension for non-payment of dues and the vote thereon is a subject for local legislation.

Jour., 1874, 902, 909.
1888, 4126, 4655, 4656, 4665, 4666.

528. On an appeal against the action of the Grand Lodge of Kentucky, the facts were these: A member who had been suspended for non-payment of dues, having paid up all his arrearages, claimed that he was thereby reinstated without any written application to the Lodge or further action on his part. His claim was allowed by the Lodge, and upon appeal to the Grand Lodge such action was sustained and the appeal dismissed. An appeal was taken from the decision of the Grand Lodge. The provision of the local law on this subject was as follows, to-wit: "Provided, however, a brother suspended for non-payment of dues shall be reinstated by paying up all arrearages." *Held*, that the appeal should be dismissed, and the action of the Grand Lodge was sustained.

Jour., 1872, 566, 588.

NOTE.—The Supreme Lodge, however, declined to make the rule of the case general. *Jour., 1872, 589.*

4—With Revival of Suspended Lodge—Part of Membership may be Reinstated, Part, for Cause, Refused.

529. Where a Lodge in Massachusetts received applications for membership from persons residing in the Jurisdiction of New Hampshire, in a city where a Lodge existed, and initiated them after being informed that they were not residents of Massachusetts, and with a protest in their hands against such act, whereupon charges were preferred against such Lodge, and the Lodge suspended; the Grand Lodge, on appeal, sustained the suspension, and provided for the reinstating said Lodge by those members who were innocent, but declaring that no one implicated in the cause of this complaint, should ever be received into membership; against this latter action of the Grand Lodge, in shutting out the guilty members from any participation in the reinstitution, appeal was taken. The Supreme Lodge sustained the Grand Lodge.

Jour., 1872, 538-551, 573.

REPORTS.

1. Of Supreme Officers to the Supreme Lodge (530).
2. Of Supreme Officers to the Pythian Press (531).

1—Of Supreme Officers to the Supreme Lodge.

530. The Reports of the Supreme Chancellor and Supreme Keeper of Records and Seal are to be printed previous to the sessions.

Jour., 1870, 219.

NOTE.—While this only specifies the two officers, the Constitution requires reports also from the Supreme Master of Exchequer and Major General, but does not define their printing.

2—Of Supreme Officers to the Pythian Press.

531. The Supreme Keeper of Records and Seal, acting in conjunction and with the approval of the Supreme Chancellor, shall cause the quarterly reports of the Supreme Keeper of Records and Seal, of the Supreme Secretary of the Endowment Rank, of the Supreme Master of Exchequer, and of the Major General of the Uniform Rank, or a synopsis thereof, to be published in several Pythian papers of influence and the largest circulation, not exceeding five in number; said papers to be selected with geographical reference, and with a view to disseminate the information contained in the said reports so that the publication may reach the largest number of Pythians in the several Jurisdictions.

That the compensation for said publication of Reports shall in no case exceed one dollar per inch (nonpareil type) to each paper, excepting where the circulation exceeds 2,500 *bona fide* subscribers, and then an additional compensation may be allowed, of fifty cents per inch for each 1,000 subscribers in excess of the 2,500 named.

Jour., 1888, 4636.

NOTE.—This legislation has never been repealed, but has so fallen into disuse as to be practically obsolete. It is given by the compiler simply because it is law.

REPRESENTATIVE.

532. A Representative to a Grand Lodge is not an officer of his Lodge.

Jour., 1886, 3522, 3555.

RESIDENCE.

1. Applicants—For membership, six months required (533); local law may increase (534); exception, where Grand Chancellor of sister Jurisdiction consents (535).
2. Ranks—Not conferred, on non-resident, without consent (536).
3. Grand Officers—Must be residents of their Jurisdiction (537).

1—Applicants—For Membership, Six Months Required —Local Law may Increase—Exception, Where Grand Chancellor of Sister Jurisdiction Consents.

533. No person shall be initiated into a Lodge of this Order unless he has been a resident of the Grand Jurisdiction in which he makes application for at least six months next preceding. (Obligatory.)

Const., Art. VIII, Sec. 2, Sub. h.

534. A Grand Lodge has a right, by constitutional provision, to prescribe that applicants for membership by initiation shall have resided for a definite period in the Jurisdiction previous to applying. This was decided on an appeal, and afterward the Supreme Lodge so amended the Constitution as to require a residence of at least six months.

Jour., 1890, 5299-5303, 5328, 5329.

535. A candidate for membership, residing in a Grand Jurisdiction other than the one in which his proposition is offered, shall not be initiated without the written consent of the Grand Chancellor of such Grand Jurisdiction. (Obligatory.)

Const., Art. VIII, Sec. 2, Sub. o.

NOTE.—This would seem to conflict with the provisions of Sections 533, 534, and can only be construed to mean that the consent of the Grand Chancellor is a waiver of the requirement of actual residence in the Jurisdiction where applying.

2—Ranks—Not Conferred, on Non-resident, without Consent.

536. No rank shall be conferred on a brother who is a non-resident of the Jurisdiction, or who is a member of another Lodge, without first obtaining the permission of the Lodge to which the brother is attached. (Obligatory.)

Const., Art. VIII, Sec. 2, Sub. p.

3—Grand Officers—Must be Residents of Their Jurisdiction.

537. In cases where a Grand Officer (except Sitting Past Grand Chancellor) of a Grand Jurisdiction acquires permanent residence in another Jurisdiction, his position thereby becomes vacant, unless the local law otherwise provides, and the vacancy may be filled in such manner as may be provided by the laws of such Grand Jurisdiction.

Jour., *1888*, *4125*, *4655*, *4656*.

NOTE.—By the Constitution of 1890, Article VI, Section 3, Supreme Representatives were made Grand Officers, but *their* removal of residence works a forfeiture of office, irrespective of any "local law."—Article II, Section 2.

RETURNS.

1. Form of—From Grand Lodges, prescribed (538).
2. Delinquent—Representation forfeited, if not made and tax paid (539, 540), but Supreme Lodge may excuse (540, 541, 542).

1—Form of—From Grand Lodges, Prescribed.

538. The blank forms, submitted by the Supreme Keeper of Records and Seal, and now used by him, were approved, and it was ordered: "That they be the Official Forms for Returns from Grand Jurisdictions, and the Grand Keeper of Records and Seal of each Jurisdiction must comply with said forms in *each* and *every* particular item specifically called for.

Jour., *1880*, *2044*.

2—Delinquent—Representation Forfeited, if Not Made and Tax Paid, but Supreme Lodge may Excuse.

539. Each Grand Lodge shall make out and forward to the Supreme Keeper of Records and Seal, on the blank furnished by him for that purpose, and in strict accordance with the forms therein prescribed, on or before the first day of April of each year, a report of its work and business. For every day which shall elapse between the said first day of April and the date of the reception of a correct report (as herein prescribed) and the correct amount of Supreme Representative tax (as prescribed by Article X, of this Constitution), said delinquent Grand Lodge shall be fined the sum of one dollar; and said Grand Lodge shall not be allowed representation in the

Supreme Lodge until the amount of Supreme Representative tax due, as well as the total amount of such fine, shall have been paid.

Const., Art. XVI.

540. The proper construction of Article XVI of Supreme Lodge Constitution is, that by the failure to do the act before described in said Article, a delinquent Grand Lodge *forfeits its right* to representation in the Supreme Lodge, but the Supreme Lodge *may*, by special vote, *permit* as a *privilege* (but not as a *right*) the said Grand Lodge, through its representatives, to be heard on the floor of the Supreme Lodge.

Jour., 1875, 1160, 1164.

541. The question as to whether any Grand Jurisdiction can obtain representation at any session of the Supreme Lodge while any representative tax remains unpaid, is a matter which the Supreme Lodge at any session, is competent to determine for itself. A request for the remission of the tax must come over the seal of the Grand Lodge.

Jour., 1877, 1426.
1878, 1529, 1621, 1641, 1642.

542. Notwithstanding that a Grand Lodge was indebted to the Supreme Lodge, time being given to make payment, also where no time was given, the Supreme Representatives from the Jurisdictions were conceded like privileges in the Supreme Lodge as others.

Jour., 1872, 447, 538.

RITUALS.

1. Set of—Five constitute; is all a Lodge should have (543).
2. Translation of—Only by authority of Supreme Lodge (544).
3. Where Kept—In Lodge room, under control of Chancellor Commander (545).
4. Language of—Must be adhered to (546, 547, 548).
5. Memorizing—Of "Amplified Third," compulsory (549); otherwise, Subordinate Lodges may require (550, 551); cannot be taken away after certain time allowed for (552).
6. Copying—Strictly forbidden (553).
7. Foreign Countries—Transmittal of, to, by Supreme Chancellor (554).

1—Set of—Five Constitute—Is All a Lodge shall Have.

543. A Lodge is only entitled to one set of five Rituals, and it is improper and illegal to furnish any one Lodge with more than that number, or for a Lodge to be in possession of more than the regular set.

Jour., 1884, 2776, 2988.
1888, 4120, 4575, 4581.

Rituals. 139

2—Translation of—Only by Authority of Supreme Lodge.

544. No translations of the Rituals of the Order can be made without the direction of the Supreme Lodge.

Jour., 1888, 4561, 4645.

3—Where Kept—In Lodge Room, under Control of Chancellor Commander.

545. The proper place for the keeping of the Rituals and other private work is in the Castle Halls of the Order ; and it is the duty of the Lodge to provide a suitable box or other receptacle, with a sufficient lock, the key of which shall be in the charge and keeping of the Chancellor Commander; and it is his duty to prevent their removal from the Castle Hall.

Jour., 1875, 1106, 1149, 1150, 1152.

4—Language of—Must be Adhered to.

546. The language and instructions of the Revised Ritual as promulgated must be strictly followed in exemplifying and explaining the unwritten work.

Jour., 1884, 2777, 2988.

547. The Prelate and all other officers of a Lodge must conform to the language of the Ritual in the opening and closing ceremonies. They have no right to make any interpolations of their own, and a Lodge is correct in preventing this.

Jour., 1884, 2777, 2988.

548. No Subordinate Lodge has any right to alter, amend or in any way omit or add to any part of the ritualistic work in any rank, and the Supreme Lodge explicitly forbids any such work.

Jour., 1886, 3756.

5—Memorizing—Of "Amplified Third," Compulsory ; Otherwise, Subordinate Lodges may Require ; Cannot be Taken Away after Certain Time Allowed for.

549. The Third, or Knight's rank, shall in no instance be conferred according to the Second or Amplified Ritual of said rank as adopted, unless the various parts have been memorized by all the persons officiating therein; so that the same can be conferred without the use of the book.

Jour., 1872, 637.

550. While it is essential to the welfare and influence of the Order that all of the lectures and charges should, where the same is practicable, be memorized, yet there are times and seasons when the same (if made imperative) would hinder and delay the business of Subordinate Lodges; and it is recommended that the several Grand Jurisdictions be requested to use their best efforts to procure the memorizing of all lectures and charges upon the part of officers of Subordinate Lodges.

Jour., 1875, 1106, 1153.

551. There being no general law bearing upon the memorizing of the ritualistic charges, it rests clearly in the province of the Subordinate Lodge to declare in what space of time the officer *shall*, by memorizing, be able to deliver the same "orally."

Jour., 1873, Appendix 37.

552. Under the decision of the Supreme Chancellor, on page 37 of his report, Journal, 1873, regarding the memorizing of charges by officers, it will not be competent for a Grand Chancellor to require that the officers of Lodges in his Jurisdiction shall memorize the ritualistic charges of their office within a specified time after their installation, and that at the expiration of that time the Rituals shall be delivered by the Lodges to their District Deputy Grand Chancellors, to be retained by them until the next installation of officers.

Jour., 1873, 756.

6—Copying—Strictly Forbidden.

553. All officers and members of Subordinate Lodges are prohibited from copying in any manner, any part or parts of their several charges or other ritualistic ceremonies.

Jour., 1875, 1134.

7—Foreign Countries—Transmittal of, to, by Supreme Chancellor.

554. The Supreme Chancellor is fully authorized and empowered to enter into negotiations with the Secretary of State, with a view to securing the right to send through the mails or express service of any foreign government the rituals and other secret work of the Order, as the Supreme Chancellor may deem wise and expedient at the time when the emergency or necessity may arise.

Jour., 1886, 3281, 3754.

RULES OF ORDER OF THE SUPREME LODGE.

Provision having been made at the session of 1890 for a complete revision of the Rules of Order of the Supreme Lodge, under instructions of the Special Committee on Digest, the existing rules have been omitted, as they have no bearing and make no law for either Grand or Subordinate Lodges.

SANITARIUM.

555. The Supreme Lodge recommended, approved and endorsed a proposition emanating from Montefiore Lodge, No. 2, of Jacksonville, Florida, and unanimously approved of by the Grand Lodge of Florida, for the establishment in that city of a suitable edifice to be dedicated and devoted as a sanitarium and home for visiting brothers and for Pythian uses.

Jour., 1890, 5274, 5275, 5387, 5422.

SEALS.

1. Of Supreme Lodge—Description (556); copyright (557).
2. Of Supreme Chancellor—Adoption of (558).
3. Of Grand Lodges—Provision for (559).
4. Of Subordinate Lodges—Provision for (560).

1—Of Supreme Lodge—Description—Copyright.

556. The Seal of the Supreme Lodge was originally adopted and approved November 10, 1868; the explanation of the Seal is as follows: The Seal is a polygon—five-sided. The five sides represent the five Grand Lodges in existence upon the formation of the Supreme Lodge. On one side, the date of organization of the Supreme Lodge; on the other, the date of the foundation of the Order. Over the shield the word "Friendship," the cornerstone of the Order. On the shield a "flotant," with stars upon it, denoting our ascendency. The perpendicular lines denote the color "Blue," the dots "Yellow," the horizontal "Red," thus showing the colors of the Order. The *"Dirigo"* means "I guide," or "I direct." Around the shield are the initials of the mottoes F., C. and B.

Jour., 1868, 25, 45, 47.

557. The original copyrighting of the Seal was June 22, 1870, the endorsement around it being: "Entered according to Act of Congress in the Clerk's Office of the Supreme Court, District of Columbia, by C. M. Barton, June 22, 1870."

In 1875 the Supreme Chancellor reported, page 1029, that he had had a new copyright issued for the Seal, and his act was approved, page 1134; the copyright then bore the following endorsement: "Copyright, 1874, S. S. Davis, Supreme Chancellor."

In 1888, page 4139, the Supreme Keeper of Records and Seal recommended the removal of the name of C. M. Barton from the old Seal, and the engraving of a new Seal, and, page 4519, the same was approved.

2—Of Supreme Chancellor—Adoption of.

558. The use, by the Supreme Chancellor, of an individual Official Seal was in 1873 authorized, though the limits of its use do not seem to have been defined by the Supreme Lodge, though definitely marked out by the Supreme Chancellor in his recommendation.

Jour., 1873, 719, 746; Appendix 14.

3—Of Grand Lodges—Provision for.

559. Each Grand and Subordinate Lodge shall have an appropriate seal, bearing proper devices thereon, name, number and location of the Lodge, with the date of its institution thereon, a good copy or impression of which shall be deposited with the Supreme Keeper of Records and Seal.

Const., Art. XXIII.

4—Of Subordinate Lodges—Provision for.

560. Each Lodge shall have a seal with appropriate devices, which shall be affixed to such cards, as well as to all official documents emanating from the Lodge. (Obligatory.)

Const., Art. VIII, Sec. 2, Sub. u.

SUBORDINATE LODGES.

1. Composition of—Not less than seven Knights (561).
2. Meetings—Once a week, except by Dispensation (562, 563, 564); "regular" and "special," are "meetings" within the meaning of the law (565).
3. Quorum and Business—Seven constitute (566); business done in Knight's Rank (567); exception (567); officer must preside (568).
4. Opening and Closing—Ceremonies cannot be dispensed with (569); except in public (570); motion to adjourn, not in order, must close after order of business is called (571).
5. "At Ease"—During, doors must be closed (572).
6. Officers—As provided in ritual (573); elective and appointive (574); Outer Guard must be a member of the Lodge (575).
7. Addressing the Chair—Dispensed with, when (576).
8. Trustees—Must not exceed their authority (577).
9. Consolidation—Of Lodges, a matter for local legislation (578).
10. Supreme Authority—Communication with, through Grand Lodge (579); Lodges cannot pass on, except in regular way (580).

1—Composition of—Not Less than Seven Knights.

561. A Lodge shall never consist of less than seven members of the Knight Rank. (Obligatory.)

Const., Art. VIII, Sec. 2, Sub. a.

2—Meetings—Once a Week, except by Dispensation—"Regular" and "Special" Are "Meetings" within the Meaning of the Law.

562. A Lodge shall hold stated meetings at least once a week, at such an hour as may from time to time be determined upon; Provided, that each Grand Lodge may allow meetings at longer intervals by a regular dispensation. (Obligatory.)

Const., Art. VIII, Sec. 2, Sub. a.

563. A Lodge should meet at least once a week, unless it has a Dispensation from the Supreme Lodge or Supreme Chancellor, when the Lodge is working under the immediate jurisdiction of the Supreme Lodge, or from the Grand Lodge or Grand Chancellor, if the Lodge be working under a Grand Lodge Jurisdiction, to meet at longer intervals, and any persistent and continuous failure to do so renders it liable to suspension.

Jour., 1884, 2777, 2988.

564. The questions whether or not a Grand Lodge has the power to authorize a Subordinate Lodge in its Jurisdiction to meet semimonthly, until the privilege is taken away from it, and whether or not a Grand Chancellor has this power, present matters for local legislation, and are not proper for determination by the Supreme Lodge.

Jour., 1876, 1284, 1285, 1299, 1300.

565. Where the By-Laws of a Subordinate Lodge, duly approved in accordance with the law of its Grand Jurisdiction, specify fines to be charged up against officers for absence from meetings, provided always they have no valid excuse; and where, under this proviso, the Supreme Lodge was asked: Has a Subordinate Lodge the right to charge fines against officers for absence from called meetings, provided said officers have due and legal notice of said called meeting? The Supreme Lodge ruled: If the By-Laws provide for "absence from meetings," the word "meetings" includes all meetings legally called and held, whether regular or special.

Jour., 1888, 4545, 4573.

3—Quorum and Business—Seven Constitute—Business Done in Knight's Rank—Exception—Officer must Preside.

566. Not less than seven members of the Knight Rank shall constitute a quorum for the transaction of business, including one qualified to preside, and if seven members only be present, no appropriation of money shall be made unless it be by unanimous consent. (Obligatory.)

Const., Art. VIII, Sec. 2, Sub. b.

567. The Lodge shall transact all its business in the Knight Rank, except the actual conferring of the Page or Esquire Rank, and except when proceeding with the trial of a Page or Esquire. (Obligatory.)

Const., Art. VIII, Sec. 2, Sub. c.

568. All business of a Lodge, except the conferring of Ranks, or when open as a Lodge of Instruction, must be transacted with an officer of the Lodge in the chair, but a Chancellor Commander may call any duly qualified member of the Order to the chair, when conferring Ranks or to give instructions.

Jour., 1880, 1828, 2003.
1886, 3286, 3525, 3526, 3527,
Errata, page i.

4—Opening and Closing—Ceremonies cannot be Dispensed with except in Public—Motion to Adjourn, Not in Order, must Close, after Order of Business is Called.

569. A motion to dispense with the opening ceremonies of a Lodge is improper and ought not to be entertained. While no law exists enforcing a proper observance of it, yet the Ritual itself is ritualistic law and must be observed.

Jour., 1880, 1828, 2003.

570. No form of opening the Lodge in public is permitted at a *public* installation of officers, except such ceremonies as are laid down in the Installation Work for public use, with accompanying forms, etc.

Jour., 1880, 1828, 2003.

571. When a Subordinate Lodge is in session a motion to adjourn is not proper, but should be, that the Lodge proceed to close. And this motion should not be entertained until the regular order of business has been called by the Chancellor Commander.

Jour., 1878, 1508, 1607.

5—"At Ease"—During, Doors must be Closed.

572. No law has ever been passed providing for a Lodge being "at ease," nor has there been any provision made with reference to it, but the Ritual recognizes this feature; and being called upon to decide as to the manner of retiring or admission at a time when a Lodge was "at ease," it was ruled that in such cases the Lodge must be called to order and the usual course be pursued, and that when a Lodge was declared "at ease" neither the inner nor outer door should be opened unless for the purpose of admission or permitting a member to retire in the regular way.

Jour., 1888, 4122, 4579, 4581.

6.—Officers—As Provided in Ritual—Elective and Appointive—Outer Guard must be a Member of the Lodge.

573. The officers of a Subordinate Lodge shall be as provided in the Ritual. (Obligatory.)

Const., Art. VIII, Sec. 2, Sub. d.

574. The Chancellor Commander, Vice Chancellor, Prelate, Keeper of Records and Seal, Master of Finance, Master of Exchequer and Master-at-Arms *must* be elected by ballot. The Inner Guard and Outer Guard *must* be appointed.

NOTE.—The legislation of 1873, page 768, provided for the election *or appointment* of the Master-at-Arms, and in 1875, pages 1043, 1114, 1121, this view was confirmed. At the latter period the *Ritual* prescribed that the Master-at-Arms might be elected *or appointed*, and the Constitution also said that "the officers of a Subordinate Lodge shall be as prescribed in the Ritual of the Order." At the present time, the Constitution says the same thing (see Section 573 of this Digest), *but the Ritual says that the Master-at-Arms must be elected*. If, therefore, in 1875, the office was declared to be elective *or appointive*, because the Ritual, read in conjunction with the Constitution, said so, it is fair to presume that the same construction may now be placed on the proposition, though the declarations of 1873 and 1875 have not been repealed.

575. A Chancellor Commander cannot appoint as Outer Guard a person who is not a member of his Lodge, nor can a person be installed into any office in the Subordinate Lodge unless he is a member of that Lodge.

Jour., 1888, 4000.

7—Addressing the Chair—Dispensed with, When?

576. Any officer or other member retiring from the Lodge under an order from the Chancellor Commander, or entering it again after having performed the duty for which being sent out of the Lodge, is not required to give the sign on retiring or re-entering, but must work his way through the doors.

Jour., 1873, Appendix 38.

8—Trustees—Must Not Exceed Their Authority.

577. Neither an officer nor a "board of trustees" has a right to transcend instructions and expend money without authority; and if it does, the Lodge will not be liable therefor.

Jour., 1871, 374, 395.

9—Consolidation—Of Lodges, a Matter for Local Legislation.

578. The consolidation of Lodges is a proper subject for local legislation.

Jour., 1877, 1421, 1428.

10—Supreme Authority—Communication with, through Grand Lodge—Lodges cannot Pass on, except in Regular Way.

579. A Subordinate Lodge under the jurisdiction of a Grand Lodge, can communicate with the Supreme Lodge only through its Grand Body; any other course is improper and illegal.

*Jour., 1872, 618, 630.
1875, 1148.
1877, 1433, 1447.
1886, 3549, 3726.*

580. No committee of a Subordinate Lodge, acting within its own Body, has any right to pass upon the conduct of the Supreme Lodge or its officers, except in the regular way and in accordance with our law, and to permit or recognize such action in any other way would be subversive of all law and order.

Jour., 1877, 1433, 1446, 1447.

SUNDAY.

581. Neither a Grand Lodge nor a Grand Chancellor has a legal or moral right to permit the institution of new Lodges, or to permit Subordinate Lodges already instituted to hold regular convocations to transact their business and work of a Lodge of the Order of the Knights of Pythias on the first day of the week, which is known throughout the world as "Sunday." The rule established in relation to the institution of new Lodges or permitting Subordinate Lodges to hold their regular meetings for the transaction of ordinary business on Sunday, applies with much stronger force to the holding of balls or other amusements in a Lodge capacity, or using any of the emblems of the Order whatsoever on the Sabbath in connection therewith.

Jour., 1886, 3287, 3525, 3527, Errata, page i.

SUPPLIES.

1. How and by Whom Furnished (582); through the Supreme Keeper of Records and Seal (583, 584, 585, 586).
   (a) Credit System—Extends only to Grand Keepers of Records and Seal and Deputy Supreme Chancellors (587).
   (b) Rebate—Allowed to the extent of foreign duties (588).
2. Prices Charged by Grand Lodges—As a general proposition, left to them (589), but must not exceed that charged by Supreme Lodge (590).

1—How and by Whom Furnished—Through the Supreme Keeper of Records and Seal.

582. All printed or other materials furnished by the Supreme Lodge to any Grand or Subordinate Lodge, members thereof or other parties, for creating a revenue for the Supreme Lodge, shall be known under the general heading of "Supplies," which supplies shall be furnished as may be from time to time specified, changed, altered, or amended by legislation at the regular sessions.

Supreme Lodge By-Law.

583. All supplies embraced in the price list, issued by the Supreme Keeper of Records and Seal, except the jewel cases, application cards and delinquent notices, shall hereafter be legally obtainable only from his office.

Jour., 1890, 4861, 5392, 5426.

584. With the exception of Official Receipts and Official Digests, all supplies for Subordinate Lodges shall be furnished hereafter through the Grand Lodges, except to those Subordinate Lodges working under the immediate jurisdiction of the Supreme Lodge of the World.

Jour., 1884, 3031.

585. Unless properly procured from the proper officers of the Supreme Lodge, private parties have no authority to furnish blanks, etc., but this legislation does not apply to blanks, such as applications for membership, etc., which have not heretofore been furnished by or through the Supreme Keeper of Records and Seal.

Jour., 1884, 2955, 2993, 2994, 3064.

586. In order to maintain uniformity, all Charter Plates are furnished, as "Supplies" by the Supreme Lodge.

Jour., 1869, 68, 120.
1870, 166, 175, 214.

(a)—Credit System—Extends only to Grand Keepers of Records and Seal and Deputy Supreme Chancellors.

587. The Supreme Keeper of Records and Seal is authorized to furnish supplies to Grand Keepers of Records and Seal when ordered over the Seal of a Grand Lodge, and Deputy Supreme Chancellors, on credit, requiring settlement in full at the end of the month, but not to others, unless the cash accompany the order asking for such supplies.

Jour., 1871, 410,
1888, 4137, 4584, 4654.
1890, 4860, 5314, 5335.

(b)—Rebate—Allowed to the Extent of Foreign Duties.

588. It was ordered that on "supplies" furnished to Jurisdictions outside the United States, a rebate, equal to the amount of customs duties charged by the respective countries, be allowed by the Supreme Keeper of Records and Seal.

Jour., 1888, 4135, 4136, 4584.

2—Prices Charged by Grand Lodges—As a General Proposition Left to Them, but must Not Exceed that Charged by Supreme Lodge.

589. Upon the question being raised as to the right of Grand Lodges to charge Subordinates for Installation Books, the Supreme Lodge ruled:

It is entirely within the power of each Grand Lodge to prescribe the terms upon which they will furnish supplies to their Subordinate Lodges.

Jour., 1878, 1612, 1620.

590. On a question involving the price to be charged by Grand Lodges, to their Subordinates, for articles furnished by the Supreme Lodge as "supplies," the laws of the Grand Lodge prescribing a much higher rate, and being in conflict with the rate prescribed by the Supreme Lodge, it was held:

Special legislation would take precedence, and the special act fixing price of Cards as referred to, becomes the law from date of passage and publication, and laws of Grand or Subordinate Lodges in conflict therewith are void ; and further, that powers previously delegated to Grand Lodges, fixing the price of supplies, etc., to Subordinate Lodges, would be abrogated by such special acts of the Supreme Lodge.

Jour., 1880, 1827, 2003.

SUPREME CHANCELLOR.

1. General Powers of (591, 592, 593, 594, 595, 596, 597, 598, 599, 600).
2. Parades—Cannot order a general demonstration (601).
3. Decisions—Stand as law till reversed (602).
4. Revision of Constitutions—Legislation regarding (603).
5. Salary and Expenses—Both paid by Supreme Lodge for the general work (604); latter paid by Grand or Subordinate Lodges, for instituting (605).

1—General Powers of.

591. The Supreme Chancellor shall exercise, as occasion may require, all the rights appertaining to his high office, in accordance with the usages of the Order. He shall have a watchful supervision over all Grand Lodges and Subordinate Lodges under the immediate jurisdiction of the Supreme

Lodge, and require all the constitutional enactments, rules and edicts of the Supreme Lodge to be duly and promptly observed, and that the dress, work and discipline of the Order everywhere are uniform.

Const., Art. III, Sec. 2.

592. Among his special prerogatives are the following :
To call special sessions of the Supreme Lodge, or conventions of Supreme Officers in council.

Const., Art. III, Sec. 2.

593. To visit any Grand or Subordinate Lodge under the immediate jurisdiction of this Supreme Lodge, and to give such instructions and directions as the good of the Order may require.

Const., Art. III, Sec. 2.

594. To cause to be executed and securely to preserve and keep the official bonds and securities of the Supreme Master of Exchequer and Supreme Keeper of Records and Seal.

Const., Art. III, Sec. 2.

595. To grant warrants of dispensation, during the recess of the Supreme Lodge, for the institution of new Subordinate Lodges, which dispensations shall be in force until taken up by charters granted in lieu thereof by a properly instituted Grand Lodge, and to promptly notify the Supreme Keeper of Records and Seal of the issuing of said warrants of dispensation.

Const., Art. III, Sec. 2.

596. To grant warrants of dispensation, during the recess of the Supreme Lodge, for the institution of Grand Lodges, in States, countries, districts or Territories where the same have not been established.

Const., Art. III, Sec. 2.

597. To suspend or remove any derelict or contumacious officer for cause, he having right of appeal to the Supreme Lodge, and to fill any vacancy by appointment until filled by regular election.

Const., Art. III, Sec. 2.

598. To appoint and commission a Deputy Supreme Chancellor for special purposes of instituting Grand Lodges and installing their officers, or otherwise as may be required, in all States, districts, Territories or countries where Lodges are established, and not having any Grand Lodge.

Const., Art. III, Sec. 2.

599. He shall, at the next regular session, present a full report of his acts during the recess of the Supreme Lodge.

Const., Art. III, Sec. 2.

600. He may hear and decide such questions of law as may be submitted to him by Grand or Subordinate Lodges under the immediate jurisdiction of this Supreme Lodge, and all such decisions shall be binding upon the bodies submitting the same until fully passed upon and disaffirmed or reversed by this Supreme Lodge.

Const., Art. III, Sec. 2.

2—Parades—Cannot Order General Demonstration.

601. The Supreme Chancellor has no power to order a grand demonstration or parade of the Order, nor is it a matter upon which the Supreme Lodge should legislate. Any Subordinate Lodge desiring to appear at such a time should obtain a dispensation from the Grand Chancellor of its Jurisdiction.

Jour., 1874, 899, 933.

3—Decisions—Stand as Law till Reversed.

602. A decision of a Supreme Chancellor stands as law until repealed.

Jour., 1875, 1034, 1045.

4—Revision of Constitutions—Legislation Regarding.

603. In 1888 the Supreme Chancellor stated, that upon entering upon the duties of his office: "I discovered from the varied questions which came to me in connection with your jurisprudence that a vast diversity of opinion existed in regard not only to the construction, but also the provisions of the laws both in Grand and Subordinate Constitutions in the various Jurisdictions. I at once concluded that the better plan would be to thoroughly revise these laws and inform the several Grand Lodges of the points wherein they differed with your Constitution and enactments"; he then set forth the changes which he had ordered. This action of the Supreme Chancellor being referred to a committee, they reported as follows, and their report was adopted:

They find that this is a report by the Supreme Chancellor of his efforts to cause the revision of the Grand Lodge Constitutions and Subordinate Lodge Constitutions in the various Jurisdictions, and specifying the parts of said Constitutions which he required should be changed, and the steps taken by him to cause such changes to be made.

Your committee do not think the Supreme Chancellor has the direct power to revise a Grand Lodge or other Constitution, but they have no doubt that under Section 2, Article III, of Supreme Lodge Constitution, he has the power and should "see that all the constitutional enactments, rules and edicts of the Supreme Lodge are duly and promptly observed"; and in performing his duties he should call attention to any and all provisions of Constitutions that are in conflict with Supreme law; and though he cannot, in direct terms, compel revision, he may take such steps under the circumstances as the law permits.

Jour., 1888, 3991-4008, 4407, 4494, 4656-4658, 4660.

NOTE.—This is the action of the Supreme Lodge, and is given *verbatim*, because of its ambiguity, the compiler being unable to digest or condense it.

5—Salary and Expenses—Both Paid by Supreme Lodge for the General Work—Latter, Paid by Grand or Subordinate Lodges, for Instituting.

604. The Supreme Chancellor shall receive an annual salary of two thousand dollars, in addition to which his necessary expenses, while in the discharge of the functions of his office, shall be paid by the Supreme Lodge.

Const., Art. III, Sec. 2.

605. The necessary expenses incident to traveling to any point and back to original starting point, for the purpose of instituting any Subordinate or Grand Lodge, by the Supreme Chancellor or his Deputy, shall be paid by the Lodges instituted.

Const., Art. XX.

SUPREME INNER GUARD.

606. The duties of the Supreme Inner Guard are such as are appropriate to his station, or such as may be assigned him by the Supreme Lodge.

Const., Art. III, Sec. 9.

SUPREME KEEPER OF RECORDS AND SEAL.

1. Duties of—Constitutional provisions (607-622).
2. Duties of—Legislative provisions.
   - (a) Reports of Expense—In detail (623); of supplies on hand (624); duplicate bills of supplies and printing (625).
   - (b) Approval of Laws—Shall notify Grand Lodges of (626).
   - (c) Committees, Etc.—Furnish each with Digest and Journals (627); Committee on Credentials with list of delinquent Jurisdictions (628); Representatives with Constitution (629).
   - (d) Journals of Grand Lodges—Preserve and bind (630).
   - (e) Jewels—Of Supreme Lodge, have charge of (631).
3. Board of Audit—To examine books of accounts of, ruled unconstitutional (632).

1—Duties of—Constitutional Provisions.

607. The Supreme Keeper of Records and Seal shall keep a just and true record of all the proceedings of the Supreme Council and Lodge at each session, and transmit to each Grand Lodge as many copies thereof as the Lodge has Past Grand Chancellors and Officers, and one copy for each Subordinate Lodge in their several Jurisdictions, and one to each Lodge under the immediate jurisdiction of the Supreme Lodge.

Const., Art. III, Sec. 6.

608. He shall collect all the revenues of the Supreme Lodge, and pay over the amount to the Supreme Master of Exchequer monthly.

Const., Art. III, Sec. 6.

609. He shall preserve the archives, have charge of the seal, books, papers and other properties of the Supreme Lodge, and deliver the same to his successor when required so to do by the Supreme Lodge.

Const., Art. III, Sec. 6.

610. He shall prepare all charters for Grand Lodges, notify officially all Grand Lodges and officers and members of the Supreme Lodge of all sessions of the Supreme Lodge.

Const., Art. III, Sec. 6.

611. He shall carry on the necessary correspondence of the Supreme Lodge.

Const., Art. III, Sec. 6.

612. He shall keep a Register which shall contain a list of all dispensations and charters granted to Grand Lodges, or warrants of dispensation issued by the Supreme Chancellor for Subordinate Lodges.

Const., Art. III, Sec. 6.

613. He shall keep a record of all Past Grand Chancellors and Representatives entitled to seats in the Supreme Lodge.

Const., Art. III, Sec. 6.

614. He shall attest necessary official papers and documents, perform such other duties as are required by the laws and regulations of the Order and as the Supreme Chancellor or Supreme Lodge may from time to time direct.

Const., Art. III, Sec. 6.

615. He shall be furnished with an office, and shall have regular office hours, and give notice to all Grand Lodges of the time at which he will so attend.

Const., Art. III, Sec. 6.

616. He shall at each session present a report of the general condition of the Order to the Supreme Lodge.

Const., Art. III, Sec. 6.

617. He shall have power to provide himself, at the expense of the Supreme Lodge, with such books, papers and stationery as are necessary for the fulfillment of his duties.

Const., Art. III, Sec. 6.

618. He shall keep in his office a copy of the seal of each Grand and Subordinate Lodge.

Const., Art. III, Sec. 6.

619. He shall submit a quarterly trial balance to the Supreme Chancellor for examination.

Const., Art. III, Sec. 6.

620. He shall also render to each regular session of the Supreme Lodge full and exhaustive copies of his accounts with the Grand and Subordinate Lodges, etc., of and during the whole term of recess passed.

Const., Art. III, Sec. 6.

621. He shall receive for his services, and that of any assistants he may require, such sums as the Supreme Lodge may from time to time determine.

Const., Art. III, Sec. 6.

622. For the faithful performance of his duties he shall give bond, to be executed and approved before his installation, in the sum of ten thousand dollars, with unexceptionable securities, or otherwise the office to be declared vacant and filled by election.

Const., Art. III, Sec. 6.

2—Duties of—Legislative Provisions.

(a)—Report of Expense, in Detail—Of Supplies on Hand—Duplicate Bills of Supplies and Printing.

623. In 1872 it was enacted that thereafter the appropriation for stationery, expenses, etc., of the department of the Supreme Scribe be paid by the Supreme Banker upon the drafts of the Supreme Scribe, countersigned by the Supreme Chancellor, and that a detailed and vouched account of the expenditures of such appropriation be annually submitted by the Supreme Scribe to the Supreme Lodge.

Jour., 1872, 633.

NOTE.—By changing the titles respectively to Supreme Keeper of Records and Seal and Supreme Master of Exchequer, the law, being unrepealed, would now apply to those officers.

624. It is made the duty of the Supreme Keeper of Records and Seal to submit in detail his annual report of supplies ordered and received, in the same manner as the report on printing, etc., submitted by him at the second annual session of the Supreme Lodge (page 172, printed Journal), and that he also report in detail at each annual session such supplies belonging to the Supreme Lodge as he may have on hand.

Jour., 1872, 624.
1874, 987.

625. The Supreme Keeper of Records and Seal is required to furnish the Supreme Chancellor at the expiration of each fiscal year, or as early thereafter as practicable, with a list of all business firms and manufacturers that have furnished any supplies or printing; and that the Supreme Chancellor obtain from each of those firms and manufacturers, duplicate invoices of all such, transmitting the same to the Finance Committee.

Jour., 1882, 2573.
1884, 3032.

(b)—Approval of Laws—Shall Notify Grand Lodge of.

626. The Supreme Keeper of Records and Seal is required to inform Grand Jurisdictions, through their Grand Keeper of Records and Seal, of the approval of Grand Lodge Constitutions, as they may be approved by the Supreme Lodge, with instructions to notify their Subordinates, over the seal of their Grand Lodge, of such approval.

Jour., 1869, 112.

NOTE.—The names of officers, etc, are changed in the foregoing to comport with those now used.

(*c*)—Committees, etc.—Furnish Each with Digest and Journals—Committee on Credentials with List of Delinquent Jurisdictions—Representatives with Constitutions.

627. The Supreme Keeper of Records and Seal was instructed to set apart from the stock on hand one copy of the Official Digest and a full set of the bound Journals of the Supreme Lodge Proceedings, for each of the Standing Committees of the Supreme Lodge, and that the same be furnished to the Chairmen of said committees at the beginning of each of the sessions of the Supreme Lodge.

Jour., 1882, 2421.

628. Hereafter, at the beginning of each session of the Supreme Lodge, and immediately upon the appointment of the Committee on Credentials and Returns, it shall be the duty of the Supreme Keeper of Records and Seal to place in the hands of the Chairman of said committee a complete report of all Grand Jurisdictions in arrears for Representative tax to the Supreme Lodge.

Jour., 1882, 2458.

629. The Supreme Keeper of Records and Seal was instructed to provide each member of the Supreme Lodge at its sessions hereafter with a copy of the Supreme Lodge Constitution and Laws.

Jour., 1886, 3511.

(*d*)—Journals of Grand Lodges—Preserve and Bind.

630. It is the duty of the Supreme Keeper of Records and Seal to carefully preserve all printed Journals of Proceedings, and all periodicals of the Order received by him, and at all suitable times cause the same to be bound in permanent binding for preservation in the archives of the Order.

Jour., 1876, 1275.

(*e*)—Jewels—Of Supreme Lodge, have Charge of.

631. It is made a part of the duty of the Supreme Keeper of Records and Seal to take charge of the Supreme Lodge Officers' Jewels.

Jour., 1869, 121.

NOTE.—This would seem to be greatly qualified by the legislation of 1890 permitting the retention of the Jewels by the officers.

3—Board of Audit—To Examine Books of Account of—Ruled Unconstitutional.

632. A Board of Auditors, with full powers to audit and examine the books and accounts of the Supreme Keeper of Records and Seal and Supreme Master of Exchequer, and to adopt such measures as may appear best for the investigation of the financial affairs of the Supreme Lodge, has been held to be out of order and unconstitutional.

Jour., 1873, 681, 729.

SUPREME LECTURER.

633. In 1873 a proposition was offered in regard to appointing a Supreme Lecturer to visit and instruct all Lodges desiring instruction in the Secret Work, and the committee to whom the matter was referred reported that the subject was one for local legislation, and the same was adopted, but in 1877 a resolution was passed, appointing "a Lecturer on the origin, rise and progress of the Order, in this Supreme Jurisdiction, and that he visit the various Subordinate Lodges, upon their invitation, the said Lodges defraying all expenses of such invitation."

Jour., 1873, 694, 734.
1877, 1449.

NOTE.—The Supreme Lecturer, appointed in 1877, made regular reports to the Supreme Lodge at its sessions in 1878, 1880, 1882, 1884, 1886 and 1888, but owing to his death in 1889, and no appointment being made in 1890, the position is now vacant.

SUPREME LODGE.

1. General Powers (634-645).
2. How Constituted (646).
3. Sessions—Regular (647); special (648); parades to be first day of (649); hall in which held must be suitable (650).
4. Quorum—A majority, to transact business (651).
5. The Head of the Order—No Lodge may exist except by its authority (652).
6. New Members—Their eligibility (653) and admission (654).
7. Revenue of—From Representative tax and supplies (655).

1—General Powers.

634. The Supreme Lodge is the source of all true and legitimate authority in the Order of Knights of Pythias wheresoever established; it possesses original and exclusive jurisdiction and power.

Const., Art. I, Sec. 1.

635. To establish, regulate and control the forms, ceremonies, Written and Unwritten Work, and to change, alter and annul the same, and to provide for the safe keeping and uniform teaching and dissemination of the same.

Const., Art. I, Sec. 1, Sub. a.

636. To provide, print and furnish all Rituals, forms, ceremonies, cards and odes, charts and certificates.

Const., Art. I, Sec. 1, Sub. b.

637. To prescribe the form, material and color of all regalia, emblems, jewels and charts, and to designate the uniform of the Order.

Const., Art. I, Sec. 1, Sub. c.

638. To provide for the emanation and distribution of all passwords, and regulate the mode and manner of using the same, and generally to prescribe such regulations as may be necessary to secure the safe and easy intercourse and identification of the brethren.

Const., Art. I, Sec. 1, Sub. d.

639. To establish the Order in States, districts, Territories, provinces or countries where the same has not been engrafted.

Const., Art. I, Sec. 1, Sub. e.

640. To provide a revenue for the Supreme Lodge, by means of a Representative tax on each Grand Lodge, charges for supplies furnished by it, and dues from Subordinate Lodges under its immediate jurisdiction.

Const., Art. I, Sec. 1, Sub. f.

641. To provide for annual reports from each Grand Lodge, and for semi-annual reports from each Subordinate Lodge under its immediate jurisdiction.

Const., Art. I, Sec. 1, Sub. g.

642. To hear and determine all appeals from Grand and Subordinate Lodges, when the same are properly brought before it in accordance with the regulations of the Order, and to provide by legislation for the enforcement of its decisions.

Const., Art. I, Sec. 1, Sub. h.

643. To enact laws and regulations of general application, to carry into effect the foregoing and all other powers reserved by this Constitution to the Supreme Lodge or its officers, and such as may be necessary to enforce its legitimate authority over Grand and Subordinate Lodges under its immediate jurisdiction.

Const., Art. I, Sec. 1, Sub. i.

644. To charter Grand Lodges, and to define the territorial extent of their jurisdiction, and to charter Subordinate Lodges not within the territorial jurisdiction of any Grand Lodge, and to provide a Constitution for each Subordinate Lodge under its immediate jurisdiction.

Const., Art. I, Sec. 1, Sub. k.

645. The Supreme Lodge reserves to itself the right, at any time, by proper amendments, duly adopted, to this Constitution, to resume any additional power necessary to promote the well being and harmony of the Order.

Const., Art. VII, Sec. 2.

2—How Constituted.

646. The Supreme Lodge shall consist of:
(*a*) All Past Supreme Chancellors.
(*b*) Sitting Past Supreme Chancellor.
(*c*) Supreme Chancellor (presiding officer).
(*d*) Supreme Vice-Chancellor.
(*e*) Supreme Prelate.
(*f*) Supreme Master of Exchequer.
(*g*) Supreme Keeper of Records and Seal.
(*h*) Supreme Secretary of the Endowment Rank.
(*i*) Major General of the Uniform Rank.
(*k*) Supreme Master-at-Arms.
(*l*) Supreme Inner Guard.
(*m*) Supreme Outer Guard.
(*n*) Two Supreme Representatives from each Grand Lodge under the jurisdiction of the Supreme Lodge, until there are twenty thousand members belonging to one Grand Lodge; and one Supreme Representative for each additional ten thousand members; and the number of members shall be determined by the last official reports prior to the session of the Supreme Lodge; Provided, that no Grand Lodge shall be entitled to more than four Supreme Representatives.
(*o*) All Past Grand Chancellors duly recognized by the Supreme Lodge.

Const., Art. II, Sec. 1.

Supreme Lodge. 159

3—Sessions—Regular—Special—Parades to be First Day of—Hall in Which Held must be Suitable.

647. Sessions of the Supreme Lodge shall be held biennially on the fourth Tuesday of April; Provided, that at any session of the Supreme Lodge, a month and a day of meeting other than the fourth Tuesday in April may be selected for the next succeeding session by a vote of two-thirds of the members present. The place for the holding of each biennial session shall be determined at the preceding biennial session : Provided, that if no place is determined upon by the Supreme Lodge, the biennial session shall be held in the City of Baltimore.

Const., Art. IV.

NOTE.—This is presumed to mean Baltimore, Maryland.

648. Among the "special prerogatives" of the Supreme Chancellor is the power to call special sessions of the Supreme Lodge.

Const., Art. III, Sec. 2.

NOTE.—Though according to this, among the special prerogatives of the Supreme Chancellor, he can "call special sessions of the Supreme Lodge," yet it does not anywhere designate the manner of the call or the business which can be transacted at such a session, notwithstanding the fact that under the Articles of Incorporation he is clothed with powers " to convene extra sessions of the Supreme Lodge *in the manner prescribed in the Constitution of the said Supreme Lodge.*"

649. In all future sessions of the Supreme Lodge, any and all invitations to attend public celebrations, parades, banquets or other exercises, outside the regular business of the Supreme Lodge, shall be peremptorily declined by the Supreme Lodge, except such public exercises as are fixed for the first day of the session.

Jour., 1877, 1432.

650. It is made the duty now of the Supreme Chancellor, either by personal inspection or correspondence, to satisfy himself that the room selected for holding the session of the Supreme Lodge is suitable for that purpose.

Jour., 1882. 2461.

4—Quorum—A Majority, to Transact Business.

651. Representatives of a majority of the Grand Lodges shall constitute a quorum to transact business, but a less number may meet and adjourn from day to day.

Const., Art. IX.

NOTE.—The language of Subdivision 7, of the Act of Incorporation. Section 285, of this Digest prescribes: "A Representative from a majority of the Grand Lodges * * * shall constitute a quorum."

5—The Head of the Order—No Lodge may Exist except by Its Authority.

652. As at present constituted, the Supreme Lodge is in fact what its name not only imports, but expresses, viz., *the only Head of the Order in the World;* and as a consequence, no organization, Lodge or other collection of men, claiming or pretending to act as a Lodge of Knights of Pythias, save and except under and by virtue of the authority of this "Head of the Order," can be, or have any right to claim to be, any part of the organization.

Jour., 1875, 1141, 1142.

6—New Members—Their Eligibility and Admission.

653. No one shall be eligible to any office in the Supreme Lodge, unless he has been duly admitted to the Supreme Lodge by being either a Representative or a Past Grand Chancellor.

Const., Art. II, Sec. 4.

654. New members are only admitted to the Supreme Lodge at the opening of the morning sessions of the two first days and the morning session of the last day.

Jour., 1875, 1166.

7—Revenue of—From Representative Tax and Supplies.

655. Each Grand Lodge shall pay to the Supreme Lodge the sum of fifty dollars annually for each Representative to which it is entitled, and each Grand and Subordinate Lodge shall pay for supplies such sums as may be fixed in the By-Laws of the Supreme Lodge.

Const., Art. X.

SUPREME MASTER AT ARMS.

656. The duties of the Supreme Master at Arms are such as are appropriate to his station, or such as may be assigned him by the Supreme Lodge.

Const., Art. III, Sec. 9.

SUPREME MASTER OF EXCHEQUER.

657. The Supreme Master of Exchequer shall render to the Supreme Chancellor a quarterly statement of the condition of funds in his hands.

Const., Art. III, Sec. 5.

658. He shall make to the Supreme Lodge, at its regular sessions, a true and perfect account of his doings, together with an account of all moneys received and disbursed, giving items in detail—all the earnings thereon accrued from interest or other investments.

Const., Art. III, Sec. 5.

659. He shall pay all orders drawn on him by the Supreme Chancellor, properly attested by the Supreme Keeper of Records and Seal.

Const., Art. III, Sec. 5.

660. For the faithful performance of his duties, he shall give bond, to be executed and approved before his installation, in the sum of fifty thousand dollars, with unexceptionable securities, or otherwise the office to be declared vacant and filled by election.

Const., Art. III, Sec. 5.

661. He shall receive for his services such sum as the Supreme Lodge may from time to time determine.

Const., Art. III, Sec. 5.

SUPREME OUTER GUARD.

662. The duties of the Supreme Outer Guard are such as are appropriate to his station, or such as may be assigned him by the Supreme Lodge.

Const., Art. III, Sec. 9.

SUPREME PRELATE.

663. The Supreme Prelate shall open and close the Supreme Lodge with prayer, and perform all obligatory ceremonials as prescribed in the Ritual or usages of the Order, and such other duties as comport with his office.

Const., Art. III, Sec. 4.

SUPREME REPRESENTATIVE.

1. **Eligibility.**
   (*a*) Past Grand Chancellor—Must be a, in good standing (664-669).
   (*b*) Residence and Membership—Must be *bona fide*, in both (670, 671).
2. **How Many**—Constitutional provision (672) and construction as to (673).
3. **Election of**—In Grand Lodges, when formed (674); in new Grand Lodges (675); additional Representatives (672, 673, 676, 677); terms (674, 675, 676, 677).
   Grand Lodge cannot vacate seat of, no sufficient charges being filed (681).
5. **Contested Seats**—Notice of, must be filed (682); Supreme Lodge does
4. **Vacancies**—How filled, must be for balance of term (678, 679, 680); not favor contest that only operates to create a vacancy (683).
6. **Suspended Grand Lodge**—Representation refused (684).
7. **Alternates**—Not recognized (685).
8. **Irregular Credentials**—Admitted on, cases cited (686).
9. **Credentials**—New form of, showing exact service qualifying for Past Grand Chancellor (687).

1—Eligibility—(*a*) Past Grand Chancellor—Must be in Good Standing.

664. Supreme Representatives must be Past Grand Chancellors in good standing in their respective Grand and Subordinate Lodges.

Const., Art. II, Sec. 2.

665. No one is eligible to election as Supreme Representative until he is entitled to the rank and title of Past Grand Chancellor.

Jour., 1874, 900, 908.
1875, 1035, 1113, 1121.
1876, 1194, 1266, 1267.

666. Any Grand Chancellor, who has served a full term in that office, and against whom no charges are pending, shall be entitled to the rank and title of Past Grand Chancellor as soon as his successor is installed, and is thereupon eligible to election as Supreme Representative, but not before.

Jour., 1874, 900, 908.
1875, 1035, 1113, 1121.
1876, 1194, 1266, 1267.

667. A Grand Lodge has a right at any time while in session to proceed with the election of a Supreme Representative when a vacancy in that position exists, and if the installation of officers has been completed the outgoing Grand Chancellor, being passed to the chair of

Past Grand Chancellor, is eligible to the position of Supreme Representative; the Supreme Constitution only requires that, to be elected as a Supreme Representative, the member must be a Past Grand Chancellor, and places no limit in that direction. (Jour., 1876, pp. 1266 and 1267, Root vs. Meech.)

Jour., 1888, 4123, 4580, 4581.

668. A retiring Grand Chancellor, who will be entitled to receive the Supreme Rank when the Supreme Lodge shall meet, is not eligible to election as Supreme Representative unless his successor is installed previous to such election.

Jour., 1888, 3996, 3997.

669. A Grand Chancellor who has served a full year, and in every way qualified under the law, and whose successor has been duly elected, but not yet installed, is not an eligible candidate for the position of Supreme Representative.

Jour., 1882, 2443, 2568.

(*b*)—Residence and Membership must be Bona Fide in Both.

670. Supreme Representatives must be *bona fide* residents of the Grand Jurisdictions they represent during the entire term for which they are elected, and removal of residence from their Grand Jurisdiction shall operate as a forfeiture of their positions.

Const., Art. II, Sec. 2.

671. By the action of the Supreme Lodge on the credentials of an appointed Supreme Representative, the fact developed itself, that the appointee was a member of a Lodge in a Jurisdiction other than the one which he was appointed to represent, and the Supreme Lodge decided that, on that ground, the appointment be not recognized.

Jour., 1882, 2266.

2—How Many—Constitutional Provision and Construction as to.

672. There shall be two Supreme Representatives from each Grand Lodge under the jurisdiction of the Supreme Lodge, until there are twenty thousand members belonging to one Grand Lodge; and one Supreme Representative for each additional ten thousand members; and the number of members shall be determined by the last official report prior to the session of the Supreme Lodge; Provided, that no Grand Lodge shall be entitled to more than four Supreme Representatives.

Const., Art. II, Sec. 1, Sub. n.

673. It requires 30,000 members in a Jurisdiction to entitle it to three Supreme Representatives.

Jour., 1880, 2036.
1888, 3983, 4408, 4514.

NOTE.—These arose out of the presentation of the credentials of a *third* Representative from Pennsylvania and Ohio, based on a membership of 28,120 and 20,952, respectively. it being claimed that an *excess*, over 20,000, entitled them to an extra Representative, under the terms of Article II, Section 1, Subdivision *n* of the Supreme Constitution.

3—Election of—In Grand Lodges, when Formed—In New Grand Lodges—Additional Representation—Terms.

674. Supreme Representatives shall be elected to serve for the term of four years from and after the first day of January next succeeding their election; except that, at the organization of any new Grand Lodge, two Supreme Representatives shall be elected, one to serve to the 31st day of December of the first odd-numbered year thereafter, and one to serve to the 31st day of December of the second odd-numbered year thereafter.

Const., Art. II, Sec. 2.

675. The law provides that the term of Supreme Representatives shall be for the term of four years from and after the first day of January next succeeding their election, and in no instance except in the formation of a new Grand Lodge can a Supreme Representative be elected for a shorter term of service than four years.

Jour., 1890, 5237, 5239, 5428.

676. When a Jurisdiction is entitled to more than two Supreme Representatives, the additional Representative or Representatives shall be elected, as above provided, for a term of four years, at the annual election preceding the commencement of his or their terms.

Const., Art. II, Sec. 2.

677. Where a Grand Jurisdiction having gained, since the adjournment of its Grand Lodge session, a membership entitling it to an additional Supreme Representative, and it being impossible to hold an election before the session of the Supreme Lodge, and the Grand Chancellor having appointed such additional Representative, the term of office of such appointment must be for the term of four years, counting from the first of January next preceding that session of the Supreme Lodge.

Jour., 1890, 5237, 5239, 5428.

4—Vacancies—How Filled—Must be for Balance of Term —Grand Lodge cannot Vacate Seat of, No Sufficient Charges being Filed.

678. In case of a vacancy in the position of Supreme Representative, from death, removal or any other cause, such vacancy shall be filled in such manner as may have been provided by law by the Grand Lodge which he represented.

Const., Art. II, Sec. 2.

679. The term of a Supreme Representative, under our laws (Constitution, Article II, Section 2), must end with the 31st day of December of an odd-numbered year; and a Grand Lodge has no right to elect, nor a Grand Chancellor to appoint, a Supreme Representative for a term ending at any other time: the certificates of Supreme Representatives appointed to fill vacancies should not show that such appointments were made "for the present session of the Supreme Lodge," or "until the next session of the Grand Lodge."

Jour., 1888, 3983.

680. Appointments to fill vacancies must be made for the unexpired portion of the term for which the Supreme Representatives were elected.

Jour., 1890, 5428.

681. When, at a previous session, the credentials of a Supreme Representative (W. C. Troy, N. C.) had been filed and approved; and where, at the next session it appeared that his Grand Lodge had meantime declared his seat vacant, and elected another in his place, the Supreme Lodge declared the course of his Grand Lodge illegal, their action not based on sufficient charges, and seated him.

*Jour., 1880, 1793, 1796.
1882, 2265.*

NOTE.—The report fails to show the cause for the action on the part of the Grand Lodge of North Carolina, but a reference to their record evidences that it was because he had "failed to furnish an excuse for non-attendance at the previous session of the Supreme Lodge." (Journal of North Carolina, 1882, 28.)

5—Contested Seats—Notice of, must be Filed—Supreme Lodge does Not Favor Contest that Only Operates to Create a Vacancy.

682. In matters of contest for the seat of Supreme Representative, notice of said contest shall be filed with the Supreme Keeper of Records and Seal at least thirty days prior to the session of this body: Provided, that the meeting of the Grand Lodge at which the election is had, or that the appointment which is contested, is not within thirty days of a session of this Supreme Lodge.

Jour., 1890, 5469.

683. Where, in a contested case of representation of a Grand Lodge, one of the contestants claiming to hold over, the other being elected for the term, which latter was in dispute, the Supreme Lodge, in seating the Representative who had been elected, as against the contestant who claimed, on a technical construction of the constitutional provision to hold over, ruled :

This construction, however, besides giving no effect to the precise words used, would only deprive the Grand Jurisdiction of a Representative at this session, as it could not be used to cause the term of the contestant to be so extended as to entitle him to a seat as Representative in this Body at this time. They would hesitate long before making a decision which would curtail the representation of any Grand Lodge and merely cause a vacancy. All intendments are to be in favor of giving each Grand Lodge its full voice and vote in this Body.

Jour., 1880, 1794, 1933.

6—Suspended Grand Lodge—Representation Refused.

684. The Supreme Representatives of a Jurisdiction that had been suspended by order of the Supreme Chancellor for cause, being present at the opening of the Supreme Lodge, and without the S. A. P. W., were not permitted to remain.

Jour., 1888, 3976.

7—Alternates—Not Recognized.

685. There is no law of the Order authorizing the election of alternate Supreme Representatives.

Jour., 1871, 342, 343.

8—Irregular Credentials—Admitted on, Cases Cited.

686. At different times Supreme Representatives have been recognized and admitted to a seat in the Supreme Lodge in a way other than prescribed, viz. :

On a telegram stating that the party had been appointed.

Jour., 1875, 1095, 1096.
1886, 3508, 3519.

On the Grand Lodge returns on file in the office of the Supreme Keeper of Records and Seal, showing the election, though there were no credentials.

Jour., 1878, 1481, 1482.
1888, 3982, 3983.

Where Grand Lodge had been suspended, the Representatives of new Grand Lodge were admitted to seats.

Jour., 1871, 291, 342, 386, 388.

9—Credentials—New Form of, Showing Exact Service Qualifying for Past Grand Chancellor.

687. The Supreme Keeper of Records and Seal is hereby instructed to prepare and issue a new form of Certificate for Supreme Representatives, which shall contain an explicit statement of the exact date on which the bearer attained the rank of Past Grand Chancellor, and the exact date on which he was elected Supreme Representative.

Jour., 1884, 3026.

SUPREME SECRETARY OF THE ENDOWMENT RANK.

688. The Supreme Secretary of the Endowment Rank shall perform such duties as are provided for in the laws relating to the Endowment Rank, and such other duties as he may be required to perform by the Supreme Lodge from time to time. For the faithful performance of his duties, he shall give bond, with good sureties, to be executed and approved before his installation, in such sum as the Board of Control shall determine.

Const., Art. III, Sec. 7.

SUPREME VICE CHANCELLOR.

689. The Supreme Vice Chancellor, in the event of the death, removal or physical incompetency of his superior, shall act as Supreme Chancellor; and if he so acts for the remainder of the term he shall be paid the salary to which the Supreme Chancellor would have been entitled for the time, and at the close of the term be entitled to the honors of the office. At all other times he shall perform such duties as may be assigned him by the Supreme Lodge or the Supreme Chancellor.

Const., Art. III, Sec. 3.

TERMS.

690. A term of the Supreme Lodge shall be two years, the term of Subordinate Lodges working immediately under the control of the Supreme Lodge shall be six months, and the terms of Grand Lodges shall be not less than one year, and the terms of Subordinate Lodges working under the control of Grand Lodges shall be fixed by the several Grand Jurisdictions; Provided, that no term of a Subordinate Lodge shall be less than six months.
Const., Art. XXVIII.

691. A Grand Lodge has the right to legislate upon duties for its officers and the terms of office; Provided, their legislation is in accordance with the Supreme Lodge Constitution, and the ritualistic work of the Order.
Jour., 1880, 1827, 2003.

TERRITORIAL JURISDICTION.

1. General Rulings (692, 693, 694).
2. Special Rulings—Case of Territory divided into two States (695).

1—General Rulings.

692. The Supreme Lodge cannot constitutionally confer upon a State Grand Jurisdiction authority to grant Dispensations or charters for the organization of Subordinate Lodges in other States and Territories; said Lodges to be under the immediate supervision or control of said Grand Jurisdiction until such time as there shall be five Subordinate Lodges instituted in each of said States or Territories, and all revenues whatsoever now derived by the Supreme Lodge in the institution and control of Subordinate Lodges, to appertain to and be transmitted to the Supreme Lodge as soon as received; nor will it approve a section in a Grand Lodge Constitution by which the power would be given to such Grand Lodge to assume jurisdiction of Subordinate Lodges in an adjacent State; but while extra-territorial jurisdiction, sought to be attained in that manner, has always been refused, yet the Supreme Lodge has, at times, placed such Subordinates under the jurisdiction of a neighboring Grand Lodge.
Jour., 1871, 427.
1872, 621, 627.
1873, Appendix 6, 7, 8.
1875, 1035–1037.
1876, 1310.
1878, 1514, 1515, 1623.
1880, 2025,
1882, 2412, 2427.
1884, 3023, 3044, 3045.

693. The Supreme Lodge refused to grant the prayer of a memorial of a Grand Lodge to extend its territorial limit so as to admit applicants residing outside their boundary and within that of an adjacent Jurisdiction; the Supreme Lodge expressed grave doubt as to the right of the Supreme Lodge, after the organization of a Grand Lodge to in any way interfere with the territory assigned to the jurisdiction and control of the Grand Body, without the consent and approval of such Grand Lodge.

Jour., 1886, 3507, 3543.

694. The order of a Supreme Chancellor placing any Lodge in any territory under the jurisdiction of the Grand Lodge already organized, becomes a nullity upon the organization of a Grand Lodge in the Territory or State where said Subordinate Lodge is located.

Jour., 1886, 3286, 3525, Errata, page 1.

2—Special Ruling—Case of Territory Divided into Two States.

695. Where a Grand Lodge had been regularly organized in a Territory, with jurisdiction coextensive with the limits thereof; and where, upon the admission of said Territory into the sisterhood of States the same was divided into two states; and further, where the Supreme Chancellor authorized, during recess of the Supreme Lodge, said two states to organize separate Grand Lodges, comprised of the Lodges then existing in each of the respective divisions of the former Territory now constituted as separate states, the Supreme Lodge declared the acts of the Supreme Chancellor null and void, and that the organization of a Grand Lodge covering a part of the territory included in another Grand Jurisdiction is illegal.

Jour., 1890, 4836, 4838, 5281, 5282, 5283, 5349. 5350, 5398, 5399.

TRAVELING SHIELDS.

1. Issuance (696), Form (697), and Purpose (698).
2. Responsibility—Rests on Lodge issuing (699).
3. Withdrawal Card—Holder of, not entitled to shield (700).

1—Issuance—Form and Purpose.

696. Traveling shields can only be used or recognized when procured from the Supreme Lodge of the prescribed and legal form, and under its restrictions, by Grand Lodges, and from them issued to the Subordinate Lodges for issuance to members, except it be where no Grand Lodge is in existence or recognized by this Supreme Lodge, and in such cases from the Deputy Supreme Chancellor in charge of said jurisdiction.

Const., Art. XXV.

697. The form of a Traveling Shield, prescribed in 1874, with its provisions, prescriptions, limitations and specifications, as thereon, therein and thereto appended, set forth and expressed, was adopted for use and immediate issuance.

*Jour., 1873, 696, 771-773.
1874, 969-972.*

698. Subordinate Lodges are authorized to issue Traveling Shields to applicants for any length of time from one month to the date of the next meeting of the Supreme Lodge, but no longer; the dues to be paid by the applicant are required to be paid for the length of time covered by the Shield; and said Traveling Shield is only to be regarded as evidence of the good standing of the holder in his Lodge, and as a letter of credit or relief shield indicating the amount of weekly and funeral benefits to which the holder is entitled, *and in no case should any money be paid unless the Shield is presented to any Lodge, except his own.* In case of sudden and severe sickness or death among strangers, the relief shield will be a sure evidence of membership.

*Jour., 1875, 1015-1022, 1106, 1144-1146.
1876, 1197.*

NOTE.—At the time of the legislation of 1875, bearing on the duration of a Shield, the Supreme Lodge met *annually;* it now meets bi-ennially. The question therefore arises whether or not this Section should be construed to the full extent of its wording now or held within the meaning of the legislation at the time at which it was passed.

2—Responsibility—Rests on Lodge Issuing.

699. Whenever a Subordinate Lodge shall pay money, either by itself, or through a relief committee, to a member of another Lodge, who is entitled to such relief under a Relief Shield, the Lodge of which the person relieved is a member, shall be responsible for the repayment to the Lodge, or Relief Committee, of the money so paid, and must promptly discharge such liability.

Jour., 1880, 1989, 1990, 2005, 2006.

3—Withdrawal Card—Holder of—Not Entitled to Shield.

700. A member holding a Withdrawal Card is not entitled to a Traveling Shield.

Jour., 1875, 1042, 1114, 1121.

NOTE.—Under this ruling, a member holding an unexpired Traveling Shield should be required to surrender it before a Withdrawal Card is granted, since the Lodge would be responsible for relief extended under the Shield by a sister Lodge. (See Section 699.)

TRIAL.

1. Appearance—Failure in, Lodge may proceed (701).
2. Testimony of Non-members—Competent (702).
3. Notice of—Mailing, sufficient (703).
4. Criminals—Lodge need not wait action of court regarding (704, 705).

1—Appearance—Failure in, Lodge may Proceed.

701. Where charges are brought against a member of a Lodge and the member so charged fails to appear either in person or by counsel, his Lodge has a right to proceed to trial just as if he were present.

Jour., 1878, 1619.
1888, 4120, 4575. 4581.

2—Testimony of Non-members—Competent.

702. It is legal and proper to receive the testimony of a person not a member of the Order for or against an officer or member on trial under charges.

Jour., 1877, 1380, 1428.

3—Notice of—Mailing, Sufficient.

703. In a case where a brother, though absent, was tried, convicted and sentenced, from which action he appealed on the ground that he did not receive the notice of the time and place of meeting of the Committee of Investigation, the notice, it was claimed, not being received by him, until after the meeting was held, and the charges investigated, and reported upon. The case coming before the Supreme Lodge, it dismissed the appeal, and ruled:

It does not appear that the brother made any effort to ascertain the time and place of the committee's meeting. It does appear that notice was *mailed* to him, in time to reach him; before the action of the Subordinate Lodge can be reversed or set aside. in a case of this character, upon such a ground, the brother appealing, must make out a clear and satisfactory case, showing that he was guilty of no negligence in using all proper means to obtain his mail, and inform himself of the action of his Lodge, and of the fact of notice.

Jour., 1880, 2070.

4—Criminals—Lodge Need not Wait Action of Court Regarding.

704. The simple indictment for a criminal offense by a grand jury would not justify a Lodge in proceeding against the alleged offender; but this shall not be construed to prevent the Lodge proceeding against the brother before his trial in the courts.

Jour., 1888, 4122, 4574, 4580, 4581.

705. In the case of a Knight under indictment for murder it is not obligatory on the Lodge of which he is a member to await the result of the trial in the criminal courts before proceeding to try him under our laws.

Jour., *1890, 4844, 5319, 5336.*

UNIFORM.

1. Adoption of—For Third Rank (706, 707).
2. Parades—To be used at (708).
3. Cap—Not to be worn in Lodge room, except by permission (709).
4. Baldric—Discarded (710).
5. Use of—Voluntary (711).
6. Admission—Jewel or collar necessary for, in addition to Uniform Rank uniform (712).

5—Adoption of—For Third Rank.

706. At the session of 1871 a uniform regalia was recommended for use where practicable or desirable, subject to the final adoption of the different Grand Lodges of the various Jurisdictions as controlled by their own action and legislation, or proper official orders.

The detailed specifications of such outside regalia or uniform costume for the Order are found in Journal, 1872, 486, *et seq.*

Jour., *1871, 362, 396, 409.,*
1872, 486-500.

707. At the session of 1872 it was enacted that all portions of the uniform or outside regalia, as established by the action of the Supreme Body at its session held in Philadelphia, A. D. 1871, except helmet, oriflamme, gorget and cloak, be declared in its present shape and detail the permanent uniform or outside regalia for the use of the Order, and which shall not be changed, mutilated or reduced, in any sense of substitution, for the space and term of *ten* years from the date of that session.

Jour., *1872, 630.*
1876, 1311, 1319.
1877, 1414, 1425.

NOTE.—The legislation in the last two sections is given simply because it has never been repealed, though practically obsolete, the old Knight's Uniform having been superseded by that of the Uniform Rank.

2—Parades—To be Used at.

708. The wearing in public of any regalia or uniform, except the funeral rosette, officers' shoulder straps and the regulation uniform of the Uniform Rank, or the uniform of the Knight's Rank, is strictly prohibited: provided, that an officer acting in his official capacity at a public installation, the dedication of a castle hall or the laying of a corner stone, may wear his official Jewel during such ceremony.

Jour., 1886, 3681, 3690, 3691.

NOTE.—The word "Jewels" was originally included in the prohibitory legislation given above, but the legislation of 1888 had the effect of changing the rule, hence it is left out of the text here.

3—Cap—Not to be Worn in Lodge Room, Except by Permission.

709. The uniform cap of the Order, as adopted, shall not be worn in a Lodge room during its sessions, except by order of the Chancellor Commander.

Jour., 1873, 683, 740, 742.

NOTE.—This refers to cap of old Third Rank Uniform.

4—Baldric Discarded.

710. The baldric, formerly a part of the uniform for the Knight Rank, was abolished as such, and its use in any rank prohibited.

Jour., 1884, 2939, 3045.

5—Use of—Voluntary.

711. The subject of uniforming is left entirely voluntary with the Order everywhere.

Jour., 1872, 577, 578, 600.

6—Admission—Jewel or Collar Necessary for, in Addition to U. R. Uniform.

712. The uniform of the Uniform Rank, does not of itself entitle a member to admission to a Lodge; he must either wear in addition thereto the proper Jewel, or, in Lodges where the old regalia still exists, the collar to which he is entitled.

Jour., 1888, 4121, 4576, 4581.

NOTE.—The latter portion in regard to use of old regalia and collar would not now obtain in the case of officers or past officers. (See Const., Art. XXVI.)

UNIFORM RANK.

(See Major General.)

713. Propositions looking to the organization of a higher rank were offered at the session of the Supreme Lodge in 1877, and a special Committee appointed on "Uniform Rank": this committee reported at the next session, in 1878, when their report was laid on the table, but at a subsequent period in the session (page 1676), on Saturday, August 30, 1878, the following was adopted:

Resolved, That the report of the Committee on the Uniform Rank, now on the table, be taken therefrom, and, together with the Ritual, be referred back to the same Committee, together with the Supreme Chancellor, Supreme Vice Chancellor, and Supreme Keeper of Records and Seal, to be examined by them, amended if necessary, fully perfected, and promulgated to the membership at the earliest moment.

The Committee, consisting of the Founder, Justus H. Rathbone, Supreme Representatives William Ward, of New Jersey; William B. Kennedy, of Ohio; P. H. Mulcahy, of Nevada; F. P. Dann, of California, and Charles D. Lucas, of Missouri, met at the city of Baltimore, Maryland, September 13, 1878, and, after a session of several days, completed the work assigned them, and upon reporting same to Supreme Chancellor David Benjamin Woodruff, he, on November 1, 1878, promulgated the Ritual and Laws governing the "Uniform Rank." This system provided only for bodies known as "Divisions," but, in 1882, provision was made for Grand Divisions or Regiments, and the government of the Rank so remained till 1884, when the present system was adopted, providing for a Major General, in charge of the Rank, with the state formations known as "Brigades," with Brigade Commanders in charge. In 1886, the Major General was made an officer of the Supreme Lodge.

Jour., *1877, 1408, 1442, 1457.*
1878, 1511, 1652, 1657, 1676,
1697-1704.
1880, 1829.
1882, 2492, 2493, 2538.
1884, 2962, 2979, 2985, 2986.
Appendix, 56-77.

VACANCIES.

1. **In Grand Lodge Offices**—Cannot be filled by Grand Chancellor, unless Constitution so provides (714).
2. **In Subordinate Lodge**—Constitutional provisions (715); at installation in, Grand Lodge may provide for filling (716).

1—In Grand Lodge Offices—Cannot be Filled by Grand Chancellor, unless Constitution So Provides.

714. Unless the Grand Lodge, by its constitution, *specifically* provides that the Grand Chancellor has a right to appoint to fill vacancies, both as to Grand Officers and Supreme Representatives any appointment made by him would be inoperative.

Jour., *1872, 443, 444.*
1888, 4123, 4580, 4581.

2—In Subordinate Lodge—Constitutional Provisions—At Installation in, Grand Lodge may Provide for Filling.

715. All vacancies by death, removal, suspension, resignation or otherwise, shall be filled in the manner of the original selection, to serve the residue of the term, and officers so serving shall be entitled to the honors of the term. (Obligatory.)

Const., Art. VIII, Sec. 2, Sub. g.

NOTE.—The words, "original selection," have been a source of much controversy, some claiming that under a strict construction of this law, nominations were necessary on the night preceding election, even to fill vacancy, thus necessitating a delay. Only in one place has the Supreme Lodge made any deliverance on this question, when it ruled that the "words 'original selection' can only be construed to refer to the manner of voting, to wit: by ballot." (Jour., 1872, 566, 625.)

716. The question as to whether or not, when a Grand Chancellor or his Deputy visits a Lodge for the purpose of installation of officers, he is justified in declaring vacant the office of any officer who fails to be present, is a matter for local legislation.

Jour., 1888, 4122, 4576, 4581.

VENUE.

717. A Grand Lodge has the right to legislate so as to permit a change of venue in favor of a brother, against whom there exists in his own Lodge such a prejudice that he cannot have a fair trial therein.

Jour., 1890, 5327, 5425, 5449.

VICE CHANCELLOR.

1. Eligibility—Any Knight eligible as, unless local law to the contrary (718).
2. Rights of—In absence of Chancellor Commander (719, 720).
3. Occupies the Chair—Until Chancellor Commander is legally elected and installed (721).

1—Eligibility—Any Knight Eligible as, unless Local Law to the Contrary.

718. In 1875, the then Supreme Chancellor ruled "that any member having served in an elective or appointive office was eligible to the office of Vice Chancellor," and the same was approved. (See Jour. 1875, 1033, 1124.) This law appeared in all the Official Digests to date, and in that of 1887 was numbered, "332." In 1888 the following resolution was adopted:

Resolved, That paragraph 332, page 98, Official Digest, edition of 1887, be stricken out, and the matter therein contained left to local legislation.

Jour., 1888, 4607, 4653.

NOTE.—The previous legislation, referred to in the resolution, is given here because of the irregular manner in which it was sought to repeal it. To strike out a section of a Digest is not the way to repeal a legislative enactment. The Supreme Lodge so ruled, 1880, 2034, 2038.

2—Rights of—In Absence of Chancellor Commander.

719. A Vice Chancellor has no right to communicate the S. A. P. W. to a member entitled to it, outside of the Lodge room, though the Chancellor Commander be absent from the city.

Jour., 1886, 3515, 3688.

720. In case the Vice Chancellor of a Lodge shall have presided at a meeting of the Lodge in the absence of the Chancellor Commander from the town or city wherein the Lodge is located, the former shall be empowered to discharge any duty appertaining to the office of Chancellor Commander until the next meeting of the Lodge, provided the latter does not return before that time.

Jour., 1886, 3711, 3725.

NOTE.—These last two sections were passed at the same session, and, upon careful reading, can be made to harmonize; the first refers to the rights of a Vice Chancellor *before* a meeting of the Lodge, and the second *after* the Vice Chancellor has presided, and an official announcement made of the absence of the Chancellor Commander.

3—Occupies the Chair—Until Chancellor Commander is Legally Elected and Installed.

721. An illegally elected and improperly installed Chancellor Commander is not the proper person to fill the chair of the Chancellor Commander. The Vice Chancellor should take the chair until a Chancellor Commander is legally elected and properly installed.

Jour., 1884, 2776, 2988.

NOTE.—This should not be construed so as to release the outgoing Chancellor Commander, who, by the ritualistic law, must discharge the duties till his successor is "legally elected and installed," but evidently refers to a case where the outgoing Chancellor Commander *had* been "passed" to the chair of Past Chancellor, and at some future time the election of his successor had been set aside on the ground of illegality.

VISITING.

1. By Grand Officers—Order of entrance (722).
2. Examination—Of visitors, as a general rule, if in possession of the S. A. P. W., not required (723); may be in case of doubt (724).
3. Debarred from—Member under suspension, pending appeal (725).
4. Objections—Made to visitor, cannot prevent, remedy lies in charges (726, 727).

1—By Grand Officers—Order of Entrance.

722. The order of entrance to Castle Hall by the Grand Officers when visiting is the same as provided in the case of installation of officers.

Jour., 1888, 4122, 4579, 4581.

2—Examination—Of Visitors, as a General Rule, if in Possession of the S. A. P. W., not Required—May be, in Case of Doubt.

723. A visiting member who is in possession of the S. A. P. W. cannot be required before entering a Lodge to produce a receipt for dues and be examined in the Secret Work.

Jour., 1876, 1227, 1296.

724. It is not required of a member of the Order, legally entitled to admission to a Subordinate Lodge, to have a Traveling Shield to visit outside his own Jurisdiction. A Traveling Shield is a letter of credit of good standing. A brother has the right to visit any Lodge if he is in possession of the S. A. P. W., but a Chancellor Commander can demand that the brother show an Official Receipt or the Traveling Shield, if he has any doubts concerning the admission of the brother.

Jour., 1882, 2275, 2465, 2466.

3—Debarred from—Member under Suspension, Pending Appeal.

725. Pending an appeal from a judgment of suspension, the brother so suspended has no right to visit a Subordinate Lodge.

Jour., 1886, 3286, 3525, Errata, page 1.

4—Objections—Made to Visitor, cannot Prevent, Remedy Lies in Charges.

726. Objections cannot be made to a member in good standing and otherwise correct while visiting another Lodge. If any one is satisfied he is unworthy to sit in a Lodge room, he must proceed against him under our penal laws, or keep silent.

Jour., 1875, 1042, 1114, 1121.

727. In a case where it appeared that a Grand Chancellor made the following decision, which was approved by his Grand Lodge:

A Knight in good standing and otherwise correct, who has a receipt for dues and an order properly drawn and signed for the S. A. P. W., cannot be refused the S. A. P. W., and the privilege of visiting a Lodge to whose membership he is obnoxious. If he is guilty of a violation of any Pythian law, charges should be preferred against him, and he should be dealt with as provided by our penal laws for the offense.

And, further, where appeal was taken from the action of the Grand Lodge, in the following words:

In presenting the foregoing appeal, we desire to state that we concur in the opinion expressed by the Grand Chancellor, and approved by the Grand Lodge, that "a Knight in good standing and otherwise correct, who has a receipt for dues and an order properly drawn and signed for the S. A. P. W.," cannot lawfully be refused the S. A. P. W. We do believe, however, that it is the legal right of every Lodge to refuse to receive as a visitor a Knight who is personally obnoxious to its membership—and it is on this point alone that we appeal.

The Supreme Lodge held "that the appeal be dismissed and the Grand Lodge of Tennessee be sustained."

Jour., 1890, 5320, 5321, 5338, 5339, 5405, 5447, 5448.

VOTING.

1. In the Supreme Lodge (728).
2. In Grand Lodges—Grand Officers, unless otherwise provided, vote (729); dual voting, not recognized 730); under certain conditions, all voting confined to Representatives in (731).
3. On Withdrawing Proposition—Majority vote (732).

1—In Supreme Lodge.

728. Each Officer, Supreme Representative and Past Supreme Chancellor by service, shall be entitled to one vote in determining any question before the Supreme Lodge.

Const., Art. II, Sec. 2.

2—In Grand Lodges—Grand Officers, unless Otherwise Provided, Vote—Dual Voting Not Recognized—Under Certain Conditions, all Voting Confined to Representatives.

729. Unless otherwise provided in their Constitution, Grand Lodge Officers, although not Representatives, are clearly entitled to vote upon all questions.

Jour., 1871, 361, 362, 391. 1880, 2035.

730. While the matter is a subject for local legislation, yet unless so specially authorized by the Grand Lodge Constitution, a Past Grand Chancellor, who is also a Representative to a Grand Lodge, has no right to cast two votes on all questions pending before his Grand Lodge.

Jour., 1886. 3286, 3525, Errata, page i.

781. In an appeal case involving the question as to who had the right to vote on the election of Grand Officers; and where it appeared that the Constitution of the Grand Lodge, in that Jurisdiction, provided:

The Grand Lodge shall be composed of all Past Chancellors in good standing in Subordinate Lodges in the State, who shall be permitted to vote for Grand Lodge Officers and Representatives to the Supreme Lodge, and on any subject before the Grand Lodge, except when a vote by Lodges may be called for by five Representatives, when each Lodge represented shall be entitled to one vote only through its Representatives.

The Supreme Lodge decided, that where such a provision existed, the vote by Lodges could be called for upon the election of Grand Lodge Officers.

Jour., 1884, 3038.

3—On Withdrawing Proposition—Majority Vote.

782. "Unanimous" consent is not necessary for the withdrawal of a proposition for membership after reference to a committee and before they report; in such an instance, a majority vote prevails; this was the construction placed on the word "consent," appearing in Article VIII, Section 2, Paragraph *n*.

Jour., 1888, 3993.

VOUCHING.

783. No vouching is allowed in the Order under any circumstances.

Jour., 1870, 229.

NOTE.—The term " vouching " here used, refers to a usage in another organization whereby a member " vouches " for a visitor.

WITHDRAWAL CARDS.

1. **Granted, How?**—On application, personal or written (734), but not by another (735); may be refused, how (734)? Fee may be charged (736).
2. **Reconsideration**—Of action granting, prohibited (737).
3. **Revocation**—May be had, for cause (738), but when for trial, holder becomes again subject to jurisdiction of Lodge (738, 739).
4. **Duration**—Till revoked or deposited (740).
5. **Affiliation**—Notice of, sent issuer (741).
6. **Password**—S. A. P. W., of the term in which issued, accompanies (742, 743).
7. **Rank-Honors**—Rank to be stated in the Card (744); holder does not lose honors by transfer (745); nor office in Supreme Lodge, during transfer, but cannot perform official acts till again affiliated (746).
8. **Privileges of Holder**—May visit during term in which issued, if in possession of S. A. P. W.; if without it, can obtain order for it (747, 748); Past Officer may visit in a Grand Lodge (749).
9. **Disabilities of Holder**—Not eligible for office (750); ceases to be Representative (751); cannot join the Uniform Rank (752).
10. **Defunct Lodges.**
    (a) **Form of Card**—For members of, provided (753).
    (b) **Pages and Esquires**—Of defunct Lodges, may obtain, how (754).
11. **Revived Lodges**—Hold jurisdiction over issuance to those holding membership at time of surrender, unless taken while defunct (755).
12. **Renewal**—Lost or destroyed, reissued by Lodge, on its terms (756, 757).
13. **"Clearance Certificates"** (758)—"Cards of Privilege" or "Dismissal Certificates" (759); in lieu of Withdrawal Cards, illegal (758, 759).
14. **Illegally Issued**—Where charges have been preferred, in Grand Lodge, Subordinate should not issue; if issued, must recall, or Grand Chancellor may order recall (760, 761, 762).
15. **Defunct Grand Lodge**—Former members under, receive, from new Grand Lodge (763).

1—Granted, How—On Application, Personal or Written, but Not by Another—Fee may be Charged.

734. Applications for Withdrawal Cards shall be made, either personally or in writing, to a Lodge, and a Card thereupon shall be granted; Provided, the brother be clear of the books, free from charges made or pending, and there be no other valid objection. If objection be offered, the objection shall be at once stated, and, if not sustained by a majority vote of the members present, the Card shall be granted, unless formal charges be preferred. (Obligatory.)

Const., Art. VIII, Sec. 2, Sub. r.

735. An application in open Lodge for a Withdrawal Card for a member of the Lodge not present, but made by another member, at the request of the brother desiring the Card is not valid, and on the granting of a Card on such request, the membership of the brother would not cease, as such a course would be contrary to Subdivision *r*, Section 2, Article VIII of the Supreme Constitution, requiring that the application shall be made either personally or in writing.

Jour., 1878, 1507, 1607.

736. It is legitimate and proper for Lodges to charge a fee for Withdrawal Cards.

Jour., 1880, 1826, 1827, 2003.

2—Reconsideration of Action Granting, Prohibited.

737. A Lodge cannot reconsider or rescind a vote granting a Withdrawal Card at the request of the brother holding the Card or otherwise.

Jour., 1876, 1228, 1296, 1297.

3—Revocation—May be Had, for Cause, but when for Trial, Holder Becomes Again Subject to Jurisdiction of Lodge.

738. Any Withdrawal Card may be revoked by a Lodge granting the same, or ordered vacated by the proper Grand Lodge or Grand Chancellor at any time, for cause appearing; and when so revoked for the purpose of impeachment or trial, the person holding said Card shall again become subject to the Lodge which issued the same, in so far as concerns said impeachment or trial. Refusal to comply with proper citations in this connection shall constitute contempt. (Obligatory.)

Const., Art. VIII, Sec. 2, Sub. s.

739. The Constitution of the Supreme Lodge, Article VIII, Section 2, Subdivision *s*, provides for the revocation of Withdrawal Cards, and they may be revoked for causes other than impeachment or trial, but only when the Card is revoked for the purpose of impeachment or trial, the holder becomes subject to the jurisdiction of the Lodge.

Jour., 1888, 4433, 4663, 4664.

NOTE.—The effect of this construction of the preceding section places it within the power of a Subordinate Lodge to revoke a Withdrawal Card, but not place the holder on trial for the cause for which the revocation took place.

4—Duration—Till Revoked or Deposited.

740. All Withdrawal Cards, whether issued prior to this legislation or subsequent, are to be considered good until revoked or deposited, and all legislation inconsistent herewith is repealed.

Jour., *1876, 1309, 1310.*
1877, 1371, 1410, 1423.
1890, 4846, 5319, 5337.

5—Affiliation—Notice of, Sent Issuer.

741. Hereafter when a brother affiliates with a Lodge by Card, it shall be the duty of the Lodge with which he affiliates to cause its Keeper of Records and Seal to at once send notice of such affiliation to the Grand Lodge or the Subordinate Lodge which granted and issued to such brother his Withdrawal Card.

Jour., *1886, 3512, 3525, 3526, 3527,*
Errata, page i.

6—Password—S. A. P. W. of the Term in Which Issued, Accompanies.

742. A brother having a Withdrawal Card is entitled to the password current at the time of withdrawal, and should he fail to attach himself to a Lodge during the continuance of that word, he is not entitled to receive a subsequent password until he has joined a Lodge.

Jour., *1872, 467, 613.*
1875, 1160.
1880, 1827, 2003.

743. The refusal of the Supreme Lodge to adopt a form of Withdrawal Card expressing on its face "the bearer of it shall be entitled to the S. A. P. W. for *one year*" (Jour., 1872, 536-7, 579), firmly establishes the principle that it only carries the S. A. P. W. for the term *in which issued*, but *no longer*.

Jour., *1873, Appendix 36.*

7—Rank-Honors—Rank to be Stated in the Card—Holder Does Not Lose Honors, by Transfer, nor Office in Supreme Lodge during Transfer, but cannot Perform Official Acts till Again Affiliated.

744. The rank of a brother to whom a Withdrawal Card is issued shall be stated on the Card, and the form of the Card shall be altered to conform to this legislation.

Jour., *1876, 1309.*

NOTE.—This legislation is a portion of a report of the Committee on Law and Supervision (Jour., 1876, 1309), and was the action taken on certain recommendations made by the Supreme Chancellor (Jour., 1876, 1231), wherein he stated that "the law, as now understood, does not allow the rank of a member to appear on the Withdrawal Card. Much trouble has arisen on this account, as the Keeper of Records and Seal, attesting Cards, often neglects to furnish a rank credential to accompany the Card."

This law can have no force for attaining the object sought. Within his own jurisdiction the holder does not require it; outside, it would be of no value, as in the latter instance he must furnish a "rank credential" from the Grand Keeper of Records and Seal of the Jurisdiction in which he became a past officer. While the Supreme Lodge adopted the above loose proposition, they failed to give it effect either by repealing prior well defined enactments and constitutional provisions, or by specifically stating to what extent, if any, such a Withdrawal Card would operate as a certificate of past rank. See Sections 511, 512, 513, 514, 516 of this Digest.

745. A brother cannot lose honors already obtained, by a transfer of membership. His past official rank should be stated in the Withdrawal Card.

*Jour., 1875, 1043, 1114, 1121.
1880, 1828, 2004.*

NOTE.—This is the wording of the latest ruling (1880, 1828, 2004), but the ruling of 1875, 1043, 1114, 1121, is more strictly in line with the Constitution, since it adds: "He must receive with his Card a rank credential as Past Chancellor."

746. An Officer of, or Representative to, this Supreme Lodge, taking a Withdrawal Card from his Subordinate Lodge, does not vacate his office thereby, if the same be immediately deposited in the office of the Grand Keeper of Records and Seal of his Jurisdiction, accompanying an application for a Charter for a new Lodge; or, if on occasion of the surrender of the Charter of the Lodge to which such Officer or Representative may belong, or on occasion of a change of Lodge or residence, such Card be deposited in a Subordinate Lodge in his Jurisdiction within one month from the granting of the same; Provided, that until such Card be so deposited, the Officer or Representative holding it can discharge no official act.

Jour., 1877, 1371, 1423, 1424.

8—Privileges of Holder—May Visit during Term in Which Issued, if in Possession of the S. A. P. W., if without It, can Obtain Order for It—Past Officer may Visit in a Grand Lodge.

747. Withdrawal Cards cannot and must *not* be used for or recognized in *any* sense as "visiting cards." The Supreme Obligatory Law is *imperative* on the point that "no visiting cards shall be used in the Order." (Jour., 1868, 18.) Therefore, when presented in that sense, they *must* be refused. If having the S. A. P. W., they are not required to be shown by the visitor. If not having the S. A. P. W., they are valueless to get it, *unless* accompanied by an order from the Lodge by which issued, signed by the Chancellor Commander, attested by the seal and signature of the Keeper of Records and Seal, *and then* ONLY *for the term in which the card was issued.*

Jour., 1873, Appendix 36.

748. A member holding a Withdrawal Card has an *inferential* right to visit while holding the same, but cannot be admitted without the S. A. P. W. This he of course has for the term in which the Card

was issued, but he cannot obtain the word while holding the Card after a new one has been promulgated; and, hence, the only right enjoyed is swept away by such change of S. A. P. W.

Jour., 1880, 1827, 2003.

749. A Past Chancellor or Past Grand Chancellor holding a Withdrawal Card is entitled to visit his Grand Lodge for the balance of the term during which his card was issued; Provided he is in possession of the S. A. P. W.

Jour., 1877, 1371, 1423.

9—Disabilities of Holder—Not Eligible for Office—Ceases to be Representative—Cannot Join Uniform Rank.

750. A brother holding a Withdrawal Card from his Lodge would not be eligible to any office in a Grand Lodge.

Jour., 1877, 1371, 1423.

751. The granting of a Withdrawal Card to a brother vacates his election as Representative to the Grand Lodge.

Jour., 1886, 3516, 3685, 3686.

752. A brother holding a Withdrawal Card cannot be admitted into a Division of the Uniform Rank, because he does not hold membership in any Subordinate Lodge.

Jour., 1890, 4846, 5319, 5338.

10—Defunct Lodges—(a) Form of Card—For Members of, Provided.

753. The Supreme Keeper of Records and Seal was directed to prepare a form of Card to be used by the Supreme Lodge and Grand Lodges in granting Cards to members of defunct Lodges in their Jurisdiction, said Card to be furnished to Grand Lodges at the same price now charged for Withdrawal Cards.

Jour., 1884, 3023.

(b)—Pages and Esquires—Of Defunct Lodges, may Obtain, How?

754. In case of a Subordinate Lodge being suspended or surrendering their Charter, a Grand Chancellor may issue Withdrawal Cards to Pages or Esquires, of such extinct Lodges to connect themselves with a Lodge in that or any other Jurisdiction, on such terms as are provided in the local laws.

Jour., 1876, 1311, 1314.
1878, 1508, 1607.

11—Revived Lodges—Hold Jurisdiction over Issuance to Those Holding Membership at Time of Surrender, unless Taken while Defunct.

755. A Lodge having been organized, under Dispensation, by a given name and number, thereafter and before the issuance of a charter, became defunct. Subsequently a charter from the Grand Lodge being obtained, a Lodge of the same name and number was established, many of the members having obtained Cards from the Grand Lodge as having been members of the old Lodge returning to and becoming affiliated in the new organization; ruled, sustaining the ruling of the Grand Lodge, that from the evidence appearing, the issuance of the charter by the Grand Lodge, was designed to give continuance to the body formerly under dispensation, and that Cards to members of such former body must be issued by the Lodge so subsequently chartered, and the Grand Lodge had no jurisdiction to issue such Cards.

Jour., 1878, 1618.

12—Renewal—Lost or Destroyed, Reissued by Lodge, on Its Terms.

756. Any brother who may have lost his Card can have the same renewed by applying to the source from which it emanated. (Obligatory.)

Const., Art. VIII, Sec. 2, Sub. m.

757. A Withdrawal Card can be renewed if lost or destroyed accidentally, and satisfactory evidence adduced from the holder and applicant, by the Lodge having granted the same, and upon such terms as the Lodge may determine. (Obligatory.)

Const., Art. VIII, Sec. 2, Sub. t.

13—"Clearance Certificates"—"Cards of Privilege" or "Dismissal Certificates"—In Lieu of Withdrawal Cards, Illegal.

758. A Grand Lodge has no right to issue Clearance Certificates in lieu of Withdrawal Cards, for to the Supreme Lodge alone belongs the exclusive right to furnish all Rituals, Forms, Cards, Ceremonies, Odes, Charts and Certificates.

Jour., 1882, 2274, 2465, 2466.

759. "Cards of Privilege" or "Dismissal Certificates," issued by a Grand Lodge in lieu of Withdrawal Cards, are in direct violation of Supreme law.

Jour., 1888, 4025.

14—Illegally Issued—Where Charges have been Preferred, in Grand Lodge, Subordinate should Not Issue; if Issued, must Recall or Grand Chancellor may Order Recall.

760. Any Past Chancellor against whom charges are brought in a Grand Lodge, notice of which has been given to the Subordinate Lodge of which he is a member, ought not to be granted a Withdrawal

Card; but if done, either willfully or innocently, it can be annulled or recalled by action of the Lodge or *order* of the Grand Chancellor.

Jour., *1873*, *Appendix 37.*

761. If the Card described in the last section, is procured by fraud, it is void; if through willfulness on the part of the Lodge, punish it; if issued innocently in absence of proper notice, etc., have it annulled.

Jour., *1873*, *Appendix 37.*

762. In any or all the cases described in the last two sections, the fact of holding the Withdrawal Card cannot be plead in bar of the proceedings, or the finding of same; and in *all* except the last would only add to the offenses for which already charged.

Jour., *1873*, *Appendix 38.*

15—Defunct Grand Lodge—Former Members under, Receive, from New Grand Lodge.

763. Where a Grand Lodge had for years been defunct, and where, subsequently, an entirely new Grand Lodge had been organized, on petition of the latter, all the books, papers and documents of the former were turned over, by the Supreme Lodge, to the new body and they authorized to grant Withdrawal Cards to members of the defunct Lodges formerly existing, where there were no good and valid reasons to the contrary.

Jour., *1882*, *2411*, *2412*, *2473*, *2474.*

WRITTEN AND UNWRITTEN WORK.

1. What Constitutes (764).
2. Book of Diagrams (765).
3. Uniformity in—Required on the part of Lodges (766).

1—What Constitutes.

764. The Written and Unwritten Work, which cannot be altered, except as provided in Article XXIX, Supreme Lodge Constitution, consists:

1. Of the Work and its explanations, as contained and illustrated in the Book of Diagrams in the hands of the Supreme Chancellor.

2. Of the lectures, charges, obligations and all written work contained in the Ritual, and included in the forms and ceremonies for opening and closing the Lodge, passing from rank to rank and conferring the different grades of rank.

3. The forms and ceremonies as prescribed for installation and funeral.

4. The forms and ceremonies as prescribed for opening and closing a Grand Lodge, and installing the officers thereof, as contained in the Grand Lodge Ritual, and also for conferring Past Chancellor's rank, as contained in the same.

5. The forms and ceremonies as laid down in Supreme Lodge Ritual.

Jour., 1876, 1293.

NOTE.—This is the report of the Committee on Law and Supervision, in answer to a question by Representative Cotter, of Kentucky (Jour., 1876, 1282), wherein he desired that the Written and Unwritten Work should be designated.

2—Book of Diagrams.

765. Pursuant to action of the Supreme Lodge, the whole of the Secret Work of the Order has been properly written out, and correct diagrams of the same prepared.

Jour., 1872, 465, 575, 594.
1873, 719, 720, 752, Appendix 29, 30.
1875, 1050, 1095, 1147, 1157.

3—Uniformity in—Required on the Part of Lodges.

766. The work in all Lodges should be uniform, and the properties necessary in conferring the ranks must be used in all cases. Lodges are not permitted to add to or take from the prescribed manner of conferring the work.

Jour., 1888, 4123, 4579, 4581.

INDEX.

(Reference is to the Sections; the small figures in brackets refer to subdivisions of sections.)

ABSENCE. SECTIONS.
 Supreme Officer absent at time of installation may be installed during recess.................................... 215
 At time of nomination, in Grand Lodge, not a disqualification 217
 Sitting Past Chancellor may be fined for..................... 460
 From meetings, includes all meetings, regular or special..... 565
 Accused being, Lodge may proceed with trial................. 701
 Prerogatives of Vice Chancellor, in absence of Chancellor Commander 719, 720

ACCOUNTS—(See Committee on Finance.)

ACTION AT LAW.
 Grand Lodge cannot prevent member bringing.............. 275

ADJOURN.
 Motion to, in Subordinate Lodge, not in order—should be to "close".. 571
 Supreme Lodge may, awaiting a quorum..................... 651

ADMISSION—(See Ballot; Membership.)

ADVANCEMENT—(See Ballot; Ranks.)

ADVERTISING.
 Emblems of the Order not to be used in, except by those engaged in the manufacture of Pythian goods and supplies...220, 221
 The name of the Order not to be used in, except for supplies, etc.. 397

AFFILIATION—(See Ballot; Membership; Withdrawal Card.)

AGE.
 Initiate must be of age.. 1
 Supreme Lodge fixes minimum................................. 2
 Maximum, a matter for local legislation..................... 2
 In Lodges subordinate to Supreme Lodge, Deputy can grant Dispensations to initiate applicant over fifty years of age. 319
 Applications for membership must state..................... 346
 Applicant to be legal age of majority in country where Lodge located.. 347
 Lodges of persons under, illegal............................ 353

(189)

Index.

ALTERNATES.   SECTIONS.
    Of Supreme Representatives, unauthorized 685

AMENDMENTS.
    TO CONSTITUTION OF SUPREME LODGE.
        Must be presented at a regular session................... 3
        Adopted by a two-thirds vote, at next regular session..... 3
        May be considered and adopted at same session, provided
            unanimous consent is given to consider............. 5
        Must be referred to, and reported on by Committee on
            Law before being taken up for action................ 6
        Supreme Lodge may resume additional power by. 645
        Written and Unwritten Work can only be altered by....4, 764
    TO CONSTITUTION OF GRAND LODGES.
        Power to amend exists only in Grand Lodge itself, cannot
            be delegated... 7
        Must be acted on in manner provided 8, 10
        Not operative unless approved according to law.......... 9
        Rejected, may be presented again, at same session, and lie
            over; such resubmission is not out of order, under
            the rule against a "consideration of the same subject" 11
        Require approval of Council of Administration........151, 152
        Failing requisite approval in ninety days, become law. 152, 186
        Go into effect upon approval............................. 185
        Supreme Keeper of Records and Seal shall notify Grand
            Keeper of Records and Seal of approval of.......... 626
    TO THE WRITTEN AND UNWRITTEN WORK.
        Must lie over from one session to another, and be adopted
            by a four-fifths vote 4

AMPLIFIED THIRD RANK.
    Adopted in 1872.. 12
    Bound separately..... 12
    Grand and Subordinate Lodges may order Rituals with or
        without 12
    Must be conferred without the use of the book............13, 549
    Subordinate determines for itself as to use of................ 14

ANNIVERSARY OF THE ORDER.
    February 19th, adopted as................................... 15

ANTE-ROOM.
    No one except Outer Guard allowed in, at opening........... 16
    Rank of Past Chancellor cannot be conferred in; must be in
        Grand Lodge... 271
    No one allowed in, without the S. A. P. W..........441, 444, 445
    Lodge visiting in a body may be examined in the rank password
        in, by Master-at-Arms................................. 453
    Members to be informed in, as to what rank Lodge is working in 510

Index.

APPEALS.   SECTIONS.

From action of Grand Lodge, or Lodge subordinate to
  Supreme Lodge, passed on by Supreme Lodge or Supreme
  Chancellor during recess................................ 17
Decisions in, by Grand Lodge, or Lodge, final until reversed.. 17
Consent by the Grand Lodge, to bring, required............18, 23
Consent to bring, not required, where Lodge has surrendered
  its property to its Grand Lodge........................ 18
Do not lie direct from the decision of a Grand Chancellor to
  Supreme Lodge...................................19, 20, 21
Consent to bring, must be obtained at the same session as
  cause arose... 22
The record in, must be properly attested by the Grand Chan-
  cellor and Grand Keeper of Records and Seal........22, 24, 27
It is the duty of Grand Lodges to furnish requisite testimony in 26
A simple statement is not an appeal........................ 28
When, may be heard, though officers fail to certify to the
  record.. 29
May be heard though not taken in time, in extreme cases....22, 31
As a general proposition, must be taken in time............. 30
Must be *bona fide*—must show interest....................32, 33
The manner of obtaining redress is by appeal................ 34
May be dismissed for irregularities, but not, in case final action
  is correct...35, 36
Should be forwarded one month previous to the session—
  exceptions.. 37
One hundred and fifty printed copies required, expense borne
  by appellant.. 38
May be heard during recess, by Supreme Chancellor, whose
  decision is binding, until reversed...................39, 600
The decision of the Committee on, final until reversed, and fixes
  status, until reversed................................ 41
Must be reported to the Supreme Lodge, when decided during
  recess..39, 40, 41, 642
Reports of a Committee on Appeals should be considered by
  Grand Lodge, and not referred to a special Committee.... 42
In Subordinate Lodge, may not be considered except in Rank
  of Knight... 43
Do not require a second—one member can take an appeal.... 44
Supreme Lodge may adopt additional rules governing........ 47
By a widow of a deceased member—Supreme Lodge has con-
  sidered such cases................................96, 99
Duties of Committee on................................... 161
From sentence of expulsion, reviewed by Grand Lodge, if
  demanded... 228

Index.

APPEALS—(Continued.)   SECTIONS.
  From action of Lodge subordinate to Supreme Lodge may be taken.. 326
  From the decision of Major General, may be taken to Supreme Chancellor or Supreme Lodge................................... 342

APPEALS FOR AID.
  By a Grand Lodge, require the permission of the Supreme Lodge or Supreme Chancellor.................................. 48
  By Lodges Subordinate to the Supreme Lodge, require the permission of the Supreme Chancellor....................... 48, 49
  By Lodges under the jurisdiction of a Grand Lodge, require the permission of their Grand Chancellor................. 50
  Rowena Lodge, of Gallatin, Tennessee, authorized to call on Grand and Subordinate Lodges for financial aid in building Pythian College.. 495

APPEALS AND GRIEVANCES.
  Committee on—(See Committees.)

APPLICANT.
  FOR INITIATION.
    Must be of age... 1, 347
    Supreme Lodge only fixes minimum age of, Grand Lodges the maximum.. 2
    Grand Lodges prescribe whether one or two black balls reject... 60
    If rejected, may not reapply for six months................ 61
    Separate ballot on each..................................... 63
    Ballot for, inspected by both Chancellor Commander and Vice Chancellor, announced by former........................ 64
    Ballot on, if rejected, cannot be reconsidered............ 66
    Another ballot on, if elected, may be taken, for causes appearing, if Grand Lodge permit............................ 67
    Elected, may be stopped, member objecting, if Grand Lodge so provide by Constitution................................ 68
    Rejected, at meeting preliminary to institution of Lodge, not "black-balled," but may reapply at once.............. 70
    Ballot on, by Card, same as by initiation.................. 71
    Must pay required fee....................................... 229
    No part of fee to be donated or refunded to............ 231, 232
    Opening "Charter Books" for, forbidden.................. 233
    Natives of Hawaiian Islands may not be................... 277
    Charter applicants, of new Lodge, pay in the full fee for all the ranks... 292 (5)
    Charter applicants of new Lodge, ballot collectively, the one for the other... 292 (6)
    At organization of Lodge subordinate to Supreme Lodge, need not be a member of the Order......................... 310

Index.

APPLICANT—(Continued.) SECTIONS.
  FOR INITIATION.
    Rejected, not to be accepted on Charter, for Lodge subordinate to Supreme Lodge........................... 312
    In Lodges subordinate to Supreme Lodge, minimum fee $10. 317
    Maimed, admitted in Lodges subordinate to Supreme Lodge, on Dispensation by Supreme Chancellor...... 318
    Elected, in Lodges subordinate to Supreme Lodge, may be refused subsequently by a majority vote.......... 320
    Rejected, in Lodges subordinate to Supreme Lodge, may reapply after one month........................... 321
    Rejected, in Lodges subordinate to Supreme Lodge, may not be accepted in any other Lodge, except by consent. 322
    Maimed, admitted, on Dispensation from Grand Chancellor 332
    Must sign petition, stating age, residence and occupation. 346
    Must be white, a believer in a Supreme Being and a resident at least six months of the Jurisdiction...347, 533, 534
    May not be a negro, a woman, a minor, a Chinaman nor Indian................................350–352, 353, 354, 355
    Must at least be able to write his name.............356, 357
    Must not be a member of another Lodge................ 358
    May be required to furnish medical certificate............ 359
    In the liquor traffic, legislation regarding................ 360
    Proposition of, cannot be withdrawn, except by consent, after referred to committee, and not then, after committee report.............................363, 364, 365
    Rejected, after six months, may reapply to any other Lodge.. 368
    Rejected, reapplying and concealing former rejection, is a member, but subject to trial........................ 369
    Non-resident, must have consent of his Grand Chancellor. 535
  BY WITHDRAWAL CARD.
    At formation of new Lodge must present his Card........ 362
    Proposition treated same as for initiation..............71, 370
    Becomes a member, on election, if Grand Lodge does not provide to the contrary............................. 372
    Non-resident, requires consent of his Grand Chancellor... 373
    Irregularly admitted, membership cannot be disturbed..374, 375, 376
    Rejected, may reapply to same or any other Lodge, if Grand Lodge does not provide to the contrary........ 378
    Being Pages or Esquires, transferred same as Knights. 379, 380
  FOR RANKS.
    Adverse ballot on, may not be laid over.................. 69
    Must be balloted on for each rank..................505, 506
    A member of another Lodge, must have consent of his own Lodge... 536

(193)

Index.

APPLICANT—(Continued.)   SECTIONS.
  FOR REINSTATEMENT.
    After suspension for non-payment of dues, received under provisions of local law. 384
    Being Pages or Esquires, dropped for failure to advance, received under provisions of local law............ 385, 386
    After indefinite suspension, must reapply and pass a ballot. 526

APPLICATION—(See Applicant; Ballot; Membership; Withdrawal Card.)

APPOINTED OFFICERS—(See Officers.)

APPOINTMENT.
    Inner and Outer Guards hold office by 574, 575
    Of additional Supreme Representative, to be for four years.. 677
    Of Supreme Representative, to fill vacancy, manner of, regulated by Grand Lodge, but term must end with the 31st of December of odd-numbered year...................678, 679
    Of Supreme Representative, to fill vacancy, to be for the unexpired term 680
    Made by Grand Chancellor, void, unless specific power of, given by Constitution 714

APPROPRIATIONS.
    Finance Committee recommend, for the purposes of the Supreme Lodge.. 157
    For nurse hire, can only be made in accordance with constitutional provision 243
    Of money, cannot be made, in a Subordinate Lodge, unless by unanimous consent, quorum only being present 566

APPROVAL.
    Constitutions, of Grand Lodges, and of Subordinates under their jurisdiction, and all amendments thereto, legally adopted, must be approved by the Supreme Lodge, if in session, or the Council of Administration, during recess, before going into effect........................8, 9, 185, 186
    "Appeals for Aid." from Grand Lodges, and Lodges Subordinate to the Supreme Lodge, must have, of the Supreme Chancellor, and from Subordinate Lodges, of their own Grand Chancellor..................................48, 49, 50
    Of a Constitution, void, if in conflict with Supreme law...... 183
    Constitutions failing, within ninety days after delivery to Council of Administration, go into effect without 186
    Not required, by the Supreme Lodge, for the appointment of a Deputy Supreme Chancellor 194
    Of the Supreme Chancellor, required on the application for a Grand Lodge 254

Index.

APPROVAL—(Continued.)   SECTIONS.
  Of the Supreme Chancellor, required on all laws of the Uniform
    Rank 337
  Of the Supreme Chancellor, required in regard to hall in
    which to hold Supreme session......................... 650
  Bond of Supreme Keeper of Records and Seal requires...... 622
  Bond of Supreme Master of Exchequer requires............. 660

ARREARS.
  Member, if in, to amount of one year's dues shall be declared
    suspended 51, 53, 54, 55
  Definition of 52
  Six months in, may not cause suspension................... 54
  When twelve months in, must be so notified, before suspension 55
  May pay up, even after being in, for twelve months, if declar-
    ation of suspension not made........................... 56
  Not being in, to extent required by local law, entitled to sick
    and funeral benefits..................................82, 86
  If not in, when taken sick, entitled to benefits, though in
    arrears when reported 98
  Paid during sickness, causing death, and not in, at time of
    death, entitled to funeral benefits................. 103, 104
  May not be declared in, if dues paid to first of term, though
    law requires dues in advance........................... 210
  May arise from non-payment of fines and assessments, if local
    law provides for imposition of fines..............237, 238
  Officers in, not to be installed 290
  Length of time in, before deprived of the S. A. P. W., a mat-
    ter for local legislation 440
  Not a bar to issuing certificate to a Past Chancellor 469
  Benefits paid by sister Lodge, on account of member in, not
    a valid claim on his Lodge 522

ASSESSMENTS.
  Grand Lodge may not levy, on Past Chancellors............. 57
  Compulsory, for insurance or relief, may not be levied.....58, 75
  Subordinate Lodge may levy, to meet necessary expenses, if
    Grand Lodge so provide............................... 59
  Subordinate Lodges may levy, for the purpose of paying
    benefits 78
  If Grand Lodge so provide, may be levied and operate as
    dues 237
  Aggregating a sum equal to one year's dues, render liable to
    suspension 238
  Lodges subordinate to Supreme Lodge may collect, in addi-
    tion to one year's dues, before reinstatement............ 323
  Official Receipt should be given for payment of............ 421

Index.

"AT EASE."   SECTIONS.
    A ritualistic provision...................................... 572
    When Lodge "at ease" doors should be closed.............. 572
    Members entering or retiring when Lodge "at ease," do so
        in the regular way—Lodge must be called to order....... 572

AUDIT—(See Committee on Finance.)

BADGES.
    Wearing of special, in addition to Jewel, cannot be required. 300

BALDRIC.
    As part of the uniform, abolished........................... 710

BALL BALLOT—(See Ballot; Black Ball.)

BALLOT.
    FOR MEMBERSHIP.
        Grand Lodges may prescribe one black ball for, but can-
            not exceed two...................................... 60
        Renewed immediately, if two black balls appear; same
            appearing on second, applicant rejected; three ap-
            pearing on first, no second ballot required.........61, 62
        Separate, required on each application................... 63
        Chancellor Commander and Vice Chancellor inspect,
            former announces.................................. 64
        Black cubes for, permitted 65
        Candidate rejected on, cannot be reconsidered 66
        Candidate elected on, if Grand Lodge so provide, another
            may be had, before admission, if there are objections
            to the applicant.................................... 67
        If local law provides, elected applicant may be denied
            admission on the objection of a member............. 68
        Adverse, on application for advancement cannot be laid
            over 69
        Grand Lodges provide how soon, may be renewed, on
            application for advancement....................... 69
        Adverse, on applicants at preliminary meeting for the
            organization of a Lodge, of no force afterward...... 70
        By Card, same as for initiation......................71, 370
        Supervised by instituting officer at organization of new
            Lodge 292 (6)
        Taken collectively, at organization of new Lodge; not
            being clear, then separate.... ....292 (6)
        For advancement, in Lodges subordinate to the Supreme
            Lodge, may be renewed in one month............... 321
        Applicants for initiation must pass a ballot............. 346
        Application must go to, after report of committee.363, 364, 365
        Disclosing name of person casting a black ball may con-
            stitute an offense, if Grand Lodge so provides....... 412

Index.

BALLOT—(Continued.) SECTIONS.
FOR MEMBERSHIP.
    Protest, by a sister Lodge, against applicant cannot operate as a black ball 493, 494
    For advancement, separate for each rank; same number of black balls reject, as in initiation 505, 506
    Not required for reinstatement, on termination of definite suspension 525
    Same as on initiation, on reinstatement after suspension for an indefinite period 526
    On reinstatement, after suspension for non-payment of dues, left to local legislation 527
GENERAL RULINGS.
    Election of officers, of the Supreme Lodge, is by 212, 213
    Unanimous, cast by a member of the Supreme Lodge, there being but one nominee 216
    Not void, because of excess, where such excess could not change result 219
    Required, for election of officers of Subordinate Lodge... 574

BALLOT BOX.
    Provided with black cubes, permitted 65

BALLS.
    Not to be held on Sunday in the name of the Order 581

BALTIMORE.
    Supreme Lodge holds sessions in, if no place determined.... 647

BANNER.
    For Supreme Lodge, form of and description 72
    For Grand Lodge, form of and description 72
    For Subordinate Lodge, form of and description 72

BARTENDERS.
    Legislation as to admission of 360

BENEFITS.
WEEKLY.
    Lodges must pay, in case of sickness, of a member in good standing 73, 75, 78, 80, 81, 82, 83, 84, 85, 87, 89, 90, 92
    One dollar the minimum, prescribed by the Supreme Lodge 73, 89, 91, 92
    Each Lodge to provide for payment of, out of its own funds 75
    The claim of members to, a right and not a charity 76
    The payment of, is a fundamental principle of the Order. 77
    Subordinates may tax their members in order to pay 78
    Above the minimum, the subject left to local legislation 56, 79, 80
    Lodge may not deprive Knight of all, for a probationary period 80, 81, 82

Index.

BENEFITS—(Continued.)   SECTIONS.
  WEEKLY.

    Lodge may prescribe probationary period, after attaining Rank of Knight, during which only the minimum shall be paid..80, 81, 82
    Immediately on reinstatement, member entitled to at least the minimum................................... ....82, 92
    Not necessarily payable to a suspended member......... 84
    Right to, not invalidated by law requiring dues paid in advance...86, 210
    Leaving the jurisdiction of Relief Committee, not a bar to.87, 88
    Lodge may not suspend payment of 89
    Lodge may not avoid payment of...................... 90
    Must be paid as long as disability continues............ 90
    Over the minimum, having been paid, Lodge cannot call the excess an offset against one dollar per week...... 90
    No change can be made in the manner or time of payment of, without consent of member...................... 90
    For "first week's sickness," must be paid................ 91
    Convalescent brother entitled to.......... ....93, 411
    Lodge may provide for reduction of, after certain number of weeks.. 94
    Not payable for time during which Lodge was suspended. 96
    Not payable, after Withdrawal Card granted, even though not delivered....................................... 97
    Payable, if in good standing when taken sick, even if in arrears when reported.............................. 98
    The claiming of, not of itself, a Pythian offense, unless fraud is shown.................................408, 411
    One who has taken a portion of the Knight rank, refusing to proceed, not entitled to........................... 410
    Renouncing the Order, debars from..................... 524
    Traveling Shields indicate amount of, holder entitled to, and issuing Lodge responsible for moneys paid on account of......................................698, 699

  FUNERAL.

    Lodges must pay, on the death of a member in good standing............... ...73, 75, 78, 80, 81, 82, 83, 85, 92
    Twenty dollars the minimum prescribed by Supreme Lodge... 73
    Each Lodge to provide for payment of, out of its own funds.. 75
    The payment of, is a fundamental principle of the Order. 77
    Subordinates may tax their members in order to pay..... 78
    Above the minimum the subject left to local legislation 56, 79, 80
    Lodge may not deny all, for a probationary period..80, 81, 82

Index.

BENEFITS—(Continued.) SECTIONS.
FUNERAL.
Lodge may prescribe probationary period, during which
only the minimum shall be paid.................80, 81, 82
Immediately on reinstatement, member entitled to at least
the minimum 82, 92
Payable to family or dependent relatives, if member not
in arrears at time of death...................85, 103, 104
Right to, not invalidated by a law requiring dues paid in
advance...86, 210
Full amount of, payable, though Lodge does not bury,
nor relatives at any expense,......................99, 100
If entitled to funeral benefits is thereby also entitled to
funeral assessment, or "widow's tax"............... 101
Payment of, to relatives of suicides, a matter for local
legislation 102
Entitled to, though arrears paid during sickness causing
death 103, 104
Lodge may not avoid payment of, simply on a claim that
deceased was intemperate........................... 106
Paid by sister Lodge, on account of member in arrears,
not a valid claim against his Lodge................. 522
Renouncing the Order debars from..................... 524
Traveling Shields indicate amount of, holder entitled to,
and issuing Lodge responsible for moneys paid on
account of....................................698, 699
GENERAL RULINGS.
Mean all advantages and privileges................. 74
Above the minimum the subject left to local legisla-
tion 56, 79, 80
Bound to give same general care and aid, to member of
sister Lodge as to one of their own................. 95
Nurse hire, not a legal claim on sister Lodge unless so provided..... 95
Lodge not to extend financial aid greater than provided by
laws of sister Lodge................................ 95
Lodge responsible for benefits paid or expenses incurred
by sister Lodge on strength of telegram of an officer.. 105
Maimed person, in good standing, entitled to all......... 333
Member admitted by Card, irregularly, through error of
the Lodge, entitled to............. 376

BIENNIAL SESSIONS—(See Sessions.)
BILLS—(See Committee on Finance.)
BLACK BALL.
Grand Lodges may provide that one, may reject applications
for membership 60

(199)

Index.

BLACK BALL—(Continued.)   SECTIONS.
    Grand Lodges may require two, to reject.................... 60
    Supreme Lodge has prescribed two, as a maximum in applications for membership................................... 60
    Should two appear in ballot, same renewed immediately..... 61, 62
    Two or more appearing on second ballot, candidate rejected... 61, 62
    Three appearing on first ballot, no further ballot required.... 62
    Cubes may be used in place of............................... 65
    Objections to elected candidate before admission may operate as, where local law so provides........................... 68
    Dropping name from list of applicants at preliminary meeting, has not the force of....................................... 70
    Rules regarding ballot for initiation apply to applications by card... 71
    Appearing in general ballot, on application at organization of new Lodge, separate ballot must be taken.............. 292 (6)

BLANKS.
    Contained in the list of supplies, forbidden to be furnished by private parties... 585

BLASPHEMY.
    An offense against the Order............................... 406

BOARD OF AUDIT.
    For examination of books of Financial Officers, unconstitutional.. 632

BOARD OF CONTROL.
    Of the Endowment Rank, number, election and term of....... 222
    In matters connected with Endowment Rank, have jurisdiction co-extensive with Supreme Lodge........................ 225
    Empowered to address Grand and Subordinate Lodges by circular, without interference by Grand Lodges........ 226, 227
    Fixes bond of the Supreme Secretary of Endowment Rank.... 688

BOARD OF TRUSTEES.
    Of the Supreme Lodge, set forth in Act of Incorporation... 285 (4)

BONDS.
    Sworn statement of sureties on, of Supreme Officers, to be filed... 107
    Of Supreme Officers, to remain in custody of Supreme Chancellor.. 594
    In the sum of ten thousand (10,000) dollars, given by Supreme Keeper of Records and Seal 622
    In the sum of fifty thousand (50,000) dollars, given by the Supreme Master of the Exchequer........................ 660
    In such sum as the Board of Control shall determine, to be given by the Supreme Secretary of the Endowment Rank.. 688

Index.

BOOK OF DIAGRAMS.   SECTIONS.
Containing illustrations of the work and its explanations; in
  the custody of the Supreme Chancellor 764
Authorized and prepared..................................... 765
BUSINESS.
Of a Lodge, to be transacted in the rank of Knight, except
  when conferring rank of Page or Esquire, or conducting
  their trial... 567
To be conducted with an officer of the Lodge in the chair ... 568
Regular order of, to be called before proceeding to close..... 571
Transaction of, by a Lodge on Sunday, forbidden............. 581
CANDIDATE—(See Applicant; Ballot.)
CAP.
Not worn in Lodge room, except by order of Chancellor
  Commander.. 709
"CARDS OF PRIVILEGE"—(See Withdrawal Cards.)
CASH SYSTEM.
In the sale of supplies, to apply to all except Grand Keepers
  of Records and Seal and Deputy Supreme Chancellors.. 587
CASTLE HALL—(See Lodge Room.)
CEREMONIES.
Supreme Lodge establishes and regulates........635, 636, 758,764
CERTIFIED RECORD.
Must accompany appeals to the Supreme Lodge, or Supreme
  Chancellor 22
In appeals, must be authenticated by Grand Chancellor and
  Grand Keeper of Records and Seal, and under seal 24, 25
In appeals, it is the duty of Grand Lodges to furnish 26
Grand Officers refusing to sign, in cases of appeal, must show
  cause, or the facts will be taken as admitted............. 29
Grand Chancellor and Grand Keeper of Records and Seal
  shall forward, in Writs of Error............................ 45
CHANCELLOR COMMANDER.
Makes declaration in open Lodge, for suspension for non-
  payment of dues... ....55, 56
Inspects and announces ballot, on application for membership. 64
Unless local law prevents, any Knight in good standing eligible
  to office of 108
May retire from Lodge during the session 109
May resign at will... 110
Eligible as Representative, after second installation, no local
  law existing to the contrary 111
Not eligible to election as Representative, on last night of
  term 112
(14)   (201)

Index.

CHANCELLOR COMMANDER—(Continued.)   SECTIONS.

In absence of, Knight may be selected to preside............ 113
May refuse permission to members to retire................. 114
If party to charges, cannot legally appoint committee on trial.. 119
Where the Constitution so provides, must preside at election of officers, otherwise election void................ ... 218
Possesses power to appoint a Chaplain at funerals........... 247
Chair of, must be filled at instituting of Lodge............. 292 (8)
Instituting Officer delivers Dispensation to............... 292 (14)
Has a right to exact the S. A. P. W. whenever he deems the safety of the work requires................................ 437
Empowered to instruct members of his own Lodge in the S. A. P. W 438
Communicates S. A. P. W. to members presenting proper order for same and Official Receipt........................438, 439
Must refuse admission, to Lodge or ante-room during session, those not in possession of S. A. P. W.........441, 443, 444, 445
Should satisfy himself of identity of person presenting order, before communicating S. A. P. W....................... 450
Should not instruct visitor in Rank password without a separate order...451, 452
Instructs Master-at-Arms to take Rank password in ante-room from members of Lodge visiting as a body.......... 453
Takes chair of Sitting Past Chancellor at installation of his successor.. 464
Re-elected, is entitled to past rank after second installation.467, 468
Having served full term of, entitled to certificate as Past Chancellor, irrespective of indebtedness to Lodge............. 469
Takes rank as Past Chancellor upon installation of successor, though minutes fail to show latter fact.................... 470
Not entitled to honors, charter being surrendered before expiration of term.. 471
Pages and Esquires admitted on the order of................ 507
Legal custodian of the private work........................ 545
Must not allow removal of the private work from the Lodge room.. 545
May call a qualified member to confer ranks................ 568
An elective officer of the Lodge............................ 574
Cannot permanently appoint as Outer Guard, a member of another Lodge... 575
Members retiring or entering under order of, need not give the sign... 576
May permit uniform cap to be worn in Lodge................ 709
In absence of, Vice Chancellor may not communicate S. A. P. W. outside of Lodge room................................. 719

Index.

CHANCELLOR COMMANDER—(Continued.)   SECTIONS.
  Where Lodge has official knowledge of absence of, Vice Chancellor empowered to perform any duty of.................. 720
  Illegally elected and installed, may not fill the chair.......... 721
  May demand Official Receipt in addition to S. A. P. W., having doubts concerning admission of a brother............... 724
  Order for S. A. P. W. must be signed by....... ....438, 747
CHANGE OF NAME—(See Name.)
CHANGE OF VENUE.
  In cases of trial, may be provided for, by Grand Lodge....... 717
CHAPLAIN.
  Chancellor Commander may appoint, at funerals............. 247
CHARGES.
  Member cannot be suspended for non-payment of dues while under...51, 120
  Withdrawal Card granted, if not under...............56, 734, 760
  Members under, not entitled to benefits 82
  Any one member may bring................................. 115
  Grand Lodge should entertain, against an officer............ 116
  Manner of proceeding in, in Subordinate Lodges may be used in Grand Lodge in analogous cases...................... 117
  Claim for money against a Lodge, cannot be prosecuted under a criminal charge...................................... 118
  Preferred by Chancellor Commander and Vice Chancellor, neither officer can appoint committee on trial............ 119
  Must be preferred, against Lodge, before Charter forfeited. 133, 135
  Against a Lodge, must be tried before a jury, during recess.. 135
  Procedure for trying, against Grand Officers 136-149
  Member against whom charges sustained, does not forfeit dues paid in advance.... 211
  Improper display of emblems, ground for charges........220, 221
  When preferred in Grand Lodge, that body hold jurisdiction... 261
  Giving false answers to questions before admission to membership, grounds for................................. 312, 407
  May be preferred against member suspended for non-payment of dues.. 382
  Failure to pay a debt, where no fraud is evidenced, not ground for...................................... 409
  Esquire refusing to proceed through the whole of the rank of Knight, not subject to................................. 410
  Office of Supreme Representative not vacated without sufficient charges... 482
  Sustained against a Past Grand Chancellor, may estop him from admission to Supreme Lodge...................... 483

Index.

CHARGES—(Continued.)   SECTIONS.
- Grand Chancellor not under, entitled to past rank on completion of term 473, 666
- May be prosecuted to trial, though accused absent 701
- In trial of, testimony of non-members, competent 702
- Notice of, by mail, held to be sufficient 703
- Lodge may proceed to try without waiting for verdict of Criminal Court 704, 705
- Simple indictment by Grand Jury not necessarily grounds for. 704
- If under, cannot be granted Withdrawal Card 734, 760
- Must be preferred, if objection sustained to granting Withdrawal Card 734
- The holding of a Withdrawal Card cannot prevent 762

CHART—(See Official Chart.)

CHARTERS.
- OF GRAND LODGES.
  - Issued by Supreme Lodge 121, 258, 644
  - Causes for revocation of 122, 331
  - Issuance of, revokes Dispensation 123
  - If lost or destroyed, Supreme Chancellor may only issue Dispensation in lieu of, until session of Supreme Lodge 124, 644
  - May not work without, being present 125
  - Committee of Supreme Lodge pass on 170
  - Forfeited, for resorting to raffles, lotteries, gift enterprises, etc. 331
  - Prepared by Supreme Keeper of Records and Seal 610
  - Charter Plates furnished by Supreme Lodge 586
- OF SUBORDINATE LODGES.
  - May not work without, being present 125
  - Exist by virtue of, issued by Grand Lodge 126, 595
  - Grand Lodges have exclusive right to issue, within their territorial jurisdiction 126, 595
  - Knight may ask to see; Lodge not compelled to show ... 127
  - Not allowed to surrender, if nine members willing to sustain, except by permission of Grand Lodge or Grand Chancellor 128
  - To whom reissued, a matter for local legislation 129
  - Which Grand Officers sign, matter for local legislation .. 130
  - Whose names shall appear on, matter for local legislation 131
  - Grand Lodge may order revocation of, for various causes 132, 133, 331
  - May not be forfeited, for offenses, without proper charges and trial 133, 135
  - Grand Lodges prescribe how many failures to meet work a forfeiture of 134

Index.

CHARTERS—(Continued.)   SECTIONS.
  OF SUBORDINATE LODGES.
    Grand Chancellor cannot suspend, unless specifically empowered by the Constitution 135
    Grand Lodges must provide a trial commission or jury for hearing charges, before suspension of 135
    If Charter temporarily suspended during recess, Grand Lodge must try Lodge at next session 135
    Shall be vacated, for resorting to raffles, lotteries, schemes of chance or gift enterprises 331
    Surrendered before expiration of term, officer loses honors 471
    Charter Plates furnished by Supreme Lodge—on list of "Supplies" 586
  OF LODGES SUBORDINATE TO SUPREME LODGE.
    May not work without, being present 125
    Exist by virtue of, issued by Supreme Lodge 126, 644
    Supreme Lodge may revoke, for various causes 132, 331
    Committee of Supreme Lodge passes on 170
    May be forfeited for failure to meet for three months 329
    Charter Plates furnished by Supreme Lodge—on list of "Supplies" 586

CHARTER BOOKS.
  No authority for opening 233

CHARTER PLATES.
  Furnished as supplies, by the Supreme Lodge 586

CHATTELS.
  In case of a suspension of a Subordinate Lodge, refusal to deliver up, constitutes on offense 287

CHINESE.
  Not eligible to membership in the Order 354

CIRCULARS.
  Grand Chancellor has no right to forbid issuance of, by Board of Control 226
  Board of Control may issue, to Grand and Subordinate Lodges 227

"CLEARANCE CERTIFICATES"—(See Withdrawal Cards.)
CLOSE—(See Adjourn; Closing.)
CLOSING.
  Officers must conform to the ceremonies of 547
  Lodge may not adjourn, but must "proceed to close" 571

CODE OF PROCEDURE IN TRIAL OF GRAND OFFICERS.
  Laid down by Supreme Lodge; applies where a Grand Lodge has not prescribed a code 136-149

COLLARS.
  Further purchase of red collars, unauthorized 518
  Constitutional provision with reference to wearing 518

Index.

COLLARS—(Continued.) SECTIONS.
  Not to be worn in a parade of any character.................. 519
  Not to be worn at funerals................................... 520
COLLEGE—(See Pythian College.)
COLORED PERSONS.
  Lodges composed of, not recognized................. 350, 351, 353
  Not eligible to membership in the Order......... 350, 351, 352, 353
COMMISSION.
  Form of Deputy Supreme Chancellor, prescribed............. 192
COMMITTEES.
  OF THE SUPREME LODGE—List of Standing, appointed biennially by the Supreme Chancellor................ 150
    COUNCIL OF ADMINISTRATION—(Three Members.)
      Constitutions, and amendments to Constitutions, of Grand and Subordinate Lodges, must be submitted to and approved by.......... 8, 9, 151, 152, 185
      Shall advise the Supreme Chancellor, when requested 151
      Failing, within ninety days, to report on Constitutions, or amendments to Constitutions, same go into effect...152, 186
      Must report action on Constitutions and amendments to Constitutions, to Supreme Lodge............. 152
    ON LAW—(Five members.)
      Amendments to the Constitution of the Supreme Lodge, referred to, before action................ 6
      To report on and have charge of all matters coming within the purview of that committee........... 153
      Inquiries, from Grand Lodges to be forwarded to, three weeks before the session 154
    ON FINANCE—(Five members.)
      To examine the accounts of Supreme Keeper of Records and Seal and Supreme Master of Exchequer before the session, and at other periods when required.....................................155, 158
      To examine all bills presented at the session......... 156
      To make estimates for and recommend appropriations. 157
      To audit the books on the year the Supreme Lodge does not meet, the Committee to convene on the call of the Chairman............................. 158
      Their pay to be same as Supreme Representative.... 159
      Their report to be printed and distributed........... 159
      To examine the books of the Major General, U. R. 160, 340
      Chairman of, a member of Committee on Supplies... 177
      To be furnished with duplicate bills of Supplies by Supreme Chancellor............................. 625

Index.

COMMITTEES—(Continued.)   SECTIONS.
OF THE SUPREME LODGE.
  ON APPEALS AND GRIEVANCES—(Five members.)
    Appeals must be sent in at least one month prior to the session and placed in hands of chairman of.. 37
    Decision of, when approved by Supreme Chancellor, final until reversed by Supreme Lodge........... 41
    To hear all appeals referred to them............... 161
  ON CREDENTIALS AND RETURNS—(Five members.)
    To examine returns of Grand Lodges and Lodges subordinate to the Supreme Lodge 162
    To examine the credentials of Past Grand Chancellors and Representatives........................162, 163
    To meet one day in advance of session.............. 163
    To be furnished with a report of delinquent Grand Lodges 628
  ON MILEAGE—(Five members.)
    To compute the mileage and per diem of the session—no order for same to be drawn until majority of, endorse report on................................. 164
  ON STATE OF THE ORDER—(Five members.)
    To report on the condition and progress of the Order 165
  ON WRITTEN WORK—(Five members.)
    To report on matters of a public nature, pertaining to the written work, covering regalia, jewels, charts, certificates, shields, uniforms, equipments or public ceremonials....................... 166
  ON UNWRITTEN WORK—(Five members.)
    To report on matters strictly private 167
  ON PRINTING—(Five members.)
    To have a general supervisory charge of all printing. 168
    General rules laid down for guidance of.......... 169
  ON DISPENSATIONS AND CHARTERS—(Five members.)
    To pass on the issuance of Dispensations and Charters, general Dispensations and Deputies' commissions.. 170
  ON ENDOWMENT RANK—(Five members.)
    To examine into the affairs of the rank, except those pertaining to finance........................... 171
  ON UNIFORM RANK—(Five members.)
    To pass on all matters pertaining to the rank as may be referred to them............................ 172
  GENERAL RULINGS—STANDING COMMITTEES.
    Each of the foregoing committees shall consist of five members, except the Council of Administration, of three members, serving during recess, paid mileage and per diem................................ 173

Index.

COMMITTEES—(Continued.)   SECTIONS.
OF THE SUPREME LODGE.
  GENERAL RULINGS—STANDING COMMITTEES.
    Who eligible on Committees of the Supreme Lodge... 174
    The expiration of term of Supreme Representative vacates seat on Standing Committee............. 175
    Chairman of each, to be furnished with an Official Digest and set of Journals....................... 627
  ON SEATS.
    To draw the seats for Representatives............... 176
  ON SUPPLIES.
    Composed of Supreme Chancellor, Supreme Keeper of Records and Seal, and Chairman of Committee on Finance... 177
    For the supplies of the Uniform Rank specially, the Major General takes the place of the Supreme Chancellor 177
  ON HOTELS AND TRANSPORTATION.
    Composed of the Supreme Keeper of Records and Seal and Major General, and have charge of arrangements of rates at hotels and on railroads......... 178
  GENERAL RULINGS—SPECIAL COMMITTEES.
    Only Past Supreme Chancellors, Officers and Representatives eligible on........................174, 175
    Special Committees, to meet during recess, time and place of meeting under control of Supreme Chancellor—not authorized to "send for persons and papers" unless so ordered....................... 179
    Supreme Representative, a member of, failing re-election, seat not vacated........................... 180
OF A GRAND LODGE.
  Appeals from Committee on Appeals of, should be heard by Grand Lodge, and not referred to a Special Committee. 42
  On charges against a Grand Officer, member of, how appointed and by whom; meetings of and duties
    ....142, 143, 144, 145, 146, 149
OF SUBORDINATE LODGE.
  Sick member leaving jurisdiction of Relief Committee where the necessity of the case required, would not
    · forfeit benefits..87, 88
  On trial, may not be appointed by Chancellor Commander or Vice Chancellor, if parties to the charges 119
  Subject to fine or suspension, for dereliction of duty..... 239
  Applications for membership to be referred to committee of three for investigation........................... 346
  On investigation on application may report at once, if local law does not prevent........................... 348

Index.

COMMITTEES—(Continued.) SECTIONS.
  OF SUBORDINATE LODGE.
    On investigation on application may not be questioned as
      to their report 349
    Application, once referred to Committee on Investigation,
      cannot be withdrawn, without consent...363, 364, 365, 370
    Have no right to pass on the conduct of the Supreme
      Lodge or its officers............................ 580
    Relief Committee; moneys paid by, under Traveling
      Shield, must be repaid to, by Lodge issuing Shield.... 699
    Notice *mailed* to accused, by Committee on Charges,
      deemed sufficient.................................. 703
COMMITTEE ON APPEALS AND GRIEVANCES—(See Committees.)
COMMITTEE ON CREDENTIALS AND RETURNS—(See Committees.)
COMMITTEE ON DISPENSATIONS AND CHARTERS—(See Committees.)
COMMITTEE ON ENDOWMENT RANK—(See Committees.)
COMMITTEE ON FINANCE—(See Committees.)
COMMITTEE ON HOTELS AND TRANSPORTATION—(See Committees.)
COMMITTEE ON LAW—(See Committees.)
COMMITTEE ON MILEAGE—(See Committees.)
COMMITTEE ON PRINTING—(See Committees.)
COMMITTEE ON SEATS—(See Committees.)
COMMITTEE ON STATE OF THE ORDER—(See Committees.)
COMMITTEE ON SUPPLIES—(See Committees.)
COMMITTEE ON UNIFORM RANK—(See Committees.)
COMMITTEE ON UNWRITTEN WORK—(See Committees.)
COMMITTEE ON WRITTEN WORK—(See Committees.)
CONSENT.
    Of a Grand Lodge, necessary in taking an appeal to the
      Supreme Lodge............. 18
    Not necessary, in taking an appeal when Lodge has surrendered its property, and appeals. 18
    Must be obtained at same session at which action had, against
      which appeal is taken........ 22
    By the Grand Chancellor, in the case of an appeal, insufficient.. 23
    Required before accepting rejected material, in Lodges subordinate to Supreme Lodge............ 322
    Propositions for membership cannot be withdrawn without... 363

Index.

CONSENT—(Continued.)   SECTIONS.
   Cannot be given for withdrawal of proposition, after same has
      been reported on by committee 363, 364, 365
   Of Grand Chancellor, required on application of non-resident 535
   Required of Lodge to which member is attached, before con-
      ferring ranks...... 536
   "Unanimous," not necessary for the withdrawal of proposition
      for membership..... 732
   Means "a majority vote".... 732
CONSOLIDATION.
   Of Lodges subordinate to Supreme Lodge, authorized....... 330
   Of Lodges, under a Grand Lodge, a subject for local legislation 578
CONSTITUTION.
   OF SUPREME LODGE.
      Amendments to, presented at regular session, and lie over   3
      Amendments to, come up for adoption at next succeeding
         regular session...................................... 3
      Amendments to, require a two-thirds vote to adopt...... 3
      Amendments to, disposed of at same session as presented,
         provided unanimous consent is given to consider.... 5
      Amendments to, referred to Committee on Law, and
         reported on, before action........................... 6
      Any decision of a Grand Lodge or Grand Chancellor that
         would by their operation invalidate, is ground for the
         issuance of a Writ of Error...................... . 45
      That prior to 1874, repealed........................... 181
      Obligatory on Grand and Subordinate Lodges....... ... 182
      Paramount authority..........................183, 504, 590
      Members of Supreme Lodge to be furnished with a copy
         of, at sessions 629
      Supreme Lodge may resume additional powers by amend-
         ments to... 645
   OF GRAND LODGE.
      Power to amend, exists only in itself.................... 7
      Can only be amended as therein provided................8, 10
      Amendments to, inoperative until approved..........9, 185
      Amendments to, rejected, may be resubmitted, and such
         resubmission is not a "consideration of the same sub-
         ject"............ 11
      Constitution and amendments to, submitted to Council of
         Administration.............. 151
      Council of Administration failing to act on, or amend-
         ments to, within ninety days, go into effect.... 152
      Though approved by Supreme Chancellor, of no force if in
         conflict with Supreme Lodge law................ 183
      Adopts, for itself.......................................184, 255

CONSTITUTION—(Continued.)   SECTIONS.
OF GRAND LODGE.
Must be approved by Supreme Lodge or Council of Administration 185
May not provide in, so as to debar a member from right of action 275
Supreme Keeper of Records and Seal to notify Grand Lodge of approval of 626
The following subjects must be provided for in the Constitutions of Grand Lodges before becoming operative:—(See Section 272 of this Digest.)
Objection to an elected candidate operating as a black ball 68
A "Probationary Period" during which only minimum benefits shall be paid 81
The power of a Grand Chancellor to suspend a Lodge ... 135
Charging dues during suspension for non-payment of dues 208
Adding fines and assessments to dues 237
Providing a representative system and limiting the rights of Past Chancellors on the floor 263, 264
Election and appointment of Grand Officers 267
Residence, of applicant for membership, exceeding six months 534
Filling vacancies, by Grand Chancellor 714

SUBORDINATE LODGE.
Grand Lodge provides 184, 187, 188
Must be approved by Supreme Lodge or Council of Administration 185
The following "Obligatory" general rules or principles shall be incorporated into. (See Section 188 of this Digest.)

NOTE.—The word "Obligatory" follows each of these rules, where they appear distributed through the work.

A Lodge shall never consist of less than seven members.. 561
- A Lodge shall meet weekly, unless Dispensation provides to the contrary 562
Seven constitutes a quorum 566
Seven only, present, appropriations require unanimous consent 566
Business transacted in Knight rank, except trial of Pages or Esquires 567
Officers of Subordinate Lodge, those prescribed in the Ritual 573
Nominations, on night preceding and night of election ... 404
Officers installed first regular meeting, new term 290
Officer, in debt to Lodge, not to be installed 290
Vacancies, how filled 715

Index.

CONSTITUTION—(Continued.) SECTIONS.
  SUBORDINATE LODGE.
    Initiate to be of legal age, a white male, in sound health, a believer in a Supreme Being, and six months a resident 347
    Application to be accompanied with fee ; total for all ranks not less than $10.00 unless under Dispensation....... 229
    Application signed by petitioner, endorsed by two Knights, referred and balloted on 346
    Two black balls reject................................ 61
    Six months before reapplying 61
    One week between the conferring of ranks 503
    Application by Withdrawal Card, same as initiate 370
    Proposition may be withdrawn, before report, by consent 363
    Non-resident to have consent of his Grand Chancellor ... 535
    Ranks not to be conferred on non-resident, or member of another Lodge, without consent of his Lodge...... 536
    Fee to accompany application 229, 366
    Application for Card, made personally or in writing 734
    Withdrawal Card may be revoked 738
    Withdrawal Card renewed if lost 756, 757
    Each Lodge to have a Seal............................. 560
    Amount equal to one year's dues, causes suspension..... 51
    Lodges shall pay benefits.............................. 73
  OF LODGES SUBORDINATE TO SUPREME LODGE.
    Arranged and adopted 328
CONTEMPT.
  Holder of Withdrawal Card in, for refusal to comply with citation in trial.. 738
CONTEST.
  In cases of Supreme Representatives, notice of, to be filed with Supreme Keeper of Records and Seal, thirty days before session.. 682
  Supreme Lodge will not favor, where effect would be merely to cause a vacancy................................... 683
COPYRIGHT.
  Seal of the Supreme Lodge covered by...............285 (2), 557
COUNCIL OF ADMINISTRATION—(See Committees.)
COUNTERSIGN.
  Of the Uniform Rank, promulgated by the Supreme Chancellor and issued by the Major General..................... 344
COURT MARTIAL.
  Major General reviews proceedings in 343
CREDENTIALS.
  Of Past Grand Chancellors and Representatives, passed on by Committee on Credentials and Returns................ 162

Index.

CREDENTIALS—(Continued.) SECTIONS.
   Of Supreme Representatives and Past Grand Chancellors to be forwarded twenty days before the session............. 189
   Past Grand Chancellors shall set forth date when term of Grand Chancellor began and ended...................... 190
   Past Chancellor taking Card, entitled to Rank Credential.... 461
   Of a Past Grand Chancellor, being passed on by Supreme Lodge, Grand Lodge cannot vacate Rank... 482
   Of Past Grand Chancellor, may be vacated, for cause, before approved by Supreme Lodge......... 483
   Member affiliating in another Jurisdiction, must present Rank Credential to entitle him to past rank................511, 512
   Withdrawal Cards, with past rank inserted, of no value as Rank Credentials 512, 513, 514, 515, 516
   Of Supreme Representative, shall state date of attaining rank of Past Grand Chancellor and of election as Supreme Representative.... 687
CREDENTIALS AND RETURNS—Committee on—(See Committees.)
CREDIT SYSTEM.
   Extended to Grand Keepers of Records and Seal and Deputy Supreme Chancellors.................................... 587
CRIMINAL CHARGES.
   Claim against a Lodge for money, cannot be prosecuted under 118
CRIMINAL INTENT.
   Constitutes an element in an offense....................... 407
CRIMINAL OFFENSE.
   Sinple indictment for, does not justify Lodge in proceeding against offender.. 704
   Indictment for, does not estop Lodge from proceeding....704, 705
CUBES.
   May be used in place of black balls..... 65
CUSTOMS DUTIES.
   Rebate to amount of, on supplies allowed.................... 588
DEALERS—(See Paraphernalia.)
DEATH BENEFIT ASSOCIATIONS.
   Operating under the name of the Order, declared to be illegal........................... ....399, 400, 401
DEBATE.
   In Grand Lodges, *members* have a right to, unless specifically debarred by Constitution 266
   Past Grand Chancellors not privileged to, in Supreme Lodge, unless by permission................................. 479
DEBT.
   Obtaining credit from a member, not in itself an offense..... 409

Index.

DECISION. SECTIONS.
Of a Grand Lodge, or of a Lodge subordinate to the Supreme Lodge, final until reversed.............................. 17
Appeal does not lie directly from, of Grand Chancellor, to the Supreme Lodge... 19, 20
Of Supreme Chancellor, certified by him to parties in interest.. 39, 45
Of Supreme Chancellor, is binding until reversed by Supreme Lodge.. 40, 600, 602
Of Supreme Chancellor, to be reported to the Supreme Lodge at its next session... 40
Of the Committee on Appeals, when confirmed by Supreme Chancellor, fixes status of rights of member until reversed by Supreme Lodge.. 41
Of the Committee on Appeals, of a Grand Lodge, should be heard by a Grand Lodge; improper to refer to a Special Committee.. 42
Grand Lodge making a decision which would operate so as to invalidate enactment of the Supreme Lodge, ground for Writ of Error.. 45
Charter of Lodge liable to suspension for refusal to obey..... 132
Of a Supreme Chancellor, stands as law until reversed... 600, 602
Supreme Lodge may provide legislation for enforcement of... 642

DECLARATION.
Of suspension of member twelve months in arrears, must be made in open Lodge.. 55
Of suspension of member twelve months in arrears, not being made, membership not severed.................................... 56
Member twelve months in arrears for dues, may tender amount any time before declaration; so doing, restored to membership in good standing.. 56

DEDICATION CEREMONIES.
Form of, prescribed... 199

DEFUNCT LODGE.
May appeal without consent, having surrended its property... 18
To whom Charter of, to be reissued, a matter for local legislation.. 129
Members of, Subordinate to Supreme Lodge, granted Withdrawal Cards by Supreme Chancellor................................ 324, 325
Form of Withdrawal Card for members of, ordered prepared. 753
Pages and Esquires of, may be issued Withdrawal Cards..... 754
Upon reorganization, control issuance of Withdrawal Cards to former members... 755
New Grand Lodge given possession of books and papers of defunct Lodges under old Grand Lodge............................ 763

Index.

DEGREES. SECTIONS.
The word, stricken out wherever appearing in the Ritual and
the word "rank" inserted in lieu thereof................. 500
DEPUTY SUPREME CHANCELLOR.
Commissions of, passed on by Committee on Dispensations and
Charters... 170
Commissioned by Supreme Chancellor..................... 191, 598
Must be a member of Lodge in his Jurisdiction............... 191
Form of commission prescribed by Supreme Lodge........... 192
Is the Representative of the Supreme Chancellor, subject to
removal at will 193
Appointment of, requires no approval by Supreme Lodge..... 194
Installs, or causes to be installed, Officers of Lodges in his Jur-
isdiction...195, 196
Responsible for appointee................................. 196
Has no authority to grant Dispensations to organize Lodges.. 197
Reports all Dispensations granted......................... 198
Installs the officers of new Grand Lodge.................... 255
Of the Hawaiian Islands, empowered to confer the rank of
Past Chancellor.. 278
Dispensation to organize Lodge must be approved by........ 310
Must forward all applications for institution of new Lodges,
together with objections filed, if any................... 310
Though in possession of Dispensation, may not proceed in face
of protest until authorized by Supreme Chancellor....... 311
Cannot accept rejected material in organizing Lodge......... 312
Empowered to confer rank of Past Chancellor on those entitled,
by actual service...................................... 315
Approval of, required on application to admit "maimed persons" 318
May grant Dispensation to confer rank on person over fifty... 319
To protect secret working properties of the Order from
improper exposure..................................... 431
"Supplies" furnished to, on credit......................... 587
Necessary expenses of, paid by Lodges instituted............ 605
Traveling shields issued through.......................... 696
DIGEST—(See Official Digest.)
DIPLOMAS.
For ladies, authorized................................... 303
DISHONORABLE DISCHARGE.
A penalty under proceedings in Court Martial............... 343
"DISMISSAL CERTIFICATES."—(See Withdrawal Cards.)
DISPENSATIONS.
GENERAL.
Grand Lodges require, when issuing "appeals for aid,"
outside their Jurisdiction, from Supreme Chancellor .. 48

Index.

DISPENSATIONS—(Continued.)   SECTIONS.
GENERAL.
Subordinate Lodges require, from their Grand Chancellor, when issuing "appeals for aid" 49
Lodges subordinate to the Supreme Lodge require, from the Supreme Chancellor, when issuing "appeals for aid" 49
From Supreme Chancellor, not required, when Lodge has obtained Dispensation from Grand Chancellor to issue "appeals for aid" 50
Required for holding meetings at longer intervals than one week 133, 562, 563
Deputy Supreme Chancellors to report all, issued 198
To reduce the minimum fee for ranks, cease with the officer granting them 200
To reduce the minimum fee for ranks, issued only on request of Grand Lodge in session 201
For special purposes—cases reported by Supreme Chancellor 202
May not be issued, to open so-called "charter books"... 233
Grand Chancellor may not issue, to initiate persons for less than legal fees 235
Supreme Chancellor may not issue to Lodges subordinate to Supreme Lodge, to reduce minimum fee for ranks. 317
To admit maimed persons, in Lodges subordinate to the Supreme Lodge, issued by Supreme Chancellor...... 318
To admit persons over fifty, in Lodges subordinate to the Supreme Lodge, may be granted by Deputy 319
To initiate candidate same night as reported on, in Lodges subordinate to the Supreme Lodge, may be granted by Deputy 319
Lodges subordinate to Supreme Lodge require, for failure to hold meetings for three months 329
Required, permitting committee to report on application for initiation same evening as presented 346
Required for conferring more than one rank on one person on the same evening, except on first four meetings of new Lodge 503, 504
Required for conferring rank of Page same evening as receipt of application 503
Supreme Chancellor may not issue, for general parade of the Order 601
WARRANTS OF.
Grand Lodges exist primarily, by virtue of, issued by Supreme Chancellor 121, 258, 596
Issuance of a Charter to a Grand Lodge rescinds 123

Index.

DISPENSATIONS—(Continued.)   SECTIONS.
  WARRANTS OF.
    Acts done under, after issuance of Charter are illegal.... 123
    Issued during recess, by Supreme Chancellor, in case of
      destruction of Charter............................. 124
    Must be present in Lodge or ante-room of Grand or Subor-
      dinate Lodge...................................... 125
    Lodges Subordinate to the Supreme Lodge, exist primarily,
      by virtue of, issued by Supreme Chancellor....... 126, 595
    Visiting Knight may ask to see Dispensation of a Lodge.. 127
    The Supreme or Grand Lodge may revoke, for cause..132, 133
    May not be forfeited, for cause, until Lodge duly notified
      and given opportunity to answer.................... 133
    Causes for forfeiting................................132, 133
    Issued by Supreme Chancellor during recess, passed on by
      Committee on Dispensations and Charters........... 170
    Deputy Supreme Chancellor has no authority to issue.... 197
    Delivered to Chancellor Commander of new Lodge by insti-
      tuting officer....................................292 (14)
    Supreme Keeper of Records and Seal shall keep register
      of, issued to Grand Lodges, or by Supreme Chancellor
      to Lodges subordinate to Supreme Lodge............ 612
DISPENSATIONS AND CHARTERS—Committee on—(See Com·
  mittees.)
DISTRICT DEPUTY GRAND CHANCELLOR.
  Grand Lodges may authorize, to empower another to install
    officers.. 203
  May not deputize another to institute a new Lodge........... 204
  May instruct in the secret work and communicate S. A. P. W.
    to Chancellor Commander, outside of Lodge Room....... 253
  Jewel for, adopted... 293
  May not annul the action of a Lodge....................... 375
  Grand Lodge cannot require rituals to be delivered up to, after
    a specified period..................................... 552
  At installation, may declare office of absent officer vacant, if
    local law permits...................................... 716
DONATIONS.
  Of part of the fees for membership, not to be made........231, 232
  May be made to a distressed brother........................ 242
DUES.
  Arrears for, equal to amount of one year, causes sus·
    pension 51, 53, 238
  "In arrears" for, designated 52
  Arrears for six months, does not justify suspension........... 54
  When twelve months in arrears for, should be notified, before
    suspension.. 55

Index.

DUES—(Continued.) SECTIONS.
    May pay arrears of, even though twelve months' owing, if declaration of suspension not made...................... 56
    As a general proposition, a subject for local legislation....79, 205
    Requiring payment of, in advance does not debar from benefits or the S. A. P. W.........................86, 210, 436
    If not in arrears for, when taken sick, entitled to benefits.... 98
    If not in arrears for, at death, family or dependent relatives entitled to funeral benefits, even though arrears of, paid during sickness causing death........................103, 104
    Charging of, to Pages and Esquires, a matter for local legislation 206
    New members may not be exempted from payment of........ 207
    May not be charged to members suspended for non-payment of, unless local law so provides......................208, 209
    Advance payment of, not forfeited nor returned in case of suspension for cause, but retained to credit of member...... 211
    Fines may operate as, if local law permits................... 237
    Fines, when added to, and making a sum equal to twelve months, cause suspension................................ 238
    Of officers, must be paid before installation.................. 290
    Official Receipt the only legal evidence of payment of........
    ....421, 422, 423, 424, 425
    Official Receipt is not conclusive evidence of payment of, as between the Lodge and member........................ 425
    The length of time arrears for, debar from receiving the S. A. P. W., is a matter for local legislation.................... 440
    Reinstatement after suspension for non-payment of, matter for local legislation.. 527
    Advance payment of, required before issuance of Traveling Shield... 698
    Must pay all, to entitle to Withdrawal Card.................. 734

ELECTIONS.
    IN SUPREME LODGE.
        Officers of, elected biennially on third day of session.212, 285 (5)
        A majority of votes present, necessary to a choice in..... 213
        May be held in case of officer, absent at time of installation 215
        Unanimous vote may be cast by one member, there being but one nominee 216
        Of Board of Control...................................... 222
        Installation and not election of successor, determines status of outgoing presiding officer................... 291
    IN GRAND LODGE.
        Officer nominated, eligible to, though absent............. 217
        Installation and not election of successor, determines status of outgoing presiding officer................... 291

Index.

ELECTIONS—(Continued.) SECTIONS.
IN GRAND LODGE.
    Of Supreme Representatives, to be for four years 674
    Certificate of Supreme Representative to show date of... 687
IN SUBORDINATE LODGE.
    Void if Chancellor Commander fails to preside, if Constitution so provides 218
    Tellers at, to be members of the Lodge.................. 218
    Simple excess of votes does not void 219
    Installation and not election of successor, determines status of outgoing presiding officer. 291
    Of officers in new Lodge, at preliminary meeting, ratified at institution..292 (7)
    Independent nominations may be made on night of...404, 405
    Of Sitting Past Chancellor, only a Past Chancellor eligible to 465
    What officers must be elected 574
ELECTIONEERING.
    In the Supreme Lodge, disqualifies candidate for office 214
ELECTION TO MEMBERSHIP.
    Whether membership by Card begins on, or on signing roster, a matter for local legislation................ 371
    Grand Lodge failing to determine, membership by Card begins on election 372
ELIGIBILITY.
    Any Knight in good standing, eligible to office in Subordinate Lodge, unless local law to the contrary.................. 108
    Re-elected Chancellor Commander eligible as Representative, unless disqualified by local law 111
    Chancellor Commander not eligible as Representative on last night of term.. 112
    Any Past Chancellor eligible to any office, at formation of Grand Lodge... 256
    Being maimed, not a disqualification for office 333
    Knight eligible as Past Chancellor at organization of Lodge.. 464
    Must be a Supreme Representative or Past Grand Chancellor, to be eligible to office in the Supreme Lodge 653
    To office, in Subordinate Lodge, left to local legislation...... 718
    Holder of Withdrawal Card may not hold office............. 750
EMBLEMS.
    Not to be used for advertising business, except by those engaged in the sale of Pythian goods, etc....................220, 221
    The improper use of, a Pythian offense..................220, 221
    Improper to be used in connection with entertainments held on Sunday... 581
    Supreme Lodge prescribes form of............... 637

Index.

ENDOWMENT RANK. SECTIONS.
  Committee on, duties of................................ 171
  Adoption of, and provisions for Board of Control............ 222
  Sections of, to be notified of suspensions in Subordinate
    Lodges.. 223
  To bear proportion of printing Supreme Lodge Journal....... 224
  Board of Control has territorial jurisdiction co-extensive with
    Supreme Lodge.. 225
  Grand Lodge may not forbid the circulation of matter pertain-
    ing to...226, 227
  Power to establish, under act of incorporation............285 (9)
  Organizations injurious to, prohibited...................... 399
  Organizations other than, using the name of the Order, pro-
    hibited.. 402
  Duties of Supreme Secretary of............................ 688
  Bond of Supreme Secretary of, determined by Board of Con-
    trol.. 688

ENTERING.
  Member entering when Lodge is "at ease," Lodge called to
    order... 572
  After retiring on order of Chancellor Commander, member
    does not give the sign................................. 576

ENTERTAINMENTS.
  Not to be held on Sunday in the name of the Order.......... 581

ESQUIRE.
  Adverse ballot on the application of, cannot be laid over 69
  Charging of dues to, rests with Subordinate Lodges.......... 206
  Funeral rosette for, prescribed............................. 245
  Per capita tax payable on, in Lodges subordinate to the
    Supreme Lodge.. 308
  Rejected on a ballot for advancement, may reapply in one
    month thereafter, in Lodges subordinate to the Supreme
    Lodge.. 321
  The transfer of, from one Lodge to another is only by With-
    drawal Card.. 380
  May be dropped for failure to advance..................... 386
  Manner of reinstatement after dropping, a matter for local leg-
    islation.. 385
  Not subject to charges because of refusing to proceed with all
    the work in the rank of Knight........................ 410
  Term Pass-Word not to be communicated to..............435, 437
  Grand Lodges may charge per capita tax on................. 490
  Separate ballot required for the advancement of............ 506
  Admitted while working in the ranks, by order of the Chancellor
    Commander... 507
  Rank of, conferred on, by sister Lodge on proper request..... 508

Index.

ESQUIRE—(Continued.)   SECTIONS.
  Regalia of, prescribed........................ 518
  Withdrawal Card issued to, on Lodge being suspended....... 754

EXPENSES.
  Subordinate Lodge may levy tax to meet..................... 59
  New Lodge to pay, of instituting officer..................292 (12)
  Itemized statement of, to be reported by instituting officer..292 (d)

EXPULSION.
  Subordinate Lodges authorized to impose the penalty of..... 228
  Colored person obtaining membership, upon discovery to be
    expelled.. 352
  Member irregularly admitted through no fault of his own, not
    subject to 375, 376

FEES.
  Dispensations to reduce, for all the ranks, die with the officer
    granting them... 200
  Dispensations to reduce, for all the ranks, issued only on
    request of Grand Lodge in session 201
  Minimum for membership, established by the Supreme Lodge,
    ten dollars.......................................229, 230, 234
  Supreme Chancellor may issue Dispensation to reduce minimum to six dollars....................................... 229
  Grand Lodge fixes, for membership, at or above the minimum...229, 230
  For all the ranks, above the minimum, subject to local jurisdiction................................. 230
  Lodges may not refund or donate any part of minimum ..231, 232
  Opening "Charter Books" thereby evading rule regarding
    minimum, forbidden...................................... 233
  The rule regarding minimum applies to new Lodges...:.234, 292 (5)
  Grand Chancellor may not grant Dispensations reducing minimum...................................... 235
  The division of, for all the ranks, left to each Grand Jurisdiction.. 236
  Minimum, for all the ranks, in Lodges subordinate to the
    Supreme Lodge, ten dollars, and the Supreme Chancellor
    may not reduce... 317
  For ranks, in case of rejection, in Lodges subordinate to the
    Supreme Lodge, must be returned....................... 320
  Must be paid, before conferring ranks 366
  Lodges have a right to charge, for Withdrawal Cards......... 736

FINANCE—Committee on—(See Committees.)

FINES.
  Where provided for by local law, may be charged up and operate as dues.. 237

Index.

FINES—(Continued.)   SECTIONS.

    Aggregating a sum equal to one year's dues, render member liable to suspension..................................... 238
    Grand Lodges may impose, on members of committees for dereliction of duty....................................... 239
    The matter of imposing, for non-attendance at meetings, a matter for local legislation................................ 240
    May be imposed on Sitting Past Chancellor, as an officer of Lodge.. 460
    Imposed on delinquent Grand Lodges, for failure to make returns.. 539
    Must be paid by delinquent Grand Lodge, before being allowed representation... 539
    Laws providing for, for non-attendance at "meetings," apply to all meetings, whether regular or special................ 565

"FIRST WEEK'S SICKNESS."
    Benefits payable to member during......................... 91

FOREIGN COUNTRIES.
    Provisions for sending secret work to...................... 554

FORMS.
    Grand Lodges must conform to, provided by Supreme Lodge. 259
    Supreme Lodge provides...........................635, 636, 758
    Of Traveling Shield, prescribed............................ 697

FRAUD.
    Claiming benefits, not a Pythian offense, unless fraudulent intent appears.......................................408, 411
    Failure to pay a debt, not an offense, unless fraud appears.... 409
    Withdrawal Card procured by, is void....................... 761

FUNDS.
    Grand Lodges may restrict the purposes for which, may be expended.. 241
    Subordinate Lodge may donate, to distressed brother........ 242
    May not be appropriated, even for nurse hire, except in the manner provided by the Constitution...................... 243
    Instituting officer turns over, upon installation of officers. 292 (12)
    Unanimous consent required to appropriate, only seven members being present..................................... 566
    Supreme Master of Exchequer renders quarterly statement of 657

FUNERALS.
    Order of march at, prescribed.............................. 244
    Rosettes to be worn at, prescribed......................245, 708
    Lodges may appear at, in citizens' dress, or in uniform, wearing rosette or jewels....................................... 246
    Chancellor Commander may appoint Chaplain to conduct exercises at... 247

Index.

FUNERALS—(Continued.)   SECTIONS.
    Ceremonies at, do not now require kneeling.................. 248
    Members excused from attendance at, where excluded from
        equal share in and control of........................ 249
    None but the prescribed ritual must be used at.... 250
    Jewels of the Order, declared legal, to be worn at............ 299
    Collars may not be worn at................................... 520

FUNERAL ROSETTE.
    Prescribed for members, officers, past officers and Grand
        Lodges...245, 708

FUNERAL SERVICE.
    Adopted by Supreme Lodge, the only one to be used......... 250

GERMAN DEPUTY GRAND CHANCELLOR.
    Provision for conferring rank of Past Grand Chancellor on,
        repealed... 486
    Acquired no vested right to rank of Past Grand Chancellor,
        because of partial service when law changed............. 486

GIFT ENTERPRISES—(See Lotteries.)

GOOD STANDING.
    Grand Lodges prescribe the limit of.......................... 52
    Though twelve months in arrears, member may place himself
        in, if no declaration made of suspension.................. 56
    Benefits payable only to a member in......................73, 85
    Minimum benefits, at least, must be paid to members in.80, 81, 83, 90
    Member reinstated after suspension for non-payment of dues,
        becomes in, so far as payment of benefits is concerned... 92
    The payment of benefits to a member in, committing suicide, a
        matter for local legislation. 102
    Local law not providing to the contrary, any Knight in, eligible
        to office of Chancellor Commander...................... 108
    All members in, of like rank and service, entitled to same priv-
        ileges, benefits and emoluments......................... 333
    Major General must be a member in......................... 334
    References on petition for membership must be Knights in.... 346
    The Official Receipt is conclusive evidence of................. 424
    Supreme Representatives must be members in................ 664
    Objections to a member in, cannot prevent his admission..726, 727

GRAND CHANCELLOR.
    Appeal from decision of, lies to Grand, not Supreme Lodge. 19, 20
    Cannot give consent to take an appeal to Supreme Lodge 23
    To certify appeal papers and Writs of Error.........24, 27, 29, 45
    Refusing to certify appeal papers, must show cause.......... 29
    Writ of Error may issue, against decision of, during recess...45, 46
    Permission of, required, in cases of "Appeals for Aid".....49, 50

Index.

GRAND CHANCELLOR—(Continued.)   SECTIONS.

May grant Lodge permission to surrender, even though nine members are willing to continue 128
Possesses no power to suspend a Chartered Lodge, unless specifically conferred on him, nor then without trial....... 135
Charges, during recess, against Grand Officer, presented to, if not himself under charges................................ 140
Appoints majority of trial committee, on charges against Grand Officer, if not himself under charges..................... 142
Provision for contingencies arising, in charges against Grand Officer, where the Grand Chancellor is under charges. 140, 143
Not empowered to request Dispensation for reducing the fee for conferring all the ranks................................ 201
May not forbid Board of Control circulating Endowment matter... 226
Has no authority to grant Dispensations to reduce prescribed fees.. 235
Shall send list of Grand Officers, to Supreme Keeper of Records and Seal, at once....................................... 251
May commission a member of the Knight rank to institute a Lodge, or for other purposes............................ 252
May instruct a Chancellor Commander in the secret work, outside the Lodge room................................ 253
Is an elective officer of a Grand Lodge.......................... 255
May not order the Past Chancellor's rank conferred in the Grand Lodge ante-room................................. 271
Report of, may not be mutilated by the Grand Lodge........ 274
May present hypothetical questions, to the Supreme Chancellor and have them answered............................ 282
Takes past rank, on *installation* and not *election* of his successor..291, 473, 474
Report of instituting officer to be forwarded to.............. 292
May issue Dispensations to initiate "maimed persons"....... 332
May grant permission for deposit of Card in a sister Jurisdiction... 373
To take action to prevent exposure or sale of the secret paraphernalia, by unauthorized persons 431
Service as, one of the qualifications for Past Grand Chancellor's rank.. 472
Notwithstanding service, may be debarred from honors, for cause... 483
In case of re-election of, Grand Lodge does not elect a Past Grand Chancellor..484, 485
Protest from, must be received by Grand Lodge.............. 492
Non-resident applicant for initiation must have written consent of his own... 535

Index.

GRAND CHANCELLOR—(Continued.)　　　SECTIONS.
Must be a resident of his Jurisdiction........................ 537
Cannot require officers of Lodges to memorize charges, and
　　return Rituals within a specified time..................... 552
May issue Dispensations to hold meetings at longer intervals
　　than one week, if local law so provides.............. 563, 564
May not permit institution of Lodges, nor their transaction of
　　business, on Sunday...................................... 581
Eligible to election as Supreme Representative, when successor
　　installed, but not before.................... 666, 667, 668, 669
Appointments by, of additional Supreme Representative, must
　　be for four years... 677
All appointments by, of Supreme Representatives, must be for
　　a term ending with December 31st of an odd-numbered
　　year.. 679
Appointments by, of Supreme Representative, to fill vacancy,
　　must be for balance of term............................... 680
Has not the power to appoint, to fill vacancies, in Grand
　　Offices, unless Constitution so specifically provides....... 714
May declare office of absent officer vacant, on night of installa-
　　tion, if local law so empowers............................ 716
May order the revocation of a Withdrawal Card, for cause, 738, 760
May issue Withdrawal Cards to Pages and Esquires of defunct
　　Lodges.. 754

GRAND INNER GUARD.
A Grand Lodge Officer....................................... 255

GRAND KEEPER OF RECORDS AND SEAL.
Signature of, necessary to authenticate appeal records...... 24, 25
Refusing to authenticate appeal record, must show cause, or
　　facts to be considered as admitted........................ 29
Must certify to record in Writs of Error...................... 45
Notice of charges against Subordinate Lodge to be certified
　　by... 133, 135
Charges against a Grand Officer to be forwarded by, unless
　　himself under charges.................................... 141
Questions on law, from Jurisdictions, forwarded through..... 154
To forward credentials of Supreme Representatives and Past
　　Grand Chancellors, twenty days before the session....... 189
Address of, to be forwarded to Supreme Keeper of Records and
　　Seal.. 251
An elective officer of the Grand Lodge....................... 255
Paraphernalia used in conferring ranks, to be ordered through 429
Must comply with forms for returns in every particular...... 538
Supplies to be furnished to, on credit........................ 587
Should notify subordinates of approval of Constitution....... 626

Index.

GRAND LODGES.
                                                                SECTIONS.
Determine maximum age for applicants for membership......	2
The power to amend their Constitution exists in themselves; cannot be delegated......................................	7
Cannot amend their Constitution except in the manner provided...	8, 10
Appeals must be from action of, and by their consent	17, 18, 19, 20, 21, 22, 23
Consent of, not necessary, where suspended Lodge surrenders its property and appeals...............................	18
Appeal papers from action of, should be properly authenticated...	24, 25
Duty of, to furnish testimony and papers in appeal cases.....	26
Action of, will not be disturbed for irregularity in procedure, final action being correct.............................	35
Writ of Error may issue against action of	45, 46
"Appeals for Aid" by, rules regarding.................	48
Limit of "good standing" prescribed by..	52
May not levy assessments on Past Chancellors...............	57
May not provide a system of compulsory insurance	58
May permit Lodges to tax their members, to meet expenses....	59
Prescribe how many black balls reject—not exceeding two....	60
May permit Lodges to take new ballot for elected candidate, for causes arising after election........................	67
May provide for an "objection" made to admission of elected candidate operating as a black ball.....................	68
Prescribe the limit for renewal of application for advancement...	69
Description of Banner for	72
May prescribe "probationary period," before paying full benefits	80
May not prescribe that no benefits shall be paid during "probationary period"—minimum, at least must be paid......	82
Control the payment of benefits to suicides	102
Must entertain charges against Grand Officer, and fairly try..	116
In trials, may adopt rules in use in Subordinate Lodges, in analogous cases......................................	117
Exist by virtue of a Charter from Supreme Lodge...........	121, 258, 285 (8), 286, 644
Charters of, may be revoked	122
Issuance of Charter to, annuls Dispensation.................	123
Charter to, issued by Supreme Lodge—not Supreme Chancellor	124
Charter of, must be in Lodge or ante-room	125
When organized, have exclusive right to issue Charters within their territorial limit	126

Index.

GRAND LODGES—(Continued.)   SECTIONS.

May grant permission to Subordinate, to surrender, though nine members willing to sustain the Lodge.............. 128
Decide as to whom Charter may re-issue..................... 129
Regulate which set of officers sign Charters.................. 130
May provide for revocation of Charters...................... 132
Must prescribe how many failures to meet, will cause suspension of Subordinate Lodge...................................... 134
Must provide tribunal for trial of offending Lodges........... 135
Code of Procedure in trial of Grand Officers—Grand Lodge may provide one for itself, but failing must use the one prescribed................................136, 137, 138–149
May suspend the functions of Grand Officer, pending charge. 139
Review report of Committee on Charges against Grand Officer 147
Officer of, may not preside in, pending charges.............. 149
Constitution of, in conflict with that of Supreme Lodge, void 182, 183
Have power to adopt Constitution for selves and subordinates...184, 187, 188
May in session, request Dispensation to confer the ranks for six dollars...201, 229
May empower District Deputies to delegate their powers to install officers... 203
Regulate dues, as a general proposition...................... 205
May provide for charging dues during suspension, and the collecting same before reinstatement...................208, 209
In cases of expulsion, for cause, may review the testimony, on appeal... 228
Prescribes minimum fee for all the ranks—not less than Supreme minimum 229
Cannot authorize Grand Chancellor to issue Dispensations to reduce fee for initiation................................... 235
Prescribe the division of fees for ranks 236
Prescribe imposition of fines and assessments........237, 239, 240
May regulate the expenditure of Lodge funds................ 241
Funeral rosette for officers of, prescribed.................... 245
May provide for excusing members from attendance at funerals, where participation by the Order is refused.......... 249
List of officers of, to be forwarded to Supreme Keeper of Records and Seal, within twenty-four hours after election. 251
Organization of... · 254
Officers of... 255
At formation of, any Past Chancellor eligible to office in 256
Notice of organization of, to be sent to the Supreme Keeper of Records and Seal... 257

Index.

GRAND LODGES—(Continued.)   SECTIONS

  Must conform to the Ritual, forms, ceremonies, work, regalia, jewels, etc... 259
  Have original jurisdiction over its subordinates and their members... 260, 261
  Supreme Lodge powers, not reserved, are delegated to....... 262
  Composed, primarily, of Past Chancellors 263
  May provide for a representative system................263, 264
  Are judges of the qualifications of their own members, but Supreme Lodge may correct violations...................... 265
  Members of, entitled to debate in, unless specifically precluded 266
  Prescribe terms of Grand Officers, not less than one year, also when nominated and elected................267, 268, 280, 691
  Prescribe when and how often sessions shall be held......268, 280
  Determine the status of a Grand Officer, while his membership is passing from one Lodge to another...................... 269
  May depose a Grand Officer by summary methods, for cause. 270
  Past Chancellor's Rank, conferred by, in Grand Lodge, not in ante-room... 271
  Rights given to, by Supreme Lodge, not operative, unless taken advantage of by statutory enactment...................... 272
  Prescribe the names to appear on "Obituary Tablet"........ 273
  Must not mutilate reports of officers, if containing no objectionable language.. 274
  May not debar member from bringing action at law. 275
  Change of time of holding session of, does not vacate "honors" of office.. 280
  Hypothetical questions must be submitted by, but, for this purpose, the Grand Chancellor is recognized, during recess, as the Grand Lodge.................................281, 282
  Incorporation of, has no bearing except as to outsiders........ 286
  The power of, to seize and possess the goods of Subordinates, exists only through a fraternal bond, unless devolved on it by State law—refusal to surrender, however, constitutes an offense.. 287
  Officers of, installed by Supreme Chancellor, Sitting Past Grand Chancellor, or a Past Grand Chancellor, in the order named.. 288
  Officer of, may not be installed by proxy..................... 289
  Cannot require Representatives to wear special badges in addition to jewel.. 300
  Journal of Proceedings of, to be sent to Supreme Keeper of Records and Seal.. 302
  On request of Supreme Chancellor, may confer rank of Past Chancellor on member of Lodge subordinate to Supreme Lodge... 316

Index.

GRAND LODGES—(Continued.)   SECTIONS.

Lotteries and gift enterprises, Grand Lodge permitting, forfeits Charter.. 331
Power to grant Dispensations admitting "maimed persons".. 332
Member who is maimed is eligible to office in................ 333
May require all applicants for new Lodges to be members of the Order.. 361
Prescribe when membership by deposit of Card begins....... 371
Cannot annul action of Lodge, without trial................. 375
Cannot compel a Lodge to readmit a member who withdrew... 377
May prescribe time within which a rejected applicant by Card may reapply—not exceeding six months.................. 378
Prescribe the status and manner of reinstatement of members suspended for non-payment of dues............... 383, 384, 527
Prescribe rule for dropping of Pages and Esquires and their reinstatement 385, 386
New Grand Lodge controls reinstatement of members of defunct Grand Lodge............................... 390, 763
May not organize and control a "Pythian Death Benefit Fund"... 401
Forbidden to aid, encourage, endorse, supervise or manage any outside insurance association using the name of the Order... 402
Must not name Lodges after living persons................... 403
Determine whether or not "disclosing the name of a brother who may speak or vote against a candidate for membership," is a Pythian offense............................. 412
Not to affix Official Seal to any other than Official Charts... 414
Official orders from, to be acted on, at once, and obeyed..... 419
Password of, changed annually—uniform everywhere......... 454
Visitors to, must be in possession of current password....... 455
Controls the creation of Past Chancellors............456, 457, 458
Regulate the status and duties of Sitting Past Chancellor.... 459
May not vacate Credential of Past Grand Chancellor after approval of Supreme Lodge............................. 482
May not vacate office of Supreme Representative after credential approved by Supreme Lodge, except for sufficient cause 482
May withdraw credential of Past Grand Chancellor, before approval, for cause..................................... 483
May appropriate portion of per capita tax to build Castle Hall 489
May charge per capita tax on Pages and Esquires............ 490
Must receive a protest from a Grand Chancellor............. 492
May provide for establishment of Schools for Knights' children.. 496

Index.

GRAND LODGES—(Continued.)   SECTIONS.

Documents issuing from, shall bear the date of the " Pythian Period "... 497
Issue credential evidencing past official rank................ 516
Regalia of, prescribed by Supreme Lodge 517, 518
Regulate the organization of "Relief Bureaus ".............. 523
May, for sufficient cause, exclude portion of former membership from participation in reorganization of Subordinate Lodge... 529
May prescribe period of residence of applicant, not less than six months..533, 534
May permit Grand Officer to be a non-resident............. 537
Returns of, to Supreme Lodge, must be made on prescribed form...538, 539
Delinquent in making returns, subject to fine—lose representation in Supreme Lodge until tax and fine are paid...539, 540
Must have appropriate seal................................. 559
May allow meetings at longer intervals than one week. 562, 563, 564
May provide rule for consolidation of Lodges................ 578
Subordinate Lodges must communicate with Supreme Lodge only through... 579
Must not permit the institution or meeting of Subordinate Lodges, for business on Sunday......................... 581
Supreme Lodge supplies, furnish through.................... 584
Regulate sale of "supplies" to Subordinates, but governed by prices charged by Supreme Lodge 589, 590
Entitled to as many copies of Journal of Proceedings of Supreme Lodge, as there are Lodges, Past Grand Chancellors and Officers in................................... 607
May provide for Lecturers................................... 633
Entitled to two Supreme Representatives, up to 20,000 members, and one additional for each extra 10,000, but not more than four in all...............285 (3), 646 (*n*), 672, 673, 676, 677
Shall pay, annually, a Supreme Lodge tax of fifty dollars.... 655
May proceed with election of Supreme Representative at any time... 667
Term of, not less than one year............................. 690
May not assume jurisdiction over Lodges in adjacent State... 692
May not extend territorial limit, so as to accept applicant from adjacent State... 693
Organization of two, in existing Jurisdiction, illegal.......... 695
Relief Shields issued through............................... 696
Must provide in its Constitution for filling vacancies, otherwise appointments are inoperative............................ 714
May provide for "Change of Venue" in trial 717
May order Withdrawal Card vacated, for cause.............. 738

Index.

GRAND LODGES—(Continued.)   SECTIONS.
    Holder of Withdrawal Card, not eligible to office in.......... 750
    Granting of Withdrawal Card, vacates election of Representative to... 751
    Have no right to issue "Clearance Cards," "Dismissal Certificates" or "Cards of Privilege," in lieu of Withdrawal Cards...758, 759
    New Grand Lodge authorized to issue Cards to members of Lodge becoming defunct under old Grand Lodge 763

GRAND MASTER-AT-ARMS.
    A Grand Lodge Officer.. 255

GRAND MASTER OF EXCHEQUER.
    A Grand Lodge Officer.. 255

GRAND OUTER GUARD.
    A Grand Lodge Officer.. 255

GRAND PRELATE.
    Appoints minority of Trial Committee, if Grand Chancellor under charges... 143
    An officer of the Grand Lodge................................. 255
    May not confer Grand Lodge Rank in ante-room 271

GRAND REPRESENTATIVES.
    Re-elected Chancellor Commander eligible as, unless disqualified by local law... 111
    Chancellor Commander not eligible as, the last night of term. 112
    Jewel for, provided.. 293
    Grand Lodge may not require, to wear special badges in addition to Jewel 300
    Are not officers of a Lodge 532
    Taking Withdrawal Card vacates election 715

GRAND VICE CHANCELLOR.
    Charges against Grand Chancellor to be presented to 140
    Appoints majority of Trial Committee, if Grand Chancellor under charges... 143
    An officer of the Grand Lodge................................. 255
    Clothed with no authority, unless representing Grand Chancellor 276
    Serving out unexpired term of Grand Chancellor, entitled to rank of Past Grand Chancellor........................... 472

HAWAIIAN ISLANDS.
    Natives of, and their descendants, not eligible to membership in the Order.. 277
    The Deputy Supreme Chancellor in, empowered to confer rank on Past Chancellor....................................... 278

HEAD OF THE ORDER.
    The Supreme Lodge is... 652

Index.

HONORS. SECTIONS.
    Can be given to but one person for the same term............. 279
    Not lost by reason of change of time of session of Grand Lodge 280
    Attained by first officers of Lodge Subordinate to Supreme
        Lodge.. 313
    Past Chancellor taking Withdrawal Card, does not forfeit..461, 745
    Past Chancellor of new Lodge entitled to, at end of term
        ....462, 463, 464
    Entitled to, though minutes fail to show installation........... 470
    Lost by reason of suspension of charter, prior to expiration of
        term... 471
    Of rank of Past Grand Chancellor, only attained as provided in
        the Supreme Constitution................................. 472
    Of Past Grand Chancellor, attained after installation of suc-
        cessor..473, 474, 476, 666
    Supreme Vice Chancellor entitled to honors of Supreme Chan-
        cellor, by reason of filling vacancy....................... 689
    Officers filling vacancies, in Subordinate Lodge, entitled to... 715
HOTELS.
    Committee on, of the Supreme Lodge, prescribed............ 178
HYPOTHETICAL QUESTIONS.
    Not to be answered by the Supreme Chancellor or Supreme
        Lodge unless coming from a Grand Lodge or Lodge
        subordinate to the Supreme Lodge, under seal, or from a
        Grand Chancellor..............................281, 282, 283
IMPOSTORS.
    Grand Officers authorized to give notification regarding....... 284
INCORPORATION.
    Act of, for Supreme Lodge, as amended 285
    Of a Grand or Subordinate Lodge, has no bearing on matters
        connected with the Order............................286, 287
INDIANS.
    Not eligible to membership in the Order..................... 355
    Descendants of, not eligible to membership in the Order 355
INITIATION—(See Applicant; Ballot; Membership; Residence.)
INNER DOOR.
    Should be closed when Lodge is "at ease" 572
INNER GUARD.
    An appointive officer of the Lodge.......................... 574
INSTALLATION.
    Of Grand Lodge Officer, may be deferred on presentation of
        charges... 139
    Of officers of Lodges subordinate to Supreme Lodge, per-
        formed by Deputy, or his appointee 195

Index.

	SECTIONS.
INSTALLATION—(Continued.)	
District Deputies may deputize others to perform	203
Supreme Lodge Officer absent at time of, may be installed during recess	215
Of Grand Lodges, by Supreme Chancellor, retiring Past Grand Chancellor, or a Past Grand Chancellor in the order named	288
Of Grand Officer, may not be done by proxy	289
Of officers of Subordinate Lodge, to take place at first regular meeting of new term	290
Of Subordinate Lodge officers, not to be performed unless they are clear on the books	290
Installation and not election of successor, determines status of outgoing officer	291, 464
Re-elected Chancellor Commander entitled to past rank after.	467
Though minutes fail to evidence, officer loses no rights	470
Grand Chancellor entitled to past rank on installation of successor	473, 666
Grand Chancellor re-elected and entitled to past rank after second installation	474
No ceremony of, for Past Grand Chancellor	478
Of officers in public, no form of opening Lodge	570
Officer installed must be a member of the Lodge in which installed	575
Outgoing Grand Chancellor eligible for Supreme Representative, after installation of officers, but not before	667, 668, 669
Grand Lodges may empower Deputy to declare office vacant, of officer absent at installation	716
Chancellor Commander improperly installed, may not fill the chair	721
INSTITUTING OFFICER.	
Grand Lodge may appoint member of Knight rank as	252
Instructions to, in organizing new Lodges	292 (1 to 14)
Expenses of, to be paid by new Lodge	292 (12)
To make a detail report, showing certain data	292 (*a, b, c, d*)
To report expenses in detail	292 (*d*)
INSURANCE—(See Life Insurance.)	
INTEMPERANCE.	
Cannot be set up, after death, as cause for not paying funeral benefits	106
INTOXICATING LIQUORS.	
Dealers, or persons engaged in the traffic of, legislation regarding	360
INVESTIGATING COMMITTEE.	
Application for membership to be referred to	346

(16) (233)

Index.

INVESTIGATING COMMITTEE—(Continued.)   SECTIONS.
  To consist of three members, none of whom recommend the
    candidate 346
  May report at same meeting, if Dispensation granted 346
  When to report, a matter for local legislation............... 348
  Cannot be questioned as to their conclusions................. 349
  Propositions cannot be withdrawn after referred to, unless by
    consent 363
  Proposition when reported on by, cannot be withdrawn, even
    by unanimous consent...........................363, 364, 365
  Application for membership, by Card, to be referred to 370
  Unanimous consent not necessary to withdraw proposition
    after referred to; only a majority vote required.......... 732

IRREGULARITIES.
  Action of Grand Lodge will not be disturbed on account of,
    final action being correct................................ 35
  Case may be remanded on account of.......................... 36

JEWELS.
  A subject for consideration by Committee on Written Work.. 166
  Permitted to be used at funerals............................ 246
  Original legislation providing for use of................... 293
  All other than those prescribed, illegal.................... 293
  The sale of, under control of the Supreme Lodge............. 294
  Manufacture of, smaller in size than originally adopted,
    approved...295, 297, 298
  Supreme Officers authorized to retain....................... 296
  Seal of Supreme Lodge stamped on special jewels upon pay-
    ment of $2.. 297
  Under present arrangement, special jewels must be obtained
    from contractor... 297
  Legal, to be worn on funeral or Pythian public occasions only. 299
  Grand Lodges may not require badges to be worn in addition to 300
  Future contracts for, to provide for manufacture of presenta-
    tion jewels by others than contractor..................... 301
  For ladies, ordered prepared................................ 303
  Past Officers to wear respective jewels of rank at all meetings,
    except when acting in an official capacity................ 518
  Of Supreme Officers, in charge of Supreme Keeper of Records
    and Seal.. 631
  Supreme Lodge prescribes form of............................ 637
  Must be worn in visiting in addition to uniform.............. 712

JOURNAL OF PROCEEDINGS.
  OF SUPREME LODGE.
    Bids for printing of, to be obtained..................... 169
    Endowment Rank to bear its share of cost of.............. 224

Index.

JOURNAL OF PROCEEDINGS—(Continued.)   SECTIONS.
  OF SUPREME LODGE.
    Laws become of force, from date of publication in........ 305
    Appeal cases to be printed to conform to size of............ 326
    Record for, to be made by Supreme Keeper of Records
      and Seal................................. 607
    Grand Lodges to be furnished with copies of, sufficient for
      Lodges, Past Grand Chancellors and Officers......... 607
    Each Lodge subordinate to the Supreme Lodge to be furnished with....................................... 607
    Supreme Lodge Committees to be furnished with bound
      set of.......................... 627
  OF GRAND LODGE.
    Two copies of, to be forwarded each year to Supreme
      Keeper of Records and Seal......................... 302
    To be bound and preserved by him...................... 630
JURISDICTION—(See also Territorial Jurisdiction.)
  Lodge has, over a member suspended for non-payment of
    dues, for the purpose of trial 382
  Lodge resumes, over holder of Withdrawal Card, upon Card
    being revoked for the purpose of trial 738, 739
JURY.
  Grand Lodge must provide, to try charges against a Lodge,
    during recess 135
KEEPER OF RECORDS AND SEAL.
  Signs orders for S. A. P. W..............................438, 747
  An elective officer of the Lodge........ 574
  Sends notice of member affiliating........................... 741
KNEELING.
  In funeral ceremonies, dispensed with 248
KNIGHT.
  Appeals regarding all questions, must be taken in the rank of. 43
  Adverse ballot on application for the rank of, cannot be laid
    over 69
  Eligible to office of Chancellor Commander, if local law does
    not prohibit... 108
  May be selected to preside, conduct the business, and confer
    ranks, proper officers being absent...................... 113
  May ask to see the Charter of a Lodge 127
  Lodge cannot exempt, from payment of dues, for specified
    period after admission.................................... 207
  Funeral rosette for... 245
  Grand Chancellor may appoint, to institute a Lodge, or for
    other purposes.. 252
  Jewel for, prescribed.. 293

Index.

	SECTIONS.
KNIGHT—(Continued.)	
Applicant rejected for rank of, in Lodges subordinate to Supreme Lodge, may reapply in one month.	321
Failure to proceed through all the rank of, not an offense.	410
Official Chart of, to be signed by Subordinate Lodge Officers.	417
Term password to be communicated only to.	435
Entitled to S. A. P. W. upon receiving rank.	436
S. A. P. W. only to be given or taken in the rank of	437
Eligible as Sitting Past Chancellor at organization of new Lodge	464
Cannot be elected or appointed to chair of Sitting Past Chancellor, in Lodge already established	466
Separate ballot to be taken on rank of	505, 506
Rank of, may be conferred by a sister Lodge, on proper request	508
Regalia for—constitutional provision	518
Lodge consists of not less than seven.	561
Business of Lodge, except conferring rank of Page and Esquire, or their trial, to be conducted in rank of	567
LADIES.	
"Diploma" and "Jewels" provided for.	303
Rank for, persistently refused by Supreme Lodge.	304, 499
Not eligible to membership in the Order	353
Allowed to establish the "Order of Pythian Sisterhood".	498
LADIES' DIPLOMAS.	
Issuance of, authorized.	303
LADIES' RANK.	
Supreme Lodge has persistently refused to establish or recognize.	304, 499
LADIES' JEWELS.	
Issuance of, authorized.	303
LAW—Committee on—(See Committees.)	
LAWS AND LEGISLATION.	
Of Supreme Lodge, obligatory on all Grand and Subordinate Lodges.	182, 591
Supreme Lodge has power to correct violation of, by Grand Lodge.	265
Right of, adopted by Grand Lodges, must be taken advantage of, before becoming operative.	272
Of the Supreme Lodge, of force from date of publishing of Official Journal.	305
Obligatory, when in accord with Supreme Constitution.	306
Official Digest, a mere compilation of.	418
Ritualistic provisions have the force of	569
Supreme Chancellor to enforce observance of.	591
Power of Supreme Lodge to enforce.	643

Index.

	SECTIONS.
LAWSUIT.	
Grand Lodge cannot prevent member bringing	275
LECTURER—(See Supreme Lecturer.)	
LIFE INSURANCE.	
Provision for compulsory assessment for, illegal	58, 75
For members of the Order, provided for by the Endowment Rank	222
Organizations providing for, other than the Endowment Rank, prohibited from using name of the Order	399, 400, 401, 402
LOCAL LEGISLATION—SUBJECTS LEFT TO.	
Maximum age of applicants	2
The right of appeal, under certain conditions	20
Good standing	52
Levying tax to meet expenses of Lodge	59
Whether one or two black balls reject	60
Ordering a new ballot on elected applicant	67
Providing for objections to elected applicant, operating as a black ball	68
How soon ballot for advancement may be renewed, in case of rejection	69
Amount of benefits, above the constitutional minimum	79
Providing for a probationary period before paying full benefits	80, 81, 82, 83, 85
Status of suspended members	83
Payment of benefits to suicide	102
Qualification for office in Subordinate Lodge, a matter for	108, 718
Election of a re-elected Chancellor Commander as Representative to his Grand Lodge	111
Issuance of Charters to Lodges within its territorial limits	126
Re-issuance of Charters—to whom issued	129
What set of officers sign Charters	130
What names appear on Charter on surrender of Dispensation	131
How many failures, by a Lodge, to hold meetings, cause suspension	134
Providing Code of Procedure in Trial of Grand Officers	136
Providing a Grand and Subordinate Constitution	184, 187, 188
Empowering District Deputies to delegate powers to install	203
Regulation of dues, as a general proposition	205
Charging dues to Pages and Esquires	206
Charging dues to members suspended for non-payment of dues, and requiring payment of same, together with arrears causing suspension, upon application for reinstatement	208, 209
Imposing the penalty of expulsion, for cause	228
Fixing amount of initiation fee	229

Index.

LOCAL LEGISLATION—(Continued.)   SECTIONS.

Amount of fee for all the ranks, above the constitutional minimum.. 230
Division of the fee for all the ranks...................... 236
The imposition of fines and assessments.................... 237
The imposition of fines or suspension, on committees, for dereliction of duty....................................... 239
The imposition of fines on members for non-attendance at regular meetings... 240
The right of Lodges to expend funds for other than the business and purposes of the Order........................... 241
Appointment of a Chaplain, at funerals..................... 247
Excusing members from attendance at funerals, where the Order is refused participation............................ 249
Grand Lodge has original jurisdiction over Lodges and members within its territorial limit, subject to Supreme law and right of appeal....................................... 260
Limiting composition of Grand Lodge 263, 264
Grand Lodge judge of its own members, subject to review. 265, 266
Terms of Grand Officers—not less than one year, also duties of 267
As to whether or no *all* the Grand Officers shall be elective. 267, 691
Questions of organization and government of Grand Lodge, the holding of sessions and when Officers shall be nominated and elected...................................... 268
The status of a Grand Officer while his membership is passing from one Lodge to another............................... 269
Deprivation of a Grand Office, by summary methods, for cause.. 270
Right of, when given by Supreme Lodge, to be operative, must be taken advantage of.................................... 272
The placing name on "Obituary Tablet"..................... 273
Manner of protecting their membership against impostors... 284
Period to elapse between application for membership and the appointment of committee on investigation................ 348
Requiring "medical certificate" with application for initiation 359
Whether or not all applicants for new Lodge shall be members... 361
As to when membership by Card shall begin, on election, or on signing the roster....................................... 371
Determining the period within which a rejected applicant by Card may re-apply—not exceeding six months............. 378
Regulating the status of members suspended for non-payment of dues and their reinstatement............. 383, 384, 527
Dropping Pages and Esquires, and their reinstatement.... 385, 386
Status of members of a defunct Grand Lodge................ 390
Selecting "Memorial Day"................................... 391

Index.

LOCAL LEGISLATION—(Continued.)   SECTIONS.
  Determining whether or not "disclosing the name of a brother who may speak or vote against a candidate" is a Pythian offense.. 412
  Length of time a member may be in arrears, not to exceed twelve months, before being deprived of the S. A. P. W.. 440
  The time when, by the failure to pay dues, a member is not entitled to the S. A. P. W., is a matter for................ 442
  The manner of creating Past Chancellors............456, 457, 458
  The status, rights and duties of Sitting Past Chancellor...... 459
  The setting aside part of the per capita tax, to build a hall... 489
  Charging per capita tax on Pages and Esquires................ 490
  The establishment of schools for children of Knights......... 496
  Organization of "Relief Bureaus"........................... 523
  Prescribing period of residence of applicant for initiation, not less than six months......................................533, 534
  Grand Lodge may permit Grand Officer to be non-resident, but if office becomes vacant by non-residence, may provide for filling vacancy.. 537
  Memorizing the Ritual... 551
  Permitting Subordinate Lodges to hold meetings at longer intervals than once a week. 562, 563, 564
  Consolidation of Lodges 578
  Furnishing "supplies" to Lodges, but not in excess of rate charged by Supreme Lodge.........................589, 590
  Appointment of Lecturers..................................... 633
  Fixing the terms of Subordinate Lodges—not less than six months.. 690
  Fixing the duties of Grand Officers........................... 691
  Power of an installing officer to declare office vacant, on account of absence of officer-elect....................... 716
  Providing for a "change of venue" in trials.................. 717
  Providing that officers of a Grand Lodge, not Representatives, are not entitled to vote.........................729, 730, 731
  Providing that Past Grand Chancellors, who are Representatives, may cast two votes.............................. 730

LODGE OF INSTRUCTION.
  Any qualified member may occupy the chair during............ 568

LODGE ROOM.
  Chancellor Commander may refuse to permit members to retire from.. 114
  Grand Chancellor or Deputy may instruct in secret work outside of... 253
  A proper place for keeping the rituals and private work...... 545
  Order of entrance to, by Grand Officers, same as at installation. 722

Index.

LODGES SUBORDINATE TO SUPREME LODGE. SECTIONS·

Appeals, and Writs of Error, lie against the action of... 17, 326, 642
Decisions of, are final until reversed by the Supreme Lodge or
    Supreme Chancellor..................................... 17
Appeals from decision of, must be printed—one hundred and
    fifty copies...38, 326
"Appeals for Aid," issued by, must be authorized by the
    Supreme Chancellor...................................48, 49
Charters of, may be revoked for violation of the Constitution..132, 133
Deputy Supreme Chancellor, in charge of, must be a member
    of one of the Subordinates under his Jurisdiction. 191
Deputy Supreme Chancellor shall install, or cause to be
    installed, the officers of............................195, 196
Must recognize appointees of Deputy Supreme Chancellor.... 196
Deputy Supreme Chancellor cannot grant Dispensation to
    organize... 197
May impose fines and assessments, if provided for in Constitution 237
May submit hypothetical questions................. 281
Are under the control of the Supreme Lodge until Grand Lodge
    is formed.... 307
Shall pay a per capita tax, semi-annually, on Pages, Esquires
    and Knights......................................307, 308, 640
Shall make returns March 1 and September 1 of each year..307, 641
Failing to make returns and pay tax, S. A. P. W. to be withheld 309
Applicants for organization of, not necessarily members of the
    Order... 310
May be organized, where Lodge already exists, notwithstanding objections by latter, but such objections should be forwarded 310
Applications for organizing, must be approved by the Deputy
    in charge 310
Objections to organization of, estop proceedings for the time
    being, though Dispensation issued..... 311
Rejected material should not be accepted on application for
    organizing 312
Certain officers at the institution of, become Past Chancellors .... ··313, 314
Supreme Chancellor empowered to authorize his Deputy to
    confer Past Chancellor's rank 315
Rank of Past Chancellor conferred by a Grand Lodge, on
    members of, on request of Supreme Chancellor 316
Fee for all the ranks in, not less than $10, nor can the Supreme
    Chancellor lower........................ .... · 317

(240)

Index.

LODGES SUBORDINATE TO, ETC.—(Continued.) SECTIONS.
  "Maimed Persons" admitted to membership in, under Dispensation from Supreme Chancellor 318
  Dispensations to confer the ranks in, on persons over fifty, and the Page rank upon applicant the same night as ballot, may be granted by the Deputy 319
  Elected applicant, for Page rank may be refused admission .. 320
  Rejected applicant for advancement may reapply in one month 321
  May not accept rejected material, without consent of rejecting Lodge 322
  Members of, suspended for non-payment of dues, desiring reinstatement, must pay one year's dues and all assessments... 323
  Provisions for granting Withdrawal Cards to members of defunct Lodges.......................................324, 325
  Name of, is the one designated in Charter ; may not be changed without authority 327
  Constitution for, uniform in character, provided by Supreme Lodge 328
  Regular meetings to be held ; failure to hold, for three months, render liable to suspension 329
  Consolidation of, permitted.................................. 330
  Must meet weekly, unless granted a Dispensation............ 563
  Dispensations for institution of, issued by Supreme Chancellor. 595
  Supreme Chancellor hears all questions coming from 600
  Charters for, issued by the Supreme Lodge.................. 644
  Terms of, shall be six months 690
  May be placed under adjacent Grand Lodge, but same becomes a nullity, upon the organization of a Grand Lodge in that territory 692, 694
  Traveling Shields issued to, by the Deputy Supreme Chancellor 696
LOTTERIES.
  Resorting to, instituting or promoting, forbidden............. 331
  Grand Lodges and Subordinate Lodges resorting to, instituting or promoting, forfeit their Charter 331
  Members resorting to, in the name of the Order, shall be suspended 331
MAIMED PERSONS.
  Dispensations to admit, in Lodges subordinate to Supreme Lodge, granted by Supreme Chancellor.................. 318
  Applications for Dispensations to admit, in Lodges subordinate to Supreme Lodge, require a vote of the Lodge...... 318
  Grand Chancellors empowered to issue Dispensations for the admission of 332
  When once admitted, are entitled to all benefits, emoluments and right to hold office 333

Index.

MAJOR GENERAL.
SECTIONS.
To submit his books for examination to the Committee on
  • Finance 160, 340
A member of the Committee on "Supplies" for Uniform Rank 177
A member of the Committee on Hotels and Transportation... 178
Appointed and commissioned by the Supreme Chancellor. 212, 334
Must be a Past Grand Chancellor and a member of the
    Supreme Lodge and the Uniform Rank, in good standing. 334
Holds office for four years from date of appointment......... 334
Has general charge of the Uniform Rank 335
Appoints his individual staff 336
When present may preside in meetings of Brigades, Divisions
    or Regiments 336
At general assembling of Uniform Rank, takes command..... 336
In conjunction with Supreme Chancellor, examines all laws .. 337
Shall keep a register of all warrants 338
Shall provide himself with stationery, at the expense of the
    Supreme Lodge.. 339
Prepares forms and blanks for the Uniform Rank............ 341
Decides tactical questions pertaining to the Uniform Rank ... 342
Reviews all Court Martial proceedings....................... 343
Sends out the countersign 344
Salary of, determined at each Supreme Lodge session 345
Report of, to be published................................. 531
An officer of the Supreme Lodge ....646 (*i*)

MASTER-AT-ARMS.
Chancellor Commander may instruct, to take Rank password
    from visiting Lodge in ante-room 453
An elective officer of the Lodge............................ 574

MASTER OF EXCHEQUER.
An elective officer of the Lodge 574

MASTER OF FINANCE.
Must notify Endowment Rank sections of suspended members 223
An elective officer of the Lodge 574

MEDICAL CERTIFICATE.
Subordinate Lodge may require, from applicant for member-
    ship.. 359

MEETINGS.
Neglecting to hold, renders Lodge liable to suspension ... 133, 563
Grand Lodge must designate how many failures to hold, render
    Lodge liable to suspension............................... 134
Fining members for non-attendance at, a matter for local legis-
    lation 240
Failure to hold for three months, renders Lodge, subordinate
    to Supreme Lodge, liable to suspension................. 329

Index.

MEETINGS—(Continued.)   SECTIONS.
  To be held at least once a week 562
  Dispensations may issue to hold, at longer intervals than one
    week 562, 563
  Grand Lodges may prescribe for their subordinates holding,
    at intervals longer than one week 564
  Fines for absence from, cover all meetings, regular or special. 565
  May not be held on Sunday 581

MEMBERSHIP.
  BY INITIATION.
    Applicant for, must be of age 1, 347
    Supreme Lodge fixes minimum age of applicant for 2
    Grand Lodge fixes maximum age of applicant for 2
    Ballot for, one black ball may reject—not more than
      two 60, 292 (6)
    Applicant rejected; cannot re-apply for six months 61
    Separate ballot must be had on each application for 63
    A fee to accompany application—for the three ranks, fee
      to be not less than ten dollars 229, 233, 234, 235, 292 (5)
    No part of the fee can be refunded or donated 231, 232
    Natives, or descendants of natives, of Hawaiian Islands
      ineligible for 277
    Ladies are not eligible to 304, 353, 499
    "Maimed Persons" eligible to, by dispensation 332
    Applications for, must be signed by the candidate 346
    Application for, must state age, residence and occupa-
      tion 346
    Application for, must be endorsed by two members 346
    Applicant for, must be of age, must be a white male and a
      believer in a Supreme Being 347
    Applicant must be a resident of the Jurisdiction for at
      least six months 347, 533, 534
    Colored persons not eligible to 350, 351, 352, 353
    Minors are not eligible to 353
    Chinamen, even though naturalized, not eligible to 354
    Indian blood, persons of, not eligible to 355
    Persons not able to write are not eligible to 356
    Persons who can write their name are entitled to 357
    A person may not hold, in two Lodges 358
    Lodge may require certificate of health 359
    Liquor traffic—legislation regarding admission of persons
      engaged in 360
    Application for, cannot be withdrawn without consent of
      the Lodge 363, 732
    Application for, cannot be withdrawn after report of com-
      mittee 363, 364, 365

Index.

MEMBERSHIP—(Continued.)

SECTIONS.

BY INITIATION.

Soliciting candidates for, forbidden...................... 367
Applicant rejected for, may, after six months, re-apply to any other Lodge, subject to local laws as to residence... 368
Protest against application for, by sister Lodge, has not force of adverse ballot........................493, 494
Non-resident applicant must obtain consent of his Grand Chancellor... 535
The vote on the withdrawal of an application for, after being referred to a committee, is a majority one...... 732

BY WITHDRAWAL CARD.

Same ballot on application for, by Withdrawal Card, as by initiation... 71
The granting a Withdrawal Card severs, whether the Card is taken or not...................................... 97
Application for, by Card, referred to committee and balloted on, same as in case of initiate................. 370
When membership by Card begins is a matter for local legislation—no local provision being made, it begins on election..371, 372
Non-resident depositing Card must have consent of Grand Chancellor of Jurisdiction where residing............ 373
Where membership by Card is obtained irregularly, but through no fault of the applicant, cannot be disturbed................................374, 375, 376
Lodge not compelled to re-admit to...................... 377
Applicant rejected on Card, if local law does not forbid, may re-apply at any time........................... 378
Pages and Esquires transfer their membership by Withdrawal Card..................................379, 380
Act of severing, by granting Card, may be revoked for cause, and if revoked for purpose of trial, membership revived... 739

BALLOT FOR.

Grand Lodge may provide that *one* black ball will reject application for, but cannot exceed *two*............... 60
Rejected initiate cannot re-apply before six months...... 61
Separate ballot on each application for............63, 292 (6)
Same ballot on application for, by Withdrawal Card, as by initiation.. 71
Collective ballot, at institution of Lodge.............292 (6)
Protest against application for, from sister Lodge, has not force of adverse ballot........................493, 494

(244)

MEMBERSHIP—(Continued.)

SECTIONS.

FEES FOR.

Applications for, by initiation, to be accompanied by such fee as Grand Lodge may provide—for all three ranks, not less than ten dollars..........229, 233, 234, 235, 292 (5)
No part of the fee can be refunded or donated........231, 232

IN LODGE SUBORDINATE TO SUPREME LODGE.

Rejected material not to be accepted for.............312, 322
Minimum fee for the three ranks ten dollars............ 317
Elected applicant found to be unworthy may be denied admission by majority vote......................... 320
Rejected applicant for advancement may re-apply in one month.. 321

ARREARS.

Shall be suspended from, if in arrears, for amount equal to twelve months' dues.................51, 53, 54, 237, 238
Must be notified of arrears before suspension from....... 55
Declaration of suspension must be made before suspension from, otherwise delinquent may pay up and prevent suspension from 55, 56

SUSPENSION FROM.

Arrears for amount equal to twelve months' dues, cause..51, 53, 54, 237, 238
Must be notified of arrears before...................... 55
Declaration of, must be made before, otherwise delinquent may pay up and prevent..........................55, 56
Upon, ceases to be a member till reinstated.............. 381
The act of, may be revoked for purpose of trial.......... 382
Manner of reinstatement after, for non-payment of dues, a matter for local legislation..................383, 384, 527
Reinstatement of Pages and Esquires after, a matter for local legislation.... 385
Grand Lodges may provide for, in case of Pages and Esquires who fail to advance, after one year......... 386
In case of, owing to suspension of Grand Lodge, the new Grand Lodge controls reinstatement to.............. 390
Regained without any action of Lodge, after termination of definite suspension for cause....................... 525
Regained through regular ballot, where suspension is for an indefinite period................................. 526

MAIMED PERSONS.

Eligible to, under dispensation from the Grand Chancellor 332
When received into, entitled to all benefits and emoluments and right to hold office....................... 333

Index.

MEMBERSHIP—(Continued.)   SECTIONS.
   GENERAL RULINGS.
      Deputy Supreme Chancellor must hold, in Jurisdiction of
         which he has charge................................... 191
      Status of a Grand Officer, while passing from one Lodge to
         another, a matter for local legislation................ 269
      Not disturbed, though applicant concealed former rejection 369
      Revived by revival of the Lodge to which formerly belong-
         ing, unless previously granted Card..........388, 389, 755
      Not severed by the granting of a Withdrawal Card, applied
         for by another member................................ 735

MEMORIAL DAY.
   Date set apart for observance of 391
   Lodge choosing may select day other than the one set apart.. 391
   Service for use on, prescribed............................... 392

MEMORIAL DAY SERVICE.
   Prescribed by Supreme Lodge.. 392

MEMORIAL SERVICE.
   For use in Subordinate Lodges, prescribed.................. 393

MEMORIZING RITUAL.
   Amplified Third, when used, must be memorized.. ....13, 549
   Not obligatory, as a general rule, but each Subordinate Lodge
      may adopt a rule requiring...........................550, 551
   Deputy may not require, and take up Rituals after certain time
      elapsing... 552

MILEAGE—(See Mileage and Per Diem.)

MILEAGE AND PER DIEM.
   Committee on Mileage, duties of............................ 164
   To be computed by the Committee on........................ 164
   Committees paid same as Representatives.................... 173
   Officers, Representatives and Past Supreme Chancellors by
      service, to be paid..................................... 394
   Members not to receive, unless present at close of session,
      unless excused... 395
   Not to be paid for both, to person holding two offices......... 396

MINIMUM BENEFITS—(See Benefits.)

MINIMUM FEES—(See Fees.)

MINORS.
   Lodges composed of, illegal.................................. 358

NAME.
   Of the Order not to be used in advertising, except by dealers
      in supplies, periodicals, etc..........................221, 397
   Of Supreme Lodge, appearing in act of incorporation........ 285

Index.

NAME—(Continued.)   SECTIONS.

    Of a Lodge subordinate to Supreme Lodge, is the one designated in its warrant.................................... 327
    Provision whereby member may change..................... 387
    Of the Order, may not be used without the permission of the Supreme Lodge.. 398
    Of the Order, if used without permission of the Supreme Lodge, Supreme Chancellor may take necessary steps to prevent. 398
    Use of, by Benefit or Insurance Associations, strictly forbidden... 399, 400, 401, 402
    Of living persons, not to be used in naming Lodges........... 403

NEGROES.
    Not eligible to membership............................. 352, 353
    Lodges composed of, not recognized................. 350, 351, 353

NEW LODGES.
    Dropping the name from list of applicants for, at preliminary meeting, not a black ball................................ 70
    The requirement as to paying minimum fee for all the ranks, applies to applicants for........................ 234, 292 (5)
    Instructions for instituting.................................. 292
    Applicants for, subordinate to Supreme Lodge, not necessarily members of the Order................................. 310
    Deputy Supreme Chancellor may not institute, in face of protest, until passed on by the Supreme Chancellor......... 311
    Rejected material cannot be accepted on the Charter of, by Deputy Supreme Chancellor........................... 312
    Certain first officers of, made Past Chancellors........... 313, 314
    Grand Lodges regulate whether or not, at the institution of, all applicants must be members........................ 361
    At the institution of, office of Past Chancellor filled from among charter members..................................... 462

NOMINATIONS.
    In the Supreme Lodge, there being but one nominee, unanimous vote may be cast by one member.................... 216
    Absence at time of, in Grand Lodge not a disqualification for office... 217
    For election of subordinate officers, to be made on the night preceding and the night of election—independent nominations may be made on the latter night............... 404, 405

NON-PAYMENT OF DUES—(See Suspension for Non-payment of Dues; Dues; Membership.)

NON-RESIDENCE—(See Residence.)

NOTICE.
    Of arrears, must be given member before suspension......... 55
    Of organization of Grand Lodge, to be sent to Supreme Keeper of Records and Seal.................................. 257

Index.

NOTICE—(Continued.)   SECTIONS.
   Mailing of, deemed sufficient in case of trial.................. 703
   Of deposit of Card, to be sent to the Body issuing............ 741

NURSE HIRE.
   Lodge not responsible for, paid by sister Lodge, unless their laws so provide... 95
   Appropriations for, can only be made in accordance with constitutional provision..................................... 243

OBITUARY TABLET.
   What names shall appear on, a matter for local legislation.... 273

OBJECTION.
   May be interposed and prevent admission of elected candidate, if local law so provides 68
   May not interpose and prevent a member in good standing from visiting...726, 727
   To the granting of a Withdrawal Card, majority vote necessary to sustain... 734

OBLIGATORY RULES.
   Prescribed in Constitution of Supreme Lodge, must be incorporated in Subordinate Constitutions 188

ODES.
   Supreme Lodge has the exclusive right to furnish.........636, 758

OFFENSES.
   By GRAND LODGE.
      Non-conformity to the work, ceremonies or Ritual, disobedience to legal mandate and improper conduct.... 122
      The enforcement of laws contrary to those of the Supreme Lodge.. 182
      Resorting to, instituting or promoting any scheme of raffle, gift enterprise, lottery or chance..................... 331
   By SUBORDINATE LODGE.
      Failure to reimburse sister Lodge for benefits legally paid 105
      Violation of Supreme Constitution, orders, enactments, legislation or decisions............................... 132
      Violation of Grand Lodge Constitution, local laws, or Grand Chancellor's official mandate 132
      Improper conduct, neglecting to make reports, neglecting to hold regular stated meetings..................133, 134
      The enforcement of laws contrary to those of the Supreme Lodge.. 182
      Refusal to deliver up goods and chattels upon suspension of Charter.. 287
      Resorting to, instituting or promoting any scheme of raffle, lottery, gift enterprise or chance..................... 331

Index.

OFFENSES—(Continued.)   SECTIONS.
  BY SUBORDINATE LODGE.
    Failure to insert in its laws a provision against the admission of any but "white males" 352
    Initiating non-residents against the protest of sister Lodge 529
    Passing on the conduct of the Supreme Lodge or its officers 580
  BY A MEMBER.
    The improper display or use of the emblems of the Order 220, 221
    Giving untrue answers to questions at time of admission 312, 407
    Resorting to, instituting or promoting any scheme of raffle, lottery, gift enterprise or chance. 331
    Concealing the fact of former rejection of application..... 693
    The use of the name of the Order publicly for pecuniary profit 397
    Blasphemy 406
    Claiming benefits with intent to defraud the Lodge....... 408
    Fraudulently obtaining money 409
    Disclosing name of a member voting against a candidate, if local law so provides 412
    The exposure or sale of the secret properties of the Order to non-members 431
    Refusal to comply with citation, constitutes 738
OFFICE.
  Any Knight eligible to, of Chancellor Commander, if local law does not forbid 108
  Electioneering for, in Supreme Lodge, disqualifies candidate. 214
  Any Past Chancellor eligible to, at organization of Grand Lodge 256
  Member being maimed, not a disqualification for 333
  Supreme Officer taking Withdrawal Card, does not thereby vacate 746
  Holder of Withdrawal Card disqualified for, in Grand Lodge. 750
OFFICERS.
  OF SUPREME LODGE.
    Eligible on standing and special committees 174
    Elected biennially by ballot, except the Major General.. 212
    A majority of all votes necessary to elect 213
    Absent at time of installation, may be installed during recess 215
    Designated in act of incorporation 285 (5)
    Retain their Jewels during recess 296
    Entitled to mileage and per diem, if present at close of session or excused 394, 395

Index.

OFFICERS—(Continued.)   SECTIONS.
- OF SUPREME LODGE.
  - Reports of, to be printed 530
  - Reports of, to be published in Pythian press 531
  - May be called in Council by Supreme Chancellor 592
  - May be suspended or removed by Supreme Chancellor, for cause... 597
  - Jewels of, in charge of Supreme Keeper of Records and Seal 631
  - Only Supreme Representatives or Past Grand Chancellors eligible as.. 653
  - Term of, two years..................................... 690
  - Entitled to one vote in determining questions before Supreme Lodge 728
  - Office of, not vacated by taking Withdrawal Card, if immediately deposited................................ 746
- OF GRAND LODGES.
  - May not issue "Appeals" for aid, sent out of Jurisdiction, without permission of Supreme Lodge or Supreme Chancellor 48
  - Any one member may bring charges against.......... 115, 116
  - Grand Lodge must entertain charges against 116
  - Which set of, sign charters, a matter for local legislation.. 130
  - Code of procedure in trial of........................136-149
  - May not be excluded from nomination, because of absence 217
  - Funeral rosettes for..................................... 245
  - Prescribed in Supreme Constitution 255
  - All Past Chancellors, in good standing, eligible as, at formation of Grand Lodge............................ 256
  - Shall hold office for not less than one year............... 267
  - Each Grand Lodge prescribes its own rule regarding nomination and election of 268
  - Grand Lodge regulates status of, while membership passing from one Lodge to another 269
  - May be summarily deprived of official power............. 270
  - Grand Lodge must not mutilate reports of 274
  - Honors of, not abridged by change in time of holding sessions.. 280
  - May notify members of impostors 284
  - May not be installed by proxy 289
  - Maimed member eligible 333
  - To sign Past Chancellor's Charts........................ 417
  - Except Sitting Past Grand Chancellor, vacate office if becoming non-residents of Jurisdiction............... 537
  - Term of, not less than one year......................690, 691
  - Grand Lodge fixes duties of.............................. 691

Index.

OFFICERS—(Continued.) SECTIONS.
OF GRAND LODGES.
    Vacancies in, filled by Grand Chancellor, inoperative unless Constitution so empowers him................. 714
    Order of entrance by, when visiting, same as provided at installations... 722
    Entitled to vote on all questions unless local law provides to the contrary.................................729, 731
    Holders of Withdrawal Cards, not eligible as Grand Officers.. 750
OF SUBORDINATE LODGES.
    Qualified officers being absent, members may select a Knight to preside...................................... 113
    Election of, void, when conducted contrary to provision of Constitution, in regard to presiding officer and tellers... 218
    Election of, cannot be set aside, simply for excess of votes 219
    Funeral rosettes for.................................... 245
    To be installed first regular meeting in new term......... 290
    Not to be installed unless clear upon the books.......... 290
    Installation, and not election of successor, determines the status of.. 291
    At organization of new Lodge, may be selected at preliminary meeting, subject to ratification.........292 (7), (10)
    Maimed member eligible................................ 333
    Nomination of, to be made on night preceding and night of election..404, 405
    The Sitting Past Chancellor is an officer of the Lodge..... 460
    Lodge must be under control of, though work in the ranks transferred to a team............................... 509
    Grand Representative is not an officer................... 532
    Must conform to the Ritual in opening and closing........ 547
    Prohibited from copying charges......................... 553
    Absence of, from "meetings," includes all meetings, regular or special....................................... 565
    Are as provided in the Ritual........................... 573
    Who are elective and who appointive..................... 574
    No one eligible as, unless a member of that Lodge....... 575
    Retiring and re-entering under the order of the Chancellor Commander, not required to give sign................ 576
    May not expend money without authority of 577
    Term of, fixed by Grand Lodge, not to be less than six months... 690
    Filling vacancy and serving residue of term, entitled to honors.. 715

Index.

OFFICIAL CHARTS.   SECTIONS.
Under the Supervision of Committee on Written Work 166
Grand Lodge must conform to................................ 259
Promulgation of.. 413
All others rescinded and annulled 414
Seal of Grand or Subordinate Lodges, not to be attached to
  any other than 414
Present name of, adopted................................... 415
Furnished same as other supplies........................... 416
Of Past Chancellor, to be signed by Grand Lodge Officers.... 417
Of Past Grand Chancellors, signed by Supreme Lodge Officers 417
Issued by the Supreme Lodge 636, 637, 758

OFFICIAL DIGEST.
A mere compilation of laws and decisions................... 418
Not proper to repeal a section of; resolution for that purpose
  should refer to original legislation 418
Furnished to Subordinate Lodges............................ 584
Furnished to Chairmen of Committees, at Supreme Lodge
  sessions 627

OFFICIAL ORDERS.
From Supreme or Grand Lodge, take precedence over all
  other business 419
Lodge being notified of, should take cognizance of, before pro-
  ceeding... 419
Though irregular or arbitrary, must be obeyed.............. 419

OFFICIAL ORGAN.
Supreme Lodge refused to recognize......................... 420

OFFICIAL RECEIPT.
Form of adopted, and issuance authorized................... 421
An authoritative and conclusive evidence of membership and
  good standing......................................421, 424
No other receipt, for claims of the Lodge on a member,
  legal..421, 422, 439
The use of, obligatory on all Lodges....................... 423
Lodges may not evade the law by giving other evidence of pay-
  ment.. 423
As between Lodges and members is prima facie, but not con-
  clusive 425
Original indorsement on, changed to order for S. A. P. W.... 426
Form of, to be uniform in all Jurisdictions................ 427
The property of the holder, and not to be retained by Officer
  giving the S. A. P. W................................... 428
Must accompany the order for the S. A. P. W............... 439
Member in possession of, entitled to a separate order for the S.
  A. P. W... 449

(252)

Index.

OFFICIAL RECEIPT—(Continued.)   SECTIONS.
    Orders for the S. A. P. W. should be on the back of.......... 450
    Furnished to Lodges... 584
    Member in possession of S. A. P. W. need not produce....... 723
    Though member in possession of S. A. P. W., Chancellor Commander may demand, if in doubt......................... 724
OFFICIAL REPORTS.
    Right of Grand Lodge to additional representation based on 646 (*n*)
ONE YEAR IN ARREARS.
    A member who owes an amount equal to one year's dues is... 51
    Member owing for twelve months' dues is................... 53
    Member must be, before being subject to suspension—cannot be suspended for six months' arrears..................... 54
    Should be notified of, before suspension...................... 55
    Member being, suspension of must be declared by Chancellor Commander in open Lodge............................. 55
    Chancellor Commander failing to make declaration of suspension of member in, member may pay up arrears and restore himself to good standing......................... 56
    May accumulate by the addition to dues, of fines, and assessments, if so provided by local laws................... 237, 238
    Amount of, must be paid before reinstatement of members suspended for non-payment of dues, in Lodges subordinate to Supreme Lodge... 323
OPENING.
    No one except Outer Guard allowed in ante-room during...... 16
    S. A. P. W. to be taken at.................................... 437
    Member not in possession of S. A. P. W. cannot remain during 442
    Officers must conform to the language of ritual in........... 547
    A motion to dispense with the ceremonies of, not in order.... 569
ORDER FOR GRAND LODGE PASSWORD.
    Past Chancellors visiting Grand Lodge entitled to 455
ORDER FOR S. A. P. W.
    Form of, now on back of Official Receipt................ 426, 427
    Though on back of Official Receipt, Lodge to which presented may not retain...................................... 428
    Must be signed by Chancellor Commander and Keeper of Records and Seal................................. 438, 439
    Must be under the Seal of the Lodge.................. 438, 439
    Must be accompanied by Official Receipt.............. 438, 439
    Member entitled to, whether resident or not 446
    Not to cover a period longer than six months........... 447, 448
    Member may call for separate, officer having failed to place it on back of Official Receipt 449
    Should, as a rule, be on back of Official Receipt 450

Index.

ORDER FOR S. A. P. W.—(Continued.)   SECTIONS.
    Chancellor Commander should satisfy himself of identity of
        holder 450
    Holder of, not entitled to rank password without separate
        order 452
    Holder of Withdrawal Card entitled to, for password of term
        in which Card issued 747

ORDER OF MARCH.
    For funerals, prescribed................................... 244

ORIGINAL SELECTION.
    Vacancies in Subordinate Lodge offices to be filled in the
        manner of 715

OUTER DOOR.
    Should be closed when Lodge is "at ease" 572

OUTER GUARD.
    No one except, allowed in ante-room during opening 16
    Must refuse admission to ante-room to any person not in pos-
        session of the S. A. P. W 441, 444, 445
    Should inform members what rank Lodge is working in...... 510
    An appointive officer of the Lodge........................ 574
    Must be a member of the Lodge of which he is the officer.... 575

PAGE.
    Adverse ballot on the application of, cannot be laid over...... 69
    Charging of dues to, rests with Subordinate Lodges.......... 206
    Funeral rosette for, prescribed............................ 245
    Per capita tax payable on, in Lodges Subordinate to the
        Supreme Lodge...................................... 308
    In Lodges subordinate to the Supreme Lodge, applicant
        elected to rank of, may be refused admission for cause.... 320
    Rejected on a ballot for advancement, may reapply in one
        month thereafter, in Lodges subordinate to the Supreme
        Lodge... 321
    The transfer of, from one Lodge to another, is only by With-
        drawal Card.................................... 379, 380
    May be dropped for failure to advance...................... 386
    Manner of reinstatement after dropping, a matter for local
        legislation... 385
    Term Password not to be communicated to.............435, 437
    Grand Lodges may charge per capita tax on................. 450
    Separate ballot required for the advancement of............. 506
    Admitted while working in the ranks, by order of the Chancel-
        lor Commander...................................... 507
    Rank of, conferred on, by sister Lodge, on proper request... 508
    Regalia of, prescribed.................................... 518
    Withdrawal Card issued to, on Lodge being suspended....... 754

Index.

PARADES.   SECTIONS.
  Uniform to be worn in.. 246
  Collar may not be worn in.. 519
  Supreme Chancellor may not order a general parade 601
  Supreme Lodge will not attend, unless fixed for first day of
    session... 649

PARAPHERNALIA.
  Dealers in, permitted to use emblems of the Order in adver-
    tising.. 221
  To be purchased through Grand Keeper of Records and Seal. 429
  Dealers in, receiving orders, should obtain indorsement of
    Grand Keeper of Records and Seal, before shipping...... 429
  Supreme Chancellor may forbid purchase of, from dealers vio-
    lating law regarding sale of....................................... 430
  The exposure or sale of, by members to persons not members,
    declared a Pythian offense....................................... 431
  Necessary in conferring ranks; must be used in all cases..... 766

" PASSED " AND " RAISED."
  The use of the words, dispensed with, and the words "proved"
    and "charged" substituted therefor...................... 502

PASSWORD.
  SEMI-ANNUAL.
    Right to, not invalidated, by requiring dues in advance. 210, 436
    Grand Chancellor or Deputy may give, to Chancellor
      Commander, outside Lodge 253
    All not in possession of, excluded from hall, at institution
      of new Lodge 292 (8)
    Supreme Chancellor may withhold, from Lodges subordi-
      nate to Supreme Lodge for failure to make returns... 309
    Order for, now on back of Official Receipt...426, 427, 449, 450
    Created by the Supreme Chancellor 432, 434
    Supreme Chancellor may rescind 432, 433
    Is universal... 434
    Admits any member into any Lodge 434
    Only communicated to Knights 435, 437
    Knights entitled to, immediately on receiving rank 436
    Only used in the rank of Knight, except at opening, or at
      outer door 437
    Chancellor Commander may exact, whenever he deems
      safety requires 437
    Chancellor Commander instructs his own members in.... 438
    Chancellor Commander communicates, to member of
      sister Lodge only on proper order and Official Re-
      ceipt 438, 439
    In what length of time, deprived of, matter for local legis-
      lation.......................................440, 442

Index.

PASSWORD—(Continued.)   SECTIONS.
  SEMI-ANNUAL.
      Without, no member may remain when opening or in session............................441, 442, 443, 444, 445
      Ante-rooms must be cleared of all without............... 441
      Refusing to accept, must retire......................... 443
      Visitor without, may not pass outer door 444
      Member without, may not remain in rank of Page or Esquire 445
      Member, resident or otherwise, entitled to order for...... 446
      Order for, not to extend over six months............447, 448
      Order for, to be only on back of Official Receipt, but failing to be placed on receipt when sent, may be on a separate document 449, 450
      Though in possession of, may not receive the rank password without specific order for it 451, 452
      Each member of a Lodge, visiting in a body, must give, at the outer door...................................... 453
      Supreme Representatives, not in possession of, not permitted to remain in Supreme Lodge................. 684
      Vice Chancellor, in absence of Chancellor Commander, may not communicate, outside Lodge room, until after a meeting of Lodge.........................719, 720
      In addition to, Chancellor Commander may ask visitor to show Official Receipt or Traveling Shield............ 724
      Having Official Receipt and order for S. A. P. W., visitor cannot be refused admission because he is obnoxious. 727
      Holder of Withdrawal Card, entitled to, only for the term in which Card issued 742, 743, 747, 748
      Past officer, out on Card, visiting Grand Lodge, must have 749

RANK.
      Chancellor Commander may not instruct in, without specific order for 451, 452
      May be taken by the Master-at-Arms, in the ante-room, from the members of a visiting Lodge, in a body..... 453

GRAND LODGE.
      Universal—changed annually 454
      Visiting Past Chancellors, must give the current word.... 455

UNIFORM RANK.
      Promulgated by Supreme Chancellor, through the Major General... 344

GENERAL RULINGS.
      Creation of, the exclusive right of Supreme Chancellor— he may rescind................................432, 433
      Supreme Lodge provides for the issuance of............. 638

Index.

PAST CHANCELLORS.

SECTIONS.

Grand Lodge may not levy assessment on 57
Cannot be deputized by District Deputy Grand Chancellor to institute new Lodge 204
Funeral rosette for 245
All, in jurisdiction, to be notified of formation of Grand Lodge 254
Officers of new Grand Lodge must all be 255
Of five or more Lodges, may organize a Grand Lodge 255
All in good standing, eligible for office, at formation of Grand Lodge 256
Grand Lodges, primarily, composed of 263
Rights of, may be limited by Grand Lodge 263
Rank of, to be conferred in Grand Lodge—not in ante-room, or adjacent room 271
Deputy Supreme Chancellor of Hawaiian Islands empowered to confer rank on 278
Rank of, to be conferred on certain officers elected at the institution of new Lodge, subordinate to Supreme Lodge. 313, 314
Supreme Chancellor empowered to authorize Deputy Supreme Chancellors to confer rank on 315
At request of Supreme Chancellor, Grand Lodge may confer rank on, of Lodge subordinate to Supreme Lodge 316
Official charts for, to be signed by Grand Officers 417
Visiting Grand Lodge, must be in possession of the current Grand Lodge password 455
The manner of electing or creating left entirely to Grand Lodges 456, 457, 458
Sitting Past Chancellors, their duties and rights, a matter for local legislation 459
Sitting Past Chancellor is an officer, and as such may be fined for absence 460
Sitting Past Chancellor, taking Withdrawal Card, does not lose honors 461
Sitting Past Chancellor, at institution of new Lodge, selected from the Charter members 462
Filling chair of, at institution of new Lodge, entitled to all honors, as though he had filled the chair of presiding officer 463
At organization of new Lodge, any Knight may be elected as. 464
Only a Past Chancellor can be elected to fill that chair, in case of a vacancy 465
A Knight cannot be elected or appointed to fill the chair of... 466
Re-elected Chancellor Commander entitled to the rank of, after second installation 467
Is not, "in full," until obligated in Grand Lodge 468
May wear jewel of rank previous to admission to Grand Lodge 468
Entitled to rank of, though indebted to the Lodge 469

Index.

PAST CHANCELLORS—(Continued.) SECTIONS.
   Entitled to the rank of, after installation of successor, though
      minutes fail to show the latter fact 470
   Not entitled to honors of, charter being surrendered before
      expiration of term.. 471
   Retiring Chancellor Commander fills the chair of............ 487
   Removing to another Jurisdiction, must present rank creden-
      tial, to entitle to rank of............511, 512, 513, 514, 515, 516
   Withdrawal Card containing rank of, does not entitle holder
      to past rank in another Jurisdiction, unless accompanied
      by rank credential........................512, 513, 514, 515, 516
   Rank credential of, must be certified to, by Grand Officers.512, 516
   Should not be granted Withdrawal Card, if charges are pend-
      ing in Grand Lodge..................................... 760

PAST GRAND CHANCELLOR.
   Credentials of, to be sent to Supreme Keeper of Records and
      Seal, twenty days before session......................... 189
   Credentials of, must show date of commencement and end of
      service.. 190
   One of the component parts of the Supreme Lodge.285 (3), 646 (o)
   In absence of Supreme Chancellor and retiring Past Grand
      Chancellor, installs Grand Officers 288
   Major General of Uniform Rank must be............ 334
   Supreme Lodge Officers sign official chart of................. 417
   Rank of, conferred only upon such as are provided for in
      Supreme Constitution.................................... 472
   Grand Chancellor serving full term, against whom no charges
      are pending, entitled to rank of......................473, 475
   Re-elected Grand Chancellor entitled to rank of, after second
      installation 474
   Retiring Grand Chancellor becomes, irrespective of length of
      service.. 475
   Sitting Past Grand Chancellor, at institution of new Grand
      Lodge entitled to rank of................................ 476
   Supreme Representative becomes, at institution of new Grand
      Lodge, by virtue of election 477
   No ceremony required in passing to chair of................. 478
   Admitted to Supreme Lodge and entitled to seats therein 479
   Unless by permission, not entitled to speak in Supreme Lodge 479
   Not entitled to vote in Supreme Lodge...................... 479
   Have been admitted on evidence, without regular credentials. 480
   Rights of, not disturbed after credentials are approved...481, 482
   May be refused admission to the Supreme Lodge for cause,
      though having served full term 483
   May not elect, in case of re-election of Grand Chancellor..484, 485

Index.

PAST GRAND CHANCELLOR—(Continued.)   SECTIONS
  Grand Chancellor being re-elected, Junior Past Grand Chancellor fills past official chair 485
  Term of service of German Deputy not being completed at time law was changed, incumbent not entitled to rank of. 486
  Removing to another Jurisdiction, must present Rank Credential, to entitle to rank of............511, 512, 513, 514, 516
  Withdrawal Card containing rank of, does not entitle holder to past rank in another Jurisdiction, unless accompanied by Rank Credential 512, 513, 514, 516
  Rank Credentials of, must be certified to by Grand Officers.. .... 512, 516
  Office of Sitting Past Grand Chancellor not affected by change of residence... 537
  Record of, to be kept by Supreme Keeper of Records and Seal... 613
  When duly recognized, is a member of the Supreme Lodge 646 (*o*)
  Necessary to holding office in the Supreme Lodge 653
  Admitted to Supreme Lodge, morning sessions, first two days and last day.. 654
  Supreme Representative must be................664, 665, 666, 667
  Grand Chancellor entitled to rank of, after successor installed, if free from charges 666
  Unless Grand Lodge so provides, not entitled to additional vote because of being 730

PAST OFFICIAL CHAIR.
  To be filled by retiring executive officer, in Supreme, Grand and Subordinate Lodges................................. 487

PAST SUPREME CHANCELLORS.
  Eligible to appointment on Special or Standing Committees.. 174
  Jewels for, ordered placed on sale........................... 295
  " By service " entitled to mileage and per diem................ 394
  " Sitting," has charge of the floor work....................... 488
  An Officer of the Supreme Lodge..........................646 (*b*)
  Part of the composition of the Supreme Lodge.............646 (*a*)
  " By service " entitled to vote in the Supreme Lodge.......... 728

PAST SUPREME CHANCELLOR BY SERVICE—(See Past Supreme Chancellors.)

PAST SUPREME REPRESENTATIVE.
  Jewel for, adopted.. 293
  May wear jewel of rank at all meetings....................... 518

PENALTY.
  List of, that may be imposed, after trial, on Grand Officer..... 148
  Of expulsion, may be imposed as............................ 228
  Of fine, may be imposed on derelict member of committee..... 239

Index.

PENALTY—(Continued.)   SECTIONS.
  Of suspension or dishonorable discharge, prescribed in Court Martial proceedings in the Uniform Rank.................. 343
  Of fine, may be imposed on delinquent Jurisdiction........... 539

PER CAPITA TAX.
  Lodges Subordinate to Supreme Lodge, must pay............. 307
  Payable on Pages, Esquires and Knights, by Lodges subordinate to Supreme Lodge....................................... 308
  Must be paid by Lodges subordinate to Supreme Lodge or Password withheld... 309
  Grand Lodges may appropriate portion of, for building hall, if their Constitution so permits.............................. 489
  The charging of, on Pages and Esquires, a matter for local legislation, where Grand Lodge exists..................... 490

PER DIEM—(See Mileage and Per Diem.)

PRELATE.
  Must conform to the language of the Ritual.................. 547
  An elective officer of the Lodge............................. 574

PRESENTATION JEWELS.
  Authorized to be made, and the Supreme Keeper of Records and Seal to have seal stamped thereon, on payment of $2; must at present be manufactured by the contractor for official Jewels 297
  Future contracts for Jewels to provide for manufacture of, by others than the contractor, on payment of ten per cent on cost... 301

PRINTED APPEALS.
  One hundred and fifty copies required by Supreme Lodge ... 38

PRINTING.
  Committee on, of the Supreme Lodge.....................150, 168
  General powers of the Committee of......................... 168
  Legislative provisions governing 169
  Proportion of, of Journal of Proceedings, to be paid by Endowment Rank... 224

PROBATIONARY PERIOD.
  Neither Grand nor Subordinate Lodges may prescribe, during which no benefits shall be paid 80, 82
  Grand Lodges may prescribe, during which members may not draw full benefits..................................... 81
  During, members in good standing should receive at least minimum benefits 80, 81, 82

PROPERTY.
  Of a Lodge, when surrendered to its Grand Lodge, Lodge may appeal without consent.............................. 18

Index.

PROPERTY—(Continued.) SECTIONS.
  In case of a suspension of a Subordinate Lodge, refusal to deliver up constitutes an offense....................... 287
PROPOSITION—(See also Applicant; Ballot; Membership.)
  For membership, may be withdrawn by consent of the Lodge. 363
  For membership, may not be withdrawn after reported on by committee................................. 363, 364, 365
PROTEST.
  Of Lodge subordinate to Supreme Lodge, against organization of new Lodge, must be submitted to Supreme Chancellor. 310
  Deputy cannot proceed to organize new Lodge in face of, without orders from Supreme Chancellor................ 311
  In Supreme Lodge, may be filed by Supreme Representative. 491
  Grand Lodge must receive from Grand Chancellor........... 492
  Against admission to membership, emanating from sister Lodge, has not the force of an adverse ballot......... 493, 494
  From sister Lodge, against admission of applicant, to be considered in an advisory capacity, and receive respectful recognition 493, 494
"PROVED" AND "CHARGED."
  Used in place of the word, "passed" and "raised," in connection with the ranks.................................. 502
PROXY.
  Grand Officer may not be installed by..................... 289
PUBLIC INSTALLATION.
  No form for opening Lodge at............................. 570
PUBLIC OCCASIONS.
  Jewels of the Order authorized to be worn on Pythian....... 299
PYTHIAN COLLEGE.
  Proposition for the erection of, recommended............... 495
  The subject of establishing such schools left to local legislation 496
PYTHIAN PERIOD.
  Law designating.. 497
PYTHIAN PUBLIC OCCASIONS.
  Jewels of the Order authorized to be worn on............... 299
PYTHIAN SISTERHOOD.
  Mothers, wives, widows, sisters and daughters of members, allowed to establish an order to be known as............ 498
  Supreme Lodge refuse to express a preference, as between two organizations of................................... 499
QUARTERLY STATEMENT.
  To be furnished by Supreme Master of Exchequer........... 657
QUESTIONS—(See Hypothetical Questions.)

Index.

QUORUM. SECTIONS.
    In order to insure, Chancellor Commander may refuse permission to retire.. 114
    Charter may be suspended for membership diminishing below... 133
    Majority of Grand Lodges constitutes, in Supreme Lodge 285 (7), 651
    Not less than seven members of Knight rank constitute, in a Subordinate Lodge....................................... 566

RAFFLES—(See Lotteries.)

RANKS.
    Appeals pertaining to the work, cannot be taken in any but that of Knight... 43
    Objection may be entered to conferring, and operate as black ball... 68
    Adverse ballot on, in case of rejection, cannot be laid over... 69
    Knight duly selected, may confer, in absence of Chancellor Commander and Vice Chancellor........................ 113
    Dispensations to confer, for less than minimum, die with officer granting... 200
    Minimum fee for conferring all, $10....................229, 234
    Minimum fee for conferring on, may be reduced on proper application by Grand Lodge............................ 229
    Grand Lodges may provide a fee for conferring all, above minimum.. 230
    Lodges may not evade the law in regard to minimum fee for, by donating portion of the fee.......................231, 232
    Grand Lodges provide for the division of the fee for.......... 236
    At least four members required in conferring, at institution of Lodges... 292 (8)
    First conferred on officers, at institution of new Lodge.... 292 (9)
    Must be conferred, in full, on all initiates, at institution of new Lodge ; portion may not remain and see the work done on others... 292 (9)
    The establishing or recognition of, persistently refused by Supreme Lodge... 304
    Elected applicant for, may be refused admission by majority vote in Lodges subordinate to Supreme Lodge............ 320
    Rejected applicants for, in Lodges subordinate to the Supreme Lodge, may re-apply in one month thereafter............ 321
    Not to be conferred unless paid for........................ 366
    Refusal to proceed in, **not ground for charges**.............. 410
    Official orders, received while working in, to be acted upon at once... 419
    Paraphernalia for conferring, to be purchased through Grand Keeper of Records and Seal............................. 429

Index.

RANKS—(Continued.) SECTIONS.
    No one allowed to remain during conference of, unless in possession of the S. A. P. W............................ 445
    Chancellor Commander not to instruct visitor in password of, unless presenting separate order........................ 451
    Password of, not to be communicated to visitor without proper order.. 452
    The use of the word "Degrees" changed to "Ranks"....... 500
    The use of the words "passed" and "raised," when referring to, changed to "approved" and "charged".............. 502
    Except where Dispensation issues, or the first four meetings of a new Lodge, one week must elapse between conferring...503, 504
    A separate ballot must be taken on each of.................. 505
    Same number of black balls reject for, as for initiation...505, 506
    Pages and Esquires admitted to Lodge when working in, by order of the Chancellor Commander..................... 507
    Lodge may confer, when requested by sister Lodge.......... 508
    Lodge conferring, on request, should send notice to sister Lodge... 508
    Work of conferring may be transferred to a "team," Lodge remaining under control of an officer 509
    Outer Guard should inform members what rank Lodge is working in... 510
    Not to be conferred on non-resident, a member of another Lodge, without their permission......................... 536
    Lodge may not alter or omit any part of the work in......... 548
    Work in the "amplified third" must be conferred without books..13, 549
    Lodge business to be transacted in rank of Knight except in trial of Page or Esquire, or conferring ranks............ 567
    Chancellor Commander may call a qualified member to confer 568
RANK CREDENTIAL.
    Past officer withdrawing, must receive...................... 461
    Past officer affiliating, must present, to entitle him to rank ... 512
    Withdrawal Card, no value as 513, 514, 515, 516
RANK TEAM.
    Work of conferring ranks may be transferred to, Lodge remaining under control of an officer 509
RECONSIDERATION.
    Of adverse ballot on application, illegal 66
    Of a vote granting a Withdrawal Card, illegal 737
RED COLLARS—(See Collars.)
REFUNDING.
    Of portion of membership fee, a violation of the Supreme Lodge Constitution..231, 232

Index.

REGALIA. SECTIONS.
   Under the supervision of the Committee on Written Work... 166
   Grand Lodges must conform to............................. 259
   Shall be as prescribed by Supreme Lodge................517, 637
   Constitutional provision, prescribed........................ 518
   Collar may not be worn at parades or funerals.......519, 520, 708
   Not to be worn in public.................................. 708

REGALIA DEALERS—(See Paraphernalia.)

REINSTATEMENT.
   Benefits payable to a member upon, if otherwise qualified..82, 92
   Grand Lodge may require applicant for, to pay dues accruing
      during suspension...................................208, 209
   A member of a Lodge subordinate to Supreme Lodge desiring,
      must pay one year's dues and all accrued assessments... 323
   As a general proposition, a matter for local legislation.383, 384, 527
   Of Pages and Esquires, a matter for local legislation........ 385
   Of members of a suspended Grand Lodge, subject to control
      of new Grand Lodge..................................... 390
   Takes place without action of the Lodge, on termination of
      definite suspension...................................... 525
   Of member, indefinitely suspended, requires written application and ballot.. 526
   After suspension for non-payment of dues, member may reinstate himself, by payment of all arrears, if local law so
      provides.. 528
   Lodge may be reorganized and only a portion of former
      members reinstated...................................... 529

REJECTION—(See Ballot; Membership.)

RELIEF.
   Lodge not responsible for, furnished without authority...521, 522
   Bureaus of, their organization a matter for local legislation... 523
   Furnished by a Lodge or Committee, under a relief shield,
      Lodges issuing shield responsible for repayment......... 699

RELIEF BUREAU.
   The organizing of, a matter for local legislation............. 523

RELIEF COMMITTEE.
   Sick member leaving jurisdiction of, without consent of, does
      not thereby lose benefits................................. 88
   Assistance furnished by, to holder of relief shield, must be
      repaid by Lodge issuing shield........................... 699

RELIEF SHIELD—(See Traveling Shield.)

RENOUNCING THE ORDER.
   Member forfeits pecuniary benefits by....................... 524

Index.

REORGANIZATION. SECTIONS.
Of a Subordinate Lodge, revives all members with it, to the same standing as existed at time of suspension........... 388

REPEALING ACT.
Of old constitution and previous conflicting legislation, previous to 1874... 181

REPORTS.
Grand Lodge may not mutilate, of its Grand Chancellor..... 274
Of Supreme Officers, to be printed and published........... 530
Supreme Chancellor and Supreme Keeper of Records and Seal to make...599, 616, 620

REPRESENTATION.
Delinquent Grand Lodge forfeits, until Representative tax paid 539
Supreme Lodge may grant, to delinquent Grand Lodge. as a privilege 540, 541, 542
Right of Grand Lodges to, in Supreme Lodge, prescribed..646 (*n*)

REPRESENTATIVE—(See Grand Representative.)

REPRESENTATIVE SYSTEM.
Grand Lodges may provide for, and limit rights of, Past Chancellors 263, 264

REPRESENTATIVE TAX.
Grand Lodges must pay...................................... 539
Grand Lodges failing to pay, within specified time, fined..... 539
Grand Lodges lose representation by failure to pay.......... 539
Grand Lodge delinquent for, may be granted representation, as a privilege 540, 541, 542
List of Jurisdictions in arrears for, to be furnished Committee on Credentials 628
One of the revenues of the Supreme Lodge.................. 640
Each Grand Lodge shall pay fifty (50) dollars annually..... 655

REPRESENTATIVE TO GRAND LODGE—(See Grand Representative.)

RESERVED RIGHTS.
Supreme Lodge may at any time resume additional powers ..
....262, 590, 645

RESIDENCE.
Application for initiation must state........................ 346
Of at least six months in Jurisdiction, required of applicant for membership.................................347, 533
Non-resident, applicant by Card, must have written consent of his Grand Chancellor..................................... 373
Resident or non-resident member, entitled to order for S. A. P. W... 446

18) (265)

Index.

RESIDENCE—(Continued.)   SECTIONS.

    Admission to membership of non-residents, in face of a protest, may cause suspension of Lodge.................... 529

    Grand Lodges may prescribe a requirement of, by applicants for membership............. 534

    Non-resident applicant for initiation, must have written consent of his Grand Chancellor........................... 535

    Non-resident applicant for ranks, must have permission of Lodge to which attached............................... 536

    Grand Officer acquiring, in another Jurisdiction, vacates office 537

    Supreme Representatives must have bona fide, in Jurisdiction they represent...................................... 670

RESIGNATION.

    Chancellor Commander has a right to resign at will.......... 110

RETIRING.

    Chancellor Commander possesses right of, without leave of the Lodge... 109

    Chancellor Commander may prevent member, without leave. 114

    Member retiring when Lodge is "at ease," Lodge called to order 572

    Officer or member retiring under order of Chancellor Commander, need not give sign....................... 576

RETURNS.

    Committee on Credentials and Returns report on............ 162

    To be made semi-annually, by Lodges subordinate to Supreme Lodge 307

    Lodges subordinate to Supreme Lodge, failing to make, S. A. P. W. may be withheld.................................... 309

    Form for, to be strictly complied with...................... 538

    Grand Lodge must make, promptly.......................... 539

    Grand Lodge failing to make promptly, subject to fine....... 539

REVENUE.

    Finance Committee to make estimate of 157

    Grand Lodge may limit the right of subordinates to expend.. 241

    Of the Supreme Lodge, collected by Supreme Keeper of Records and Seal... 608

    Of Supreme Lodge, to be paid over to Supreme Master of Exchequer, monthly...................................... 608

    Supreme Lodge provides its own, by Representative tax, sale of supplies, etc....................................640, 655

REVISION OF CONSTITUTION.

    Special rule with reference to 603

REVOCATION.

    Charters of Grand Lodges may be revoked for various causes....... 122

Index.

REVOCATION—(Continued.) SECTIONS.
    Charters of Subordinate Lodges may be revoked for various
        causes 132, 133
    Declaration of suspension for non-payment of dues may be
        revoked for the purpose of trial 382
    Supreme Chancellor may revoke passwords............... 432, 433
    Withdrawal Card may be revoked by the Lodge granting same,
        for causes other than impeachment and trial..... 738, 739, 760
    Grand Lodge or Grand Chancellor may order, of Withdrawal
        Card 738, 760
    Of Withdrawal Card, for the purpose of impeachment or trial,
        holder becomes subject to his Lodge................ 738, 739
    Withdrawal Cards, good until revoked...................... 740
RITUAL.
    Changes in, laid over one session; require four-fifths vote to
        adopt 4
    Amplified Third, adopted in 1872; Lodges choose which to
        use... 12, 14
    Amplified Third, when used, must be without the books ... 13, 549
    Printing of, in charge of Committee on Printing............... 169
    That for funerals, adopted by Supreme Lodge, the only one
        to be used 250
    Grand Lodges must conform to................................ 259
    Lodge must only have a set of five Rituals.................... 543
    No translations of, to be made without direction of Supreme
        Lodge 544
    To be in charge of the Chancellor Commander, and kept in
        Castle Hall 545
    Language of, to be strictly adhered to 546, 548
    Officers to adhere to, in opening and closing................. 547
    Not to change, alter, amend, add to or omit any part of, in
        the ranks 548
    Memorizing, as a general rule, not made obligatory, but each
        Subordinate Lodge may declare in what space of time
        officer *shall* memorize ritualistic charges 550, 551
    Grand Chancellor may not empower his Deputy to take up,
        after specific time 552
    Officers and members prohibited from copying 553
    Supreme Chancellor authorized to arrange with Secretary of
        State for sending, through mails, to foreign countries 554
    Opening ceremonies in, cannot be dispensed with, by motion. 569
    Controlled by the Supreme Lodge 635, 636, 758
ROSETTE—(See Funeral Rosette.)
ROSTER.
    Whether membership by Card begins on signing, or on elec-
        tion, a matter for local legislation 371

Index.

ROSTER—(Continued.)   SECTIONS.
    Member elected on Card may come in at any time and sign... 372
    When Pages and Esquires may be dropped from, a matter for local legislation 386

SABBATH—(See Sunday.)

SALARY.
    Of Major General, determined from time to time... 345
    Of Supreme Chancellor, two thousand (2,000) dollars 604
    Of Supreme Keeper of Records and Seal, determined from time to time... 621
    Of Supreme Master of Exchequer, determined from time to time 661
    Supreme Vice Chancellor to receive, in case of vacancy in office of Supreme Chancellor.......................... 689

SALOON KEEPERS.
    Special legislation with reference to their right to admission to membership... 360

SANITARIUM.
    Proposition for establishing, approved..................... 555

SCHEMES OF CHANCE—(See Lotteries.)

SCHOOLS—(See Pythian College.)

SEAL.
    OF SUPREME LODGE.
        Copyrighted..285 (2), 557
        Must be stamped on presentation Jewels ... .297, 301
        Must be on all Official Receipts 421, 427
        Description of....... 556
        In charge of the Supreme Keeper of Records and Seal... 609
    OF SUPREME CHANCELLOR.
        The use of, authorized in 1873............................ 558
    OF GRAND LODGE.
        To be attached to papers in cases of Appeal or Writs of Error to the Supreme Lodge or Supreme Chancellor. 24, 26, 45
        To be affixed to rank credentials......................... 512
        Constitutional provision requiring 559
        To bear date of institution ,.............................. 559
        Impression of, to be deposited with Supreme Keeper of Records and Seal................................559, 618
    OF SUBORDINATE LODGE.
        Not to be affixed to other than Official Charts............ 414
        Orders for S. A. P. W. to bear.....................438, 439
        Required to have 559, 560
        To bear date of institution............................... 559

Index.

SEAL—(Continued.) SECTIONS.
    OF SUBORDINATE LODGE.
        Affixed to Withdrawal Cards and official documents emanating from the Lodge............................... 560
SEATS—Committee on—(See Committees.)
SECRET WORK—(See Written Work, Unwritten Work and Paraphernalia.)
    Exposure or sale of, by members of the Order to non-members, declared an offense against the Order.................... 431
SESSIONS.
    OF SUPREME LODGE.
        Supreme Chancellor may call special........285 (6), 592, 648
        Grand Lodges, officers, and members to be notified of... 610
        To be held biennially, on fourth Tuesday of April. 285 (6), 647
        May hold biennially, on other than fourth Tuesday of April, by two-thirds vote............................ 647
        Place of holding biennial, determined at preceding session 647
        No place being determined for holding, to be held in Baltimore.. 647
        Invitations to parades, banquets, etc., not accepted, unless on first day of.. 649
        Supreme Chancellor to pass on suitability of a room in which to hold..................................... 650
        Majority of Grand Lodges constitute a quorum for holding 651
    OF GRAND LODGES.
        Determining when held, left to Grand Lodge............ 268
SICKNESS.
    The payment of benefits to members during, is a right and not a charity—a fundamental principle of the Order....76, 77
    Benefits paid during, only to members in good standing...... 85
    Leaving the country during, does not forfeit benefits.......87, 88
    Lodge may not adopt a law during, suspending payment of benefits.. 89
    Lodge must pay benefits during "first week" of sickness.... 91
    Convalescence not a bar to benefits......................... 93
    Where clearly continuous, Lodge may apply rule reducing benefits... 94
    Member entitled to benefits on account of, if in good standing at commencement of, though in arrears when reported 98
    May pay arrears during and be entitled to funeral benefits. 103, 104
    Improperly claiming benefits during, not itself an offense, unless fraud appears.................................... 411
SIGNS.
    Not made on retiring or re-entering, by member leaving under order of Chancellor Commander...................... 576

Index.

	SECTIONS.
"SIR KNIGHT."	
Title of, not to be used in designating members of Third Rank.	501
SITTING PAST CHANCELLOR.	
Status of, a matter for local legislation....................	459
Subject to fines, same as any other officer.................	460
Taking Card, does not vacate rank.........................	461
A Knight cannot fill chair of, under any circumstances......	466
SITTING PAST GRAND CHANCELLOR.	
An officer of the Grand Lodge.............................	255
No election for, in case of re-election of Grand Chancellor.	484, 485
Office not vacated by change of residence to another jurisdiction...	537
SITTING PAST SUPREME CHANCELLOR—(See Past Supreme Chancellor.)	
SOLICITING CANDIDATES.	
Not permitted..	367
SPECIAL COMMITTEES OF THE SUPREME LODGE— (See Committees.)	
SPECIAL SESSIONS—(See Sessions.)	
SPECIFICATIONS.	
Accompanying charge against Grand Officer, must particularize place and circumstances of the alleged offense........	138
STATE OF THE ORDER—Committee on—(See Committees.)	
STANDING COMMITTEES—(See Committees.)	
STANDING COMMITTEES OF THE SUPREME LODGE— (See Committees.)	
SUBORDINATE LODGE.	
Determines for itself as to the use of Amplified Third Rank ritual....	12, 14
No one allowed in ante-room during opening of.............	16
Appeal may be taken by...................................	17
Appeal by, to Supreme Lodge, must first be acted on by Grand Lodge..	21
Appeals in, from decision of the chair, only taken up in rank of Knight...	43
"Appeal for aid" by, to be sent in or out of its own Jurisdiction, must have the approval of its own Grand Chancellor; the approval of the Supreme Chancellor is not required...	49, 50
Declaration of suspension for non-payment of dues must be made in open Lodge.....................................	55
May levy a tax to meet necessary expenses of the Lodge.....	59
May not "lay over" an adverse ballot for advancement......	69
Description of banner for use of...........................	72

Index.

SUBORDINATE LODGE—(Continued.)   SECTIONS.
Must provide for paying weekly and funeral benefits........73, 78
Must provide for paying benefits, out of its own funds, and
  not by a combination of Lodges.......................... 75
Must tax their members, if necessary, to pay benefits........ 78
May not frame a By-Law depriving Knights of benefits for one
  year after attaining that rank...................... ......80, 82
May provide a probationary period, during which only the
  minimum benefits shall be paid......................... 80
Payment of benefits by, to members *in good standing*, is obliga-
  tory..83, 92
May not pass a law "suspending the payment of all weekly
  benefits"... 89
May not avoid or evade the payment of weekly benefits...... 90
Must pay benefits for "first week's sickness"................ 91
Bound to give same care and general aid to stranger brother
  as it would to one of its own members.................. 95
May not charge for nurse hire, in caring for stranger brother,
  unless laws of sister Lodge so provide................... 95
Not bound to furnish aid to greater amount than allowed by
  sister Lodge... 95
Must pay over all unexpended or balance of funeral benefit,
  even though others provide for the burial.............99, 100
Must pay "Widow's Tax," if deceased entitled to funeral bene-
  fits.. 101
Responsible to sister Lodge for benefits paid out on telegram
  by Keeper of Records and Seal......................... 105
Cannot avoid payment of funeral benefits on plea of deceased
  being intemperate during life........................... 106
In the absence of the proper officers, the Knight selected to
  preside over, becomes "an officer of the Lodge"........ 113
Members retiring from, require permission of the Chancellor
  Commander... 114
Charter of, must be in Lodge room or ante-room............ 125
Exist by virtue of Charter.................................. 126
Not compelled to exhibit Charter, on demand of visitor...... 127
May not dissolve so long as nine members are willing to sustain,
  except by permission of Grand Lodge or Grand Chan-
  cellor 128
Dispensation or Charter may be revoked for cause.......132, 133
May not be suspended without charges and trial 133, 135
Supreme Constitution and legislative acts, obligatory on.....
  ....182, 187, 306
Grand Lodge provides Constitution for ; not operative till duly
  approved.................................184, 185, 186, 187, 188

Index.

SUBORDINATE LODGE—(Continued.)   SECTIONS

  Constitutions of, must contain obligatory general rules and principles, set forth in Article VIII, Section 2, of Supreme Constitution. (See following Sections of this Digest: 51, 61, 73, 229, 290, 346, 347, 363, 366, 370, 404, 503, 533, 535, 536, 560, 561, 562, 566, 567, 573, 715, 734, 738, 756, 757).......... 188
  May charge dues to Pages and Esquires....................... 206
  May not exempt Knights from dues, for a certain period after attaining rank.. 207
  May not charge dues, to members suspended for non-payment of dues, unless Constitution so provides..............208, 209
  May collect dues in advance, but such rule cannot invalidate right to benefits or S. A. P. W.....................86, 210
  Need not return advance dues to member suspended for cause 211
  Where the Constitution provides, that in elections, two *members* must act as tellers, it means members *of that Lodge*.. 218
  Elections in, not set aside simply on account of an excess of votes cast... 219
  Should prevent improper use of the emblems of the Order ... 220
  Should report list of suspended members to Endowment Section.. 223
  Board of Control, of Endowment Rank, may send circulars to 226, 227
  May impose penalty of expulsion, for cause.................. 228
  May not confer the ranks for a less sum than the prescribed fee...230, 234, 235
  May not refund or donate any portion of the fee for the ranks 231, 232
  May not open so-called "Charter Books"..................... 233
  May not add fines and assessments to dues, unless Constitution so provides... 237
  May fine derelict members of committees, if Grand Lodge so provides... 239
  May fine members for non-attendance, if Grand Lodge so legislates... 240
  May make donations to a distressed brother 242
  Funerals; order of formation by Lodge...................... 244
  Funeral rosette prescribed for Officers, Past Officers and members of... 245
  May appear in parade, at funerals, how..................... 246
  May appoint a Chaplain to conduct exercises at funerals..... 247
  Where excluded from share of control of funeral, members of, excused from attendance..................................... 249
  A Knight may be commissioned to institute..... 252
  Five Lodges necessary to establish a Grand Lodge........254, 255
  Has no standing unless legally chartered............. 285 (8), 652

Index.

SUBORDINATE LODGE—(Continued.)   SECTIONS.

Incorporation of, has no bearing as to its relations to the Order	286
Directions for instituting	292
Jewels of, may be worn on public Pythian occasions only	299
Must not resort to, institute or promote raffles, lotteries, gift enterprises, or schemes of chance, in the name of the Order, on pain of forfeiture of Charter	331
May initiate maimed persons, under Dispensation from Grand Chancellor	332
May elect maimed persons to office	333
May not initiate any person who is not of age, a white male, of good standing, a believer in a Supreme Being, and a resident at least six months	347, 533
Colored Lodges exist without authority	350, 351, 353
Constitutions of, must contain provision that applicants shall be "white persons"	352
Any Subordinate Lodge violating the law regarding the admission of only "white persons," subjects itself to suspension	352
Must expel any "colored person" upon discovery, obtaining membership under false representation of being a "white person"	352
May not admit ladies	353
May not admit minors	353
May not admit Chinamen	354
May not admit persons of Indian blood	355
May not admit persons unable to write	356
May admit person who can write his name	357
May not admit person belonging to another Lodge	358
May require applicant to furnish medical certificate	359
Consent of, required for withdrawal of proposition for membership	363, 365
Rejected applicant may re-apply to another	368
Cannot take advantage of its own wrong or error, to the exclusion of a member who, through no fault of his own, was irregularly admitted	374, 375, 376
Action of, may not be annulled without trial	375
May refuse to re-admit to membership one to whom they had granted Card	377
Rejected applicant by Card may re-apply to same or any other, at any time, if local law does not forbid	378
Transfer from, of Pages and Esquires, is by Withdrawal Card	379, 380
May revoke act of suspension for non-payment of dues, for purposes of trial	382

Index.

SUBORDINATE LODGE—(Continued.)   SECTIONS.

May drop Pages and Esquires who fail to advance within one year, if Grand Lodge so provides	385, 386
In case of reorganization of, all members revived with it, except those who meantime had taken Cards 388, 389,	755
Not to be named after living persons	403
Must not attach seal of, to Charts other than issued by Supreme Lodge	414
Must at once obey official orders from Supreme or Grand Lodge	419
Must give only the Official Receipt, for payment of moneys by members; its use is obligatory, and must not be evaded 421,	423
Official Receipt is not conclusive on, as between it and the member	425
May not retain Official Receipt when presented for purpose of obtaining the S. A. P. W	428
Are required to purchase "paraphernalia used in conferring ranks" through Grand Keeper of Records and Seal	429
Must refuse admission to any one not in possession of the S. A. P. W	441
Member without the S. A. P. W. cannot remain in, when opening or in session 442, 443, 444,	445
When visiting in a body, rank password taken by Master-at-Arms, in the ante-room, and all admitted together	453
May select members on whom their Grand Lodge will confer the rank of Past Chancellor 456, 457,	458
Sitting Past Chancellor is an officer of	460
Holds jurisdiction over whom it will admit, irrespective of protest 493,	494
May confer the ranks on a Page or Esquire, on request of sister Lodge 508,	536
May transfer the work, in the ranks, to a "team," provided the Lodge remains under control of a proper officer	509
Members should be informed by Outer Guard of, what rank is being worked	510
Regalia of, prescribed by Supreme Lodge 517,	518
May not use collars at funerals	520
Not responsible for unauthorized advances of money to its members	521
Not responsible for funeral expenses paid by sister Lodge, where Lodge burying him knew deceased to be non-beneficial	522
May withhold benefits where member renounces the Order	524
No action of, required to reinstate a member at termination of definite suspension for cause	525

Index.

SUBORDINATE LODGE—(Continued.)   SECTIONS.
  Members implicated in cause of suspension of, may be
    excluded from, on reorganization 529
  Representative to Grand Lodge, not an officer of 532
  Must require applicants for initiation to be residents of the
    Jurisdiction 533, 534
  Only entitled to one set of five (5) Rituals.................. 543
  Rituals belonging to, must be kept in Castle Hall 545
  Must not alter, amend nor omit any portion of the Ritual..... 548
  May itself determine within what period the officers shall be
    able to deliver the charges without the book 551
  Officers of, prohibited from copying any part of the Ritual... 553
  Shall have an appropriate seal 560
  Shall never consist of less than seven Knights 561
  Shall hold weekly meetings, unless Dispensation permits
    longer intervals........................... 562, 563, 564
  May impose fines on officers for absence from "called meet-
    ings," if the laws of its Grand Lodge permit fining officers
    for absence 565
  Not less than seven Knights constitute a quorum of.......... 566
  Transacts all business, except conferring Page and Esquire
    rank, and trial of same, in the Knight rank 567
  Transacts all business with an officer of, in the chair, except
    ranks 568
  May not dispense with opening ceremonies 569
  Opening ceremonies of, not to be used at public installation.. 570
  May not "adjourn"—'must '' close"........................ 571
  When "at ease," both the inner and outer door must be
    closed... 572
  Officers of, are as provided in the Ritual................ 573
  All officers of, are elective, except those of Inner and Outer
    Guards, which are appointive 574
  The Outer Guard cannot be a member of another Lodge..... 575
  Officer or member of, retiring, by order of the Chancellor
    Commander, need not address the chair—neither need
    they, on re-entering 576
  Not liable for unauthorized expenditures of Trustees......... 577
  May consolidate with another Lodge, if local law provides ... 578
  May communicate, with Supreme Lodge, through Grand
    Lodge 579
  May not pass on the conduct of Supreme Lodge or its officers. 580
  Prohibited from holding meetings, for the transaction of busi-
    ness, on Sunday 581
  Supreme Representatives must be members of, in good stand-
    ing 664
  Terms of, fixed by Grand Lodge, not less than six months ... 690

Index.

SUBORDINATE LODGE—(Continued.)   SECTIONS.
    Empowered to issue Traveling Shields to members, to the limit for which paid, not however to extend beyond the date of the next meeting of the Supreme Lodge 698
    Responsible for repayment for money paid under a Relief Shield 699
    Holder of a Withdrawal Card not entitled to Relief Shield from... 700
    May proceed with trial, accused being absent............... 701
    May receive testimony of non-members, in a trial........... 702
    Trial proceedings in, need not wait the action of a Court, in a case of indictment of a member on a criminal charge. 704, 705
    Third Rank Uniform Cap may not be worn in, unless by permission 709
    Uniform Rank uniform alone does not admit to 712
    Vacancies in office in, filled in the manner of original selection 715
    "Change of Venue," in case of prejudice in, permitted in trials, if the Grand Lodge so legislate.................... 717
    Not to require a visiting member to produce receipt and be examined, if in possession of the S. A. P. W............. 723
    Traveling Shield not required for purpose of visiting......... 724
    Suspended member, pending appeal, may not visit........... 725
    May not exclude a visitor, simply on account of objections offered 726, 727
    "Consent" of, for withdrawal of application for membership, means a majority vote.................................... 732
    No "vouching" in, allowed................................. 733
    Applications for Withdrawal Card must be made, either personally or in writing, to.........................734, 735
    May charge a fee for Withdrawal Card...................... 736
    May not reconsider a vote granting Withdrawal Card........ 737
    May revoke a Withdrawal Card..........................738, 739
    Must send notice of deposit of Card, to issuer............... 741
    Holder of a Withdrawal Card may visit, if having the S. A. P.W. 748
    Representative of, to Grand Lodge, vacates his right, by the granting him a Card..................................... 17
    Pages and Esquires of a defunct, may obtain Withdrawal Cards from Grand Chancellor............................ 754
    May issue new Withdrawal Cards in case of loss.........756, 757
    Not permitted to add to nor take from the prescribed work... 766

SUICIDE.
    Whether or not, benefits shall be paid to relatives of, a matter for local jurisdiction..................................... 102

SUNDAY.
    Meetings of Lodges for business strictly prohibited on....... 581

Index.

SUPPLIES.
SECTIONS.
Bills for, need not be audited before payment............... 169
Committee on, of the Supreme Lodge, composition and duties of.. 177
Diplomas and jewels for ladies, placed on list of............. 303
Memorial services placed on the list of...... ..:........... 393
Official charts placed on the list of.......................... 416
Consist of all material furnished by Supreme Lodge for creating revenue.......... ....582, 640
Shall be furnished as specified, but may be changed by legislation at regular sessions............................... 582
All on list of, except jewel cases. application cards, and delinquent notices, obtainable only from Supreme Keeper of Records and Seal... 583
To be furnished through respective Grand Lodges.......... 584
Private parties have no right to furnish..................... 585
Charter plates furnished as................................. 586
Furnished on credit to Grand Keeper of Records and Seal and Deputy Supreme Chancellors; to others, for cash only 587
Rebate on, equal to customs duties, allowed............ 588
Grand Lodges prescribe terms for furnishing................ 589
Prices of, charged by Grand Lodges, to conform to rule of Supreme Lodge.................................. 590
Supreme Keeper of Records and Seal to report supplies ordered and on hand... 624
Price of, fixed in By-laws of Supreme Lodge................ 655

"SUPREME BEING."
Belief in, required of applicant for membership............. 347
Chinaman, though a believer in, not eligible to membership... 354

SUPREME CHANCELLOR.
May not dispense with requirements as to age of initiates.... 1
May decide Appeals and Writs of Error during recess.......
....17, 22, 39, 45, 342
Certifies to parties in interest, his decisions on Appeals and Writs of Error..... ... .39, 45
Decisions of, on Appeals and Writs of Error, binding until reversed.. 40
Decisions of, on Appeals and Writs of Error, with all papers therein, to be reported to the Supreme Lodge............ 40
During recess, decisions of Committee on Appeals, of Supreme Lodge, operative only after approval of.......... 41
"Appeals for Aid," by Grand Lodges, must be approved by. 48
"Appeals for Aid," by Subordinate Lodges, require no approval by, if approved by their own Grand Chancellor... 50
"Appeals for Aid," by Lodges subordinate to the Supreme Lodge, must be approved by............ ....48, 49

(277)

Index.

SUPREME CHANCELLOR—(Continued.)   SECTIONS.

Dispensations for Grand Lodges, issued by, during recess... 121, 124, 596
Issues Dispensation, not Charter, during recess, original being lost or destroyed... 124
Has no control over what names to appear on Charters of Lodges... 131
Appoints the Standing Committees of the Supreme Lodge... 150
Council of Administration, act in an advisory capacity to.... 151
Convenes the Committee on Finance, for examination of books of financial officers... 155
Appoints Committee on Allotment of Seats, just preceding the session... 176
Member of Committee on Supplies... 177
Controls time and place of meetings of Special Committees, during recess... 179
Approval by, of Constitution, void if in conflict with Supreme law... 183
Constitutions and amendments to be submitted to, and by him referred to Council of Administration... 185
Appoints and commissions Deputy Supreme Chancellors, with power to control and remove at will.................. 191, 192, 193, 194, 195, 598
Responsible for the acts of his Deputy... 193
Dispensations issued by Deputy Supreme Chancellors must be reported to... 198
Dispensations granted by, to reduce the minimum membership fee to $6, die with the officer granting them... 200
Appoints and commissions the Major General of the Uniform Rank... 212
May, for causes arising, install a Supreme Officer, during recess... 215
Is a member, *ex-officio*, of the Board of Control, Endowment Rank... 222
May grant Dispensations to confer all the ranks for less than minimum, upon the application of a Grand Lodge....201, 229
Has the power to approve or not, the application for the formation of a Grand Lodge... 254
Installs, or causes to be installed, the Officers of a new Grand Lodge... 255
Not to answer hypothetical questions, unless coming from Grand Lodge or Grand Chancellor... 281, 282
Is one of the trustees of the Supreme Lodge... 285 (4)
If present, installs the Officers of a Grand Lodge... 288
May withhold the S. A. P. W. from delinquent Lodges subordinate to Supreme Lodge... 309

Index.

SUPREME CHANCELLOR—(Continued.)   SECTIONS.
Passes upon protests against formation of Lodges, where no
    Grand Lodge exists.. 311
Has power to authorize Deputy Supreme Chancellors to con-
    fer rank of Past Chancellor on those eligible.............. 315
On request of, Grand Lodge may confer rank of Past Chan-
    cellor on a member of a Lodge subordinate to Supreme
    Lodge.. 316
Has no power to grant Dispensation to Lodges subordinate to
    the Supreme Lodge, to reduce the minimum membership
    fee below $10... 317
Empowered to issue Dispensations to Lodges subordinate to
    the Supreme Lodge, to admit " maimed persons "........ 318
May issue Card to member of defunct Lodge, in Jurisdiction
    where no Grand Lodge exists......................... 324, 325
Appoints the Major General of the Uniform Rank............ 334
In conjunction with Major General, examines and passes on
    all laws of the Uniform Rank................................... 337
Promulgates the countersign of the Uniform Rank to the
    Major General... 344
Authorized to make public declaration touching clandestine
    bodies.. 353
Power to excuse members of Supreme Lodge from attendance 395
Fully empowered to deal with persons making improper use of
    the name of the Order... 398
Signs Official Charts issued to Past Grand Chancellors...... 417
Authorized to advertise dealers selling paraphernalia contrary
    to the rules of the Supreme Lodge, and forbid members
    and Lodges dealing with such................................... 430
Has the exclusive right of creation and promulgation and re-
    scinding of password.............................. 432, 433, 434, 454
Report of, to be presented, printed and published.... 530, 531, 599
Authorized to arrange for transmission of Rituals, through the
    mails, to foreign countries....................................... 554
Individual Official Seal of, authorized, in 1873................. 558
Issues Dispensations, to Lodges subordinate to Supreme
    Lodge, to meet at longer intervals than weekly........... 563
To see that the Constitutional enactments, rules and edicts of
    the Supreme Lodge are obeyed................................ 591
To call special sessions of the Supreme Lodge............ 592, 648
To call conventions of Supreme Officers in Council........... 592
To cause to be executed and keep the official bonds of officers. 594
To issue Dispensations for new Lodges, subordinate to the
    Supreme Lodge... 595
To suspend or remove an officer, for cause, and fill the
    vacancy... 597

Index.

SUPREME CHANCELLOR—(Continued.)   SECTIONS.
  To decide all questions of law submitted...................... 600
  May not order a general parade of the Order................ 601
  A decision of, stands as law, until reversed or repealed...600, 602
  Power to revise Constitutions defined........................ 603
  Salary of, $2,000 per annum.................................. 604
  Expenses of, to be paid...................................... 605
  Trial balance of the books, to be submitted to, by the Supreme
    Keeper of Records and Seal, quarterly.................... 619
  To be furnished every fiscal year, by the Supreme Keeper of
    Records and Seal, with list of firms furnishing supplies,
    on receiving which, the Supreme Chancellor is to obtain
    duplicate invoice for Finance Committee.................. 625
  Presiding Officer of the Supreme Lodge......................646 (c)
  To see to the selection of a suitable hall in which to hold the
    session 650
  To receive a quarterly statement from the Supreme Master of
    the Exchequer 657
  In the event of death, removal or physical incompetency of,
    Supreme Vice Chancellor succeeds to office, honors and
    salary... 689
  Order of, placing Lodge under adjacent Jurisdiction, a nullity,
    on formation of a Grand Lodge............................ 694
  Has no power to vacate Charter of Grand Lodge, for the purpose of forming two Grand Lodges, in a Jurisdiction
    formerly a Territory, but divided into two States......... 695
  Has charge of the Book of Diagrams........................ 764

SUPREME COUNCIL.
  Of Supreme Officers, called by Supreme Chancellor.......... 592
  Proceedings of, kept by Supreme Keeper of Records and
    Seal... 607

SUPREME INNER GUARD.
  Duties of.. 606
  An officer of the Supreme Lodge........................ 646 (*l*)

SUPREME KEEPER OF RECORDS AND SEAL.
  Appeals to be sent to, one month prior to session............ 37
  Shall place all appeals in hands of Chairman of Committee on
    Appeals.. 37
  Sworn statement of sureties, on bonds of Supreme Officers, to
    be filed with.. 107
  Sends notice of charges against Lodge subordinate to Supreme
    Lodge...133 (c)
  Books of, examined by Committee on Finance............155, 158
  Member of the Committee on Supplies....................... 177
  Member of the Committee on Hotels and Transportation..... 178

Index.

SUPREME KEEPER OF RECORDS, ETC.—(Cont'd.) SECTIONS.
Certificates of Past Grand Chancellors and Supreme Representatives to be sent to, twenty days before session...... 189
List of new Grand Officers to be forwarded to, immediately... 251
Issues to the Lodges, the call for the meeting to organize a Grand Lodge................................ 254
Notice of organization of Grand Lodge to be forwarded to.... 257
Deputy Supreme Chancellor of the Hawaiian Islands to forward certificates of Past Chancellors to................. 278
A Trustee of the Supreme Lodge, under the Act of Incorporation...285 (4)
To give bond for the faithful discharge of duties ; failing to do so, office to be vacated..........................285 (5), 622
To issue permits for manufacture of special jewels, with the Supreme Lodge Seal impressed thereon.............297, 301
To preserve and bind the Journals of Proceedings of Grand Lodges... 302
To prepare and sell Ladies' Diploma and Jewel.............. 303
Lodges subordinate to Supreme Lodge to pay per capita tax to 307
Furnishes the blanks for the use of the Major General....... 341
Official Charts furnished by................................. 416
Official Receipts furnished by............................... 421
May not issue but one uniform style of Official Receipt....... 427
To be furnished with reports, every two years, of the numerical and financial strength of the Sisterhood............. 498
Report of, to be printed previous to the session............. 530
To furnish quarterly reports to the press.................... 531
Returns from Grand Lodges, to be on blanks furnished by...
....538, 539
All supplies on price list, except jewel cases, application cards and delinquent notices obtainable only from..........583, 585
Authorized to furnish supplies, on credit to Grand Keepers of Records and Seal and Deputy Supreme Chancellors—others, only for cash..................................... 587
To allow amount, equal to customs duties, on Supplies....... 588
Bond of, placed in hands of Supreme Chancellor............. 594
Supreme Chancellor to notify, of issuance of Warrants 595
To keep the record of the proceedings of Supreme Council and Lodge, and transmit same to Grand Lodges and Lodges subordinate to Supreme Lodge......................... 607
To collect and pay over the revenues 608
To preserve the archives and have charge of the Seal....... 609
To prepare Charters for Grand Lodges..................... 610
To notify Grand Lodges and members of Supreme sessions.. 610
To carry on the correspondence............................ 611
To keep register of Dispensations and Charters............. 612

Index.

SUPREME KEEPER OF RECORDS, ETC.—(Cont'd.) SECTIONS.

To keep a record of Past Grand Chancellors and Representatives... 613
To attest all necessary documents........................... 614
To perform such other duties as may be required............ 614
Shall be furnished with an office............................ 615
Shall report to the Supreme Lodge........................... 616
Shall be provided with stationery............................ 617
Shall preserve copies of Seals of Grand and Subordinate Lodges...559, 618
To submit quarterly trial balance............................ 619
To report a showing of his accounts......................... 620
Salary of, determined at each session........................ 621
To report a vouched statement of expenses................... 623
To submit detail report of supplies received and on hand..... 624
To furnish Supreme Chancellor, at end of each fiscal year, list of firms furnishing supplies purchased.................... 625
To notify Jurisdictions of approval of Constitutions.......... 626
To furnish Chairmen of Committees with Digest and file of Journals... 627
To furnish Chairman of Committee on Credentials and Returns with a list of delinquent Jurisdictions..................... 628
To furnish members of Supreme Lodge with Constitution.... 629
To preserve Journals and periodicals, and have bound....... 630
To have charge of the Supreme Lodge Jewels................ 631
Books of, may not be turned over to a "Board of Auditors".. 632
An Officer of the Supreme Lodge..........................646 (*g*)
Orders on Master of Exchequer, to be attested by 659
Notice of contested seat of Supreme Representative, to be filed with... 682
To issue Supreme Representative's certificate providing for evidence of service as Past Grand Chancellor............. 687
Authorized to prepare form of Withdrawal Card, for members of defunct Lodges....................................... 753

SUPREME LECTURER.

Special appointment of, by Supreme Lodge................... 633
Appointment of, a matter for local legislation................ 633

SUPREME LODGE.

Prescribes only the minimum age of applicants for membership... 2
AMENDMENTS TO CONSTITUTION OF.
    Must be offered at regular session, and lie over............ 3
    Considered at next regular session — two-thirds vote required to adopt.. 3
    Considered and adopted at same session if unanimous vote given to consider................................... 5

(282)

Index.

SUPREME LODGE—(Continued.)   SECTIONS.
POWERS OF.

To adopt additional rules to carry out constitutional provisions regarding Appeals and Writs of Error.........	47
To revoke Charters of, and suspend Grand Lodges, for cause	122
Alone, to reissue Charter, if destroyed...................	124
To issue Charters to Lodges under control of 126,	644
To revoke Charters of Lodges under control of	132
To authorize committees to call for persons and papers..	179
To approve Constitutions, when in session...............	185
To issue Charters to Grand Lodges..................258,	644
To resume any of the powers delegated to Grand Lodges... 262,	645
To correct any abuse of discretion or violation of law by a Grand Lodge.......................................	265
To establish the Uniform Rank........................285	(9)
To establish the Endowment Rank 285	(9)
To prescribe and provide the Jewels of the Order.293, 518,	637
To control the sale of the Jewels of the Order...........	294
To control all Lodges where no Grand Lodge exists..307,	644
To provide Constitution for subordinates under control of..328,	644
To establish a "Memorial Day".........................	391
To issue Official Charts............... ...413, 414, 416, 636,	637
To issue Official Receipts..................421, 422, 423,	427
To exclude improper persons for causes arising after the issuance of their certificate.........................	483
To prescribe the regalia of the Order........... 517, 518,	637
To determine the right to representation by delinquent Grand Jurisdictions.............................541,	542
To order translations of the Rituals......................	544
To adopt a seal for itself, and an official seal for the Supreme Chancellor........................556, 557,	558
To furnish "supplies" 582,	585
To furnish Charter Plates.......................	586
To fix the price of "supplies"...........................	590
To determine the salary of the Supreme Keeper of Records and Seal	621
To establish, regulate, control, change and alter the Written and Unwritten Work of the Order...............	635
To provide, print and furnish all Rituals, forms and ceremonies 635, 636,	758
To provide Cards, Odes, Charts and Certificates......636,	758
To prescribe the emblems of the Order...................	637
To designate the Uniform of the Order...................	637

Index.

SUPREME LODGE—(Continued.)   SECTIONS.
POWERS OF.
    To provide for the emanation of all Passwords....... 454, 638
    To establish the Order where not engrafted.............. 639
    To provide its own revenue....................... 640
    To provide for annual reports from Grand Lodges, and Lodges under its own control.................... 641
    To hear and determine all appeals..................... 17, 642
    To legislate for the enforcement of its own decisions.. 642, 643
    To enact laws and regulations of general application to carry into effect its own Constitution and reserved powers... 643
    To define the territorial limit of Grand Lodges.......... 644
    To determine the salary of Supreme Master of Exchequer... 661
    To issue Traveling Shields to Grand Lodges............ 696
Description of banner for................................. 72
List of Standing Committees of.......................... 150
Duties of Standing Committees of....................... 151–172
Special Committees of, permanent in character, duties of 176–178
Appointment of Deputy Supreme Chancellor, does not require approval of.. 194
Elections in, to be held at the forenoon meeting on the third day of biennial session—majority of votes present necessary to a choice.. 212, 213
Officer absent, may be excused by, and installed during recess of... 215
May designate one member to cast unanimous vote, there being but one nominee.................................. 216
Will approve amendments to Constitutions of Grand Lodges, providing for a representative system..................... 264
Will not answer hypothetical questions, unless coming from Grand Lodge or Grand Chancellor............... 281, 282, 283
Laws and legislation of, become of force from date of the Official Journal... 305
Legislative acts of, obligatory........................... 306
Pays mileage and per diem to its Officers, Representatives and Past Supreme Chancellors by service................... 394
Orders from, take precedence over all business, and must receive immediate attention............................... 419
Has no "Official Organ".................................. 420
Does not recognize the "Pythian Sisters" or the "Pythian Sisterhood"... 499
Approved the establishment of a "Sanitarium" at Jacksonville, Florida... 555

Index.

SUPREME LODGE—(Continued.)   SECTIONS.
  Communication with, must be through a Grand Lodge, where
    one exists... 579
  Subordinate Lodges may not pass on acts of................ 580
  Is the source of all authority in the Order.............634, 652
  Composition of, Past Supreme Chancellors, Officers, Representatives and Past Grand Chancellors duly recognized..285 (3), 646
  Sessions of, held biennially, at place selected; failing to
    select, to be held at Baltimore........................... 647
  Will not attend parades, public celebrations, etc.. except held
    on first day of session................................... 649
  Majority of Grand Lodges constitute a quorum of, for business...285 (7), 651
  Only Representatives or Past Grand Chancellors eligible to
    admission to... 653
  New members admitted first two and last day of session
    of... 654
  Opened with prayer, by Supreme Prelate................... 663
  Terms of, two years....................................... 690
  Cannot empower Grand Lodges to charter Lodges in other
    States.. 692
  May place subordinates, in States where there is no Grand
    Lodge, under neighboring Jurisdiction..................... 692
  Will not grant power to a Grand Lodge to extend territorial
    limit so as to take in applicants resident in another
    Jurisdiction.. 693
  Officer of, or Representative to, taking Withdrawal Card,
    does not vacate office, if Card immediately deposited..... 746
  ACT OF INCORPORATION OF.
    Corporate name of, "Supreme Lodge of the Knights of
      Pythias"..285 (2)
    Composition of, Past Grand Chancellors, Officers and Representatives......................................285 (3)
    Board of Trustees of, Supreme Chancellor, Supreme
      Keeper of Records and Seal, Supreme Master of Exchequer and Supreme Vice Chancellor, to serve until
      the election of their successors....................285 (4)
    Officers of, and their election.......................285 (5)
    Sessions, regular and special........................285 (6)
    Quorum, majority of Representatives.................285 (7)
    Power to amend its Constitution, at will.............285 (8)
    Bodies of Knights of Pythias, not chartered through,
      are illegal..285 (8)
    Empowered to establish the Uniform Rank and Endowment Rank......................................285 (9)

Index.

SUPREME MASTER-AT-ARMS.
SECTIONS.
An officer of the Supreme Lodge............................646 (*k*)
Duties of... 656

SUPREME MASTER OF EXCHEQUER.
Accounts of, to be examined by Committee on Finance...155, 158
Report of, to be published... 531
To receive monthly revenues of the Supreme Lodge......... 608
" Board of Auditors," may not examine books of............. 632
One of the officers of the Supreme Lodge...................646 (*f*)
Makes quarterly statements of funds in his hands............. 657
Makes a report to the Supreme Lodge.......................... 658
To pay all properly drawn orders................................ 659
Gives bond, for fifty thousand (50,000) dollars, before installation... 660
To be paid a salary, determined from time to time........... 661

SUPREME OUTER GUARD.
Officer of the Supreme Lodge..............................646 (*m*)
Duties of.. 662

SUPREME PRELATE.
An officer of the Supreme Lodge..................285(5), 646 (*e*)
Opens and closes the Supreme Lodge with prayer........... 663

SUPREME REPRESENTATIVE.
Seat of, may not be declared vacant without fair trial........ 33
If seat of, unjustly declared vacant, is the only proper party to appeal.. 33
With Past Supreme Chancellors and Officers, only eligible on standing and special committees............................. 174
Position of, on standing committee, vacated if not re-elected.. 175
Position of, on special committee, not vacated by reason of failure in re-election.. 180
Credentials of, to be forwarded at least twenty days before session.. 189
Name of, newly elected, to be forwarded at once to Supreme Keeper of Records and Seal................................... 251
Two, elected at the organization of a Grand Lodge 255
Any Past Chancellor, eligible to election as, at formation of Grand Lodge... 256
Entitled to mileage and per diem, if present at close of session —may be excused by the Supreme Chancellor........394, 395
May not draw mileage both as Representative and Officer.... 396
Elected at organization of Grand Lodge, become Past Grand Chancellors.. 477
Office of, may not be vacated without sufficient charges...... 482

Index.

SUPREME REPRESENTATIVE—(Continued.)   SECTIONS.

Desiring to protest, may present same in writing, to Supreme Lodge.. 491
Loses rights in Supreme Lodge if his Jurisdiction delinquent.. ....539, 540, 541, 542
May be accorded privileges as, on the floor of the Supreme Lodge, though Jurisdiction delinquent, but cannot claim it as a right....................................540, 541, 542
Record of, kept by Supreme Keeper of Records and Seal 613
One of the component parts of the Supreme Lodge... ....646 (*n*)
One of the qualifications for office in the Supreme Lodge 653
Must be a Past Grand Chancellor 664
Must be in good standing in Lodge and Grand Lodge......... 664
No one eligible to election as, until a Past Grand Chancellor . 665
A Grand Chancellor eligible to election as, after his successor is installed, but not before 666, 667, 668, 669
Not eligible to election as, on the ground that nominee will be entitled to rank as Past Grand Chancellor at time of taking his seat 668
Must be *bona fide* resident of Jurisdiction they represent 670
Office of, vacated by change of residence 670
Must be a member of a Lodge in the Jurisdiction represented 671
Grand Lodge entitled to two, up to twenty thousand members; one additional for each additional ten thousand, but not to exceed four Representatives in all 672
Grand Lodge not entitled to additional, for fraction of ten thousand 673
To be elected for four years, except at organization of new Grand Lodge..674, 675
Term of, to begin January next succeeding election, and to end 31st day of December......................674, 675, 679
Elected at organization of Grand Lodge, service of one Representative to be for short term, and one for long term... 674
Term of additional, whether appointed or elected, to be for four years.. 676, 677
Vacancy in the position of, to be filled as provided by the law of Jurisdiction represented 678
When appointed to fill vacancy, credential should be for a period ending with December 31st, of an odd-numbered year 679
Appointment of, to fill vacancy, should be for unexpired term for which predecessor elected............................ 680
Office of, cannot be declared vacant for insufficient cause 681
Seat of, being contested, notice must be filed with Supreme Keeper of Records and Seal................................ 682

Index.

SUPREME REPRESENTATIVE—(Continued.)   SECTIONS.
  Supreme Lodge refuse to declare seat of, vacant when the effect would only be to leave Jurisdiction unrepresented.. 683
  Not in possession of S. A. P. W., compelled to retire from Supreme Lodge 684
  "Alternate," not authorized................................ 685
  Seated on irregular credentials—specific cases given 686
  Form of credential of, to show when rank of Past Grand Chancellor attained and date of election as 687
  Appointment of, by Grand Chancellor, void unless Grand Lodge Constitution specifically gives Grand Chancellor appointing power 714
  Entitled to one vote in determining all questions before Supreme Lodge... 728
  Taking Withdrawal Card, office of, not thereby vacated, if Card immediately deposited........................... 746

SUPREME SECRETARY OF THE ENDOWMENT RANK.
  Is the Secretary of the Board of Control.................... 222
  Jewel for, prescribed....................................... 293
  Synopsis of report of, to be published...................... 531
  An Officer of the Supreme Lodge........................ 646 (*h*)
  Performs such duties as may be prescribed................. 688
  To give bond in such sum as determined by Board of Control, 688

SUPREME VICE CHANCELLOR.
  A trustee of the Supreme Lodge..........................285 (4)
  An Officer of the Supreme Lodge.................285 (5), 646 (*d*)
  Performs such duties as may be assigned to him............. 689
  Acts as Supreme Chancellor in case of vacancy.............. 689
  Filling vacancy of Supreme Chancellor, paid salary and entitled to honors.. 689

SURETIES.
  On bonds of Supreme Officers, must file sworn statement showing pecuniary responsibility....................... 107

SUSPENSION.
  OF A GRAND LODGE.
    Subject to, for non-conformance of, or disobedience to, legal mandates, or improper conduct 122
    Subject to, for instituting or promoting schemes of chance, lotteries, gift enterprises, etc........................ 331
    Status of members of suspended Grand Lodge, under control of new Grand Lodge............................ 390
  OF A SUBORDINATE LODGE.
    Members not entitled to benefits during.................. 96
    Grand Lodges may provide for, for various causes, 132, 133, 134
    Cannot take place without proper charges and trial...... 135

Index.

SUSPENSION—(Continued.)   SECTIONS.
  OF A SUBORDINATE LODGE.
    Grand Chancellor possesses no inherent power of........ 135
    Under Supreme Lodge, may take place for neglecting to
      hold meetings.. 329
    Subject to, for instituting or promoting schemes of chance,
      lotteries, gift enterprises, etc......................... 331
    Invasion of Jurisdiction, a cause for.................... 529
  OF A GRAND OFFICER.
    Pending investigation of charges, requires a two-thirds
      vote of a Grand Lodge............................... 139
    May take place during recess after charges, and with con-
      sent of the majority of Grand Lodge Officers........ 146
    One of the penalties provided in the code in trial........ 148
  FOR CAUSE.
    The manner of reinstatement after, a matter for local
      legislation...83, 383
    Member under, not entitled to minimum benefits......... 84
    Advance dues paid by member under, retained by Lodge
      until expiration of suspension....................... 211
    Members subject to, for refusing to deliver up property of
      Lodge, on suspension of Charter.................... 287
    Subject to, for instituting or promoting schemes of chance,
      lotteries, gift enterprises, etc......................... 331
    Member under definite, reinstated on termination of,
      without action of Lodge............................ 525
    Member under indefinite, reinstated upon application, on
      passing regular ballot.............................. 526
    Pending appeal from, member no right to visit........... 725
  FOR NON-PAYMENT OF DUES.
    Subject to, if in arrears for an amount equal to one year's
      dues..51, 53
    Member may not be made subject to, for six months'
      arrears.. 54
    Must be notified of arrears before....................... 55
    Declaration of, must be made in open Lodge by Chancel-
      lor Commander................................... 55
    Failure to make declaration of, membership not severed. 56
    Before declaration of, though twelve months in arrears,
      member may pay arrears and prevent................ 56
    Upon being reinstated after, member entitled to benefits.82, 92
    Not liable to, if under charges.......................... 120
    Dues cannot be charged to members under, unless local
      law so provides..................................208, 209
    Fines and assessments may operate as dues and render
      member liable to, if local law so provides........... 237

SUSPENSION—(Continued.)   SECTIONS.
  FOR NON-PAYMENT OF DUES.
    Members under, in Lodges subordinate to Supreme Lodge, must pay at least one year's dues and all assessments before reinstatement.......................... 323
    A person under, ceases to be a member of the Order until reinstated.. 381
    Declaration of, may be revoked for the purpose of trial.. 382
    Status of members under, and their reinstatement or readmission, a matter for local legislation ...383, 384, 527
    A member under, may reinstate himself, by paying all arrears, if the local law so provides.................. 528
  GENERAL RULINGS.
    Status of suspended members, a matter for local legislation 83, 383
    Section of Endowment Rank to be notified of members suspended for any cause 223
    Derelict members of committee may be suspended........ 239
    Members subject to, for refusing to deliver up property of Lodge on suspension of Charter 287
    A penalty under proceedings in Courts Martial, in the Uniform Rank 343
    Brother admitted to membership, cannot be suspended without due process of law......................375, 376.
    Pending appeal from, member no right to visit........... 725

TEAM—(See Rank Team.)

TAX—(See also Representative Tax; Per Capita Tax.)
  Lodge may levy on its members, to meet necessary expenses... 59
  May be levied by Lodge to pay benefits..................... 78
  Lodges failing to pay to Supreme or proper Grand Lodge may be suspended 133

TELLERS.
  In elections, the law providing the appointment of two "members" as, means members of that Lodge 218

TERM.
  On expiration of, the Supreme Representative vacates place on Standing Committee................................. 175
  Of Supreme Lodge Officers, two years...................212, 690
  Of members of Board of Control, six years................. 222
  Of Grand Lodge Officers, not less than one year.....267, 280, 690
  Grand Lodge Officers entitled to honors of full term, though time of annual session changed......................... 280
  Of Major General, four years from date of appointment...... 334
  Chancellor Commander serving one, entitled to certificate as Past Chancellor.. 469

Index.

TERM—(Continued.) SECTIONS.
  Charter being surrendered before completion of, Chancellor Commander not entitled to honors...................... 471
  Retiring Grand Chancellor becomes Past Grand Chancellor without reference to length of service.................... 475
  Of Supreme Representatives, four years, except at organization of new Lodge..... .... 674, 675, 676. 677
  Of Supreme Representatives, must end with 31st of December of an odd-numbered year........................... 679
  Of Supreme Representatives appointed to fill vacancies, to be for unexpired portion of................................. 680
  Of Subordinate Lodges, regulated by each Grand Jurisdiction, not less than six months........................... 690
  Of Lodges subordinate to the Supreme Lodge, six months.... 690
  Of Grand Officers, Grand Lodge regulates, within the provision of the Supreme Constitution........................ 691

TERRITORIAL JURISDICTION.
  Board of Control have, co-extensive with the Supreme Lodge.. 225
  Grand Lodges have exclusive original, over all their subordinates and members...................................260, 261
  Applicants for membership in a Jurisdiction other than their own, require consent of their Grand Chancellor.......... 373
  Invasion of, a cause for suspension of Subordinate Lodge.... 529
  Supreme Lodge will not interfere with, of Grand Lodges, when established..........................692, 693, 694, 695
  Of a Grand Lodge, not to be interfered with by Supreme Chancellor—Dakota case.......... 695

TESTIMONY.
  In the trial of a Lodge, must be made of record and reported to Grand Lodge........ 135
  Competent, though witness not a member of the Order........ 702

TRANSLATIONS.
  Of the Ritual of the Order, made only under direction of Supreme Lodge..................................... 544

TRANSPORTATION.
  Committee on, of the Supreme Lodge, prescribed............ 178

TRAVELING SHIELDS.
  Under the supervision of the Committee on Written Work.... 166
  Grand Lodge must conform to.................. 259
  Only recognized when procured from the Supreme Lodge.... 696
  Must be of the prescribed legal form........................ 696
  Issued to Subordinate Lodges by their Grand Lodges 696
  Issued to Lodges subordinate to Supreme Lodge, through the Deputy Supreme Chancellor...................... 696
  Form, provisions, limitations, etc., prescribed 697

Index.

TRAVELING SHIELDS—(Continued.)   SECTIONS.
    Issued for any length of time for which dues paid, but not beyond next meeting of Supreme Lodge 698
    An evidence of good standing and a letter of credit....... 698, 724
    Shows amount of weekly and funeral benefits to which holder entitled 698
    Money paid on presentation of, by sister Lodge, issuing Lodge responsible for... 699
    Holder of Withdrawal Card, not entitled to................. 700
    Not required for purpose of visiting......................... 724
    Chancellor Commander may demand, before admission, if in doubt 724

TRIAL.
    OF A GRAND OFFICER.
        Supreme Representative entitled to, before seat can be legally vacated....................................... 33
        Grand Lodge must give fair and proper trial............. 116
        Rules governing, in Subordinate Lodge, may be used in trial in Grand Lodge, in analogous cases 117
        Code of Procedure in, where Grand Lodge fails to provide 136–149
    OF A SUBORDINATE LODGE.
        May not be held, until due notice given of offense, properly served.................................... 133 (*c*), 135
        Testimony and record in, to be reported to Grand Lodge. 135
        Must be acted on at same session as reported............ 135
        Grand Lodge must provide a commission or jury for..... 135
        Must be had, before they can be suspended.............. 135
        Grand Lodge cannot annul action of Subordinate without 375
    OF A MEMBER.
        All brothers are entitled to a fair trial.................. 33
        Committee to try may not be appointed by officers who are parties to the charges............................ 119
        Penalty of expulsion may be imposed in.................. 228
        Member irregularly admitted, entitled to, before membership can be disturbed................... 369, 374, 375, 376
        Members suspended for non-payment of dues, may be brought to 382
        Cannot be placed on trial for private debt................ 409
        Of a Page or Esquire, conducted in their respective rank. 567
        Not appearing, Lodge may proceed with.................. 701
        Non-members, competent witnesses on 702
        Notice of time of holding, by mail, sufficient 703
        Indictment for criminal offense, not of itself cause to place on 704

Index.

TRIAL—(Continued.)   SECTIONS.
  OF A MEMBER.
    Lodge need not await action of court, on a criminal charge, before proceeding with 704, 705
    Change of venue in, may be provided for, by Grand Lodges 717
    Holder of Withdrawal Card, may be placed on, after revocation of Card 738, 739

TRIAL COMMITTEE.
  Neither Chancellor Commander nor Vice Chancellor may appoint, if party to the charges 119
  Grand Lodge must provide, in case of charges against a Lodge, during recess 135
  In charges against a Grand Officer, appointment, duties and powers of 142, 143, 144, 145, 146, 147, 149

TRUSTEES.
  Of the Supreme Lodge, designated in the Act of Incorporation, ... 285 (4)
  Board of, may not exceed their instructions in expending money 577

UNANIMOUS CONSENT—(See Consent.)

UNIFORM.
  Under the supervision of the Committee on Written Work... 166
  May be worn at funerals 246
  Grand Lodges must conform to 259
  Supreme Lodge prescribes 637
  Of Third Rank, adopted 706, 707
  To be worn in parades 708
  Cap of, not to be worn in Lodge room, except by order of Chancellor Commander 709
  Baldric of, abolished 710
  Use of, entirely voluntary 711
  Of the Uniform Rank, does not of itself entitle member to admission; jewel must be worn in addition 712

UNIFORM RANK.
  Committee on, duties of 150, 172
  Committee on supplies for, prescribed 177
  Major General of, appointed and commissioned by Supreme Chancellor 212, 334
  Power to establish, under Act of Incorporation 285 (9)
  Powers and duties of Major General of 334-345
  Adoption and promulgation of 713
  Members holding Withdrawal Card, not entitled to admission to 752

UNWRITTEN WORK.
  May not be changed without lying over one session and adopted by a four-fifths vote 4, 764

Index.

UNWRITTEN WORK—(Continued.)   SECTIONS.
    Appeals regarding, from the decision of the Chair, considered only while in the Third Rank............................ 43
    Committee on, in the Supreme Lodge—duties of 150, 167
    Instruction in, may be given by Grand Chancellor or Deputy, outside Lodge room... 253
    Language of, to be strictly adhered to 546, 547, 548
    Not to be changed, altered, added to, amended, or any part omitted 548
    Transmission of, to foreign countries, authorized 554
    Under the control of the Supreme Lodge 635
    Visiting member not examined in 723
    What constitutes..764, 765
    Must be uniform in all Lodges.... 766

VACANCY.
    Absence of officer-elect, in Supreme Lodge, creates, unless excused... 215
    Occurring in office of Sitting Past Chancellor, only a Past Chancellor can be elected to fill 465
    In office of Grand Chancellor, Grand Vice Chancellor filling, entitled to honors 472
    Created, by Grand Officer acquiring residence in another Jurisdiction.. 537
    Supreme Chancellor has power to fill, caused by removal of officer 597
    Declared in office of Supreme Keeper of Records and Seal, by failure to furnish bond 622
    In office of Supreme Representative, to be filled as law of his Grand Lodge provides, for the unexpired term, ending with December 31st of an odd-numbered year....678, 679, 680
    In office of Supreme Representative, cannot be declared, except for sufficient cause 681
    Supreme Lodge refused to render decision, which would only operate to create, in office of Supreme Representative.... 683
    Appointment by Grand Chancellor to fill, inoperative, unless Constitution so provides.................................... 714
    By death or otherwise, filled in the manner of original selection 715
    Absence at installation may create, if Grand Lodge legislation so provides... 716
    In office of Representative to Grand Lodge, created by taking Withdrawal Card 751

VENUE.
    Change of, in cases of trial, may be provided for, by Grand Lodge 717

VICE CHANCELLOR.
    Inspects ballot for membership............................. 64

Index.

VICE CHANCELLOR—(Continued.)   SECTIONS.
    Takes the chair, when Chancellor Commander retires........ 109
    If a party to charges, cannot appoint Committee on Trial.... 119
    Eligibility to office of, a matter for local legislation........... 718
    Circumstances under which may or may not act, in absence of
        Chancellor Commander............................. 719, 720
    Fills the chair until Chancellor Commander is legally elected
        and installed.. 721
VISITING.
    Knight when, must be in possession of S. A. P. W....445, 724, 748
    Chancellor Commander may not instruct visiting brother in
        Rank Passwords without a separate order........... 451, 452
    Lodge visiting in a body, Master-at-Arms may take Rank pass-
        word in the ante-room................................... 453
    Past Chancellors visiting Grand Lodge, must have current
        Grand Lodge password................................. 455
    Grand Officers visiting, enter hall, in same order as in instal-
        lation... 722
    Receipt for dues and examination in secret work, not required
        of visitor.. 723
    Traveling Shield not required in........................... 724
    Chancellor Commander may require Official Receipt from
        visitor, if in doubt...................................... 724
    Pending appeal, suspended brother has not right of.......... 725
    Member cannot be debarred from, on account of objections,
        if otherwise qualified.............................. 726, 727
    Withdrawal Cards cannot be used for 747
    Holder of Withdrawal Card has privilege of, if in possession
        of S. A. P. W...................................... 748, 749
    Past Chancellor or Past Grand Chancellor holding Withdrawal
        Card has privilege of, in his Grand Lodge, if having the
        S. A. P. W... 749
VISITING CARDS.
    Not recognized in the Order................................ 747
    Withdrawal Cards cannot be used as....................... 747
VOTING.
    TWO-THIRDS VOTE.
        To amend the Constitution of the Supreme Lodge........ 3
        Required in Grand Lodge to temporarily suspend officer,
            pending investigation.............................. 139
        Required to postpone installation of Grand Officer pend-
            ing investigation.................................. 139
        When for expenditure of money, any appropriation for
            "nurse hire," would be governed by the rule......... 243
        To change the day of meeting of Supreme Lodge, from the
            fourth Tuesday in April............................ 647

VOTING—(Continued.)

SECTIONS.

FOUR-FIFTHS VOTE.
To change the Written or Unwritten Work.............. 4

UNANIMOUS VOTE.
To consider a proposition to amend the Constitution of the Supreme Lodge at the same session as presented 5
In case of one nominee for office in the Supreme Lodge, cast by one member, by a vote of the body....... 216
Required on appropriations of money, in Subordinate Lodge, only a quorum being present.................. 566
Not necessary to withdraw proposition for membership... 732

MAJORITY VOTE.
To elect officers of the Supreme Lodge.................... 213
Appropriation for "nurse hire," cannot be made by, when rule provides a two-thirds vote on expenditures of money................................. 243
To withdraw a proposition for membership............. 732
To sustain an objection to granting Withdrawal Card..... 734

GENERAL RULINGS.
An excess of votes in an election, does not void the ballot where such excess would not change the result.... 219
Disclosing name of member voting against candidate may be made an offense, by local law..................... 412
Past Grand Chancellors have not privilege of, in Supreme Lodge.................................. 479
Vote on reinstatement after suspension for non-payment of dues, a matter for local legislation........... 527
In the Supreme Lodge, confined to the Officers, Supreme Representatives and Past Supreme Chancellors by service, who have one vote each 728
Right of, inheres to Grand Officers, in their Grand Lodge, if no local law to the contrary....................... 729
Unless local law permits, Past Grand Chancellors, who are also Representatives, cannot cast two votes on questions in their Grand Lodge................... 730
Grand Lodges may provide for the exclusion from voting, even on the election of officers, of all but Representatives of Lodges... 731
"Consent" means a majority vote....................... 732

VOUCHING.
Not allowed... 733

WARRANTS—(See Dispensations.)

WHITE MALE.
Applicant for membership must be...................... 347, 352

Index.

WHITE MALE—(Continued.)   SECTIONS.
   Lodges must provide this as a qualification, in their Constitutions 352
   Lodge violating the law with reference to, subjects itself to suspension... 352

WIDOW.
   Of a member, right to bring an appeal recognized..........96, 99

"WIDOW'S TAX."
   Payable, if member entitled to funeral benefits............... 101

WITHDRAWAL CARD.
   Member, though twelve months in arrears, but not declared suspended, may pay up arrears and ask for and receive a Card.. 56
   Application for membership by, passes same ballot as by initiation.. 71
   Asked for and granted, severs the membership, whether the Card is taken or not.. 97
   Being properly granted, all responsibility in regard to Lodge paying benefits, ceases.. 97
   Properly granted, but improperly filled out, the error creates no responsibility for benefits................................. 97
   Status of a Grand Officer while out on, a matter for local legislation.. 269
   Supreme Chancellor may issue, to members of defunct Lodges in territory where no Grand Lodge exists..............324, 325
   Member joining in application for new Lodge must present... 362
   Application for membership by, same as for initiation.... 370
   Time when applicant for membership becomes a member, is a matter for local legislation, but no rule being provided, membership begins upon election...................... 371, 372
   Non-resident applicant for membership by, requires permission of his Grand Chancellor................................. 373
   Applicant for membership by, irregularly admitted, but through no fault of his own, membership cannot be disturbed, except after trial........................374, 375, 376
   Lodge not compelled to readmit member to whom they had granted 377
   Rejected applicant for membership by, may reapply, at any time, unless local law prevents............................. 378
   Local law cannot extend probationary period, before reapplication by Card, beyond six months....................... 378
   Transfer of Pages and Esquires, is by.............379, 380, 754
   Members taking, while Lodge is suspended, membership not revived with that Lodge, when reorganized.......... 388, 389
   Sitting Past Chancellor, taking, does not lose honors......... 461

Index.

WITHDRAWAL CARDS—(Continued.)

SECTIONS.

Members affiliating by, in another Jurisdiction, must evidence past rank by having a rank credential, which must issue from his own Grand Lodge; the placing of past rank on Withdrawal Card is of no force 511, 512, 513, 514, 515, 516
Printed and furnished by Supreme Lodge 636
Holder of, not entitled to a Traveling Shield 700
Applications for, to be made either personally or in writing .. 734
Applicant for, must be clear on the books and free from charges 56, 734, 760
Granted on application, no objections being made 734
Objections to granting, must be sustained by a majority vote, unless charges are preferred 734
Application for, by another member, of no binding effect 735
Lodges may charge a fee for 736
Once granted, vote on cannot be reconsidered, even at request of the holder 737
Holder of, revoked for purpose of trial, refusing to obey citation, is in contempt 738
May be revoked by Lodge granting 738, 760
When revoked, for purpose of trial, holder again becomes subject to the jurisdiction of the Lodge 738, 739
May be revoked for purposes other than impeachment and trial 739
Are good until revoked or deposited 740
Notice of deposit of, to be sent to source of issue 741
Holder of, only entitled to the S. A. P. W. current at the time the Card issued 742, 743
Rank of a brother to be stated in 744, 745
Honors not lost by taking 745
Supreme Officers and Supreme Representatives taking, do not thereby vacate office; must at once deposit; while holding, can perform no official act 746
Cannot be used as "visiting cards" 747
Holder of, desiring to obtain S. A. P. W. current at time of issue of Card, must present a proper order therefor 747
Holder of, has a right to visit, being in possession of the S. A. P. W 748
Holder of, cannot obtain S. A. P. W. of next term 748
Past Chancellor, or Past Grand Chancellor, in possession of S. A. P. W., entitled to visit Grand Lodge 749
Holder of, not eligible to any office in Grand Lodge 750
Granting of, vacates election of Representative to Grand Lodge 751
Holder of, not admissible in the Uniform Rank 752
Special form for, issued to members of defunct Lodges 753

Index.

WITHDRAWAL CARDS—(Continued.)   SECTIONS.
    Issued, by Grand Chancellor, to Pages and Esquires of defunct
        Lodges 754
    Grand Chancellor may not issue, to members of a Lodge,
        after its revival 755
    If lost or destroyed, may be renewed, by Lodge issuing... 756, 757
    Grand Lodge has no right to issue "Clearance Certificates"
        "Cards of Privilege" or "Dismissal Certificates" in lieu
        of 758, 759
    Not to be granted to Past Chancellor under charges in Grand
        Lodge 760
    Grand Chancellor may order revocation of, for cause....... 760
    If procured by fraud, is void................................. 761
    The simple fact of holding, cannot be plead in bar, in pro-
        ceedings on charges..................................... 762
    New Grand Lodge given jurisdiction over granting, to mem-
        bers of defunct Lodges organized under old Grand Lodge, 763

WITNESS:
    A person not a member may be, in trials..................... 702

WORK—(See Written Work; Unwritten Work.)

WRITE.
    Persons not able to, not eligible to membership 356
    Member able to write his name entitled to advance 357

WRITS OF ERROR.
    Lie against the action of a Grand Lodge, or during recess,
        against the decision of a Grand Chancellor, which would,
        by its operation, invalidate any enactment of the Supreme
        Lodge 17, 45, 46
    In extreme cases, may be heard later than the next following
        session... 22
    Records in, shall be certified to, by the Grand Chancellor and
        Grand Keeper of Records and Seal, who, failing to so cer-
        tify, must show cause, otherwise the facts will be admitted
        as true 29, 45
    To be passed on by the Supreme Lodge, or during recess, by
        the Supreme Chancellor 17, 45
    To be reported to the Supreme Lodge, by Supreme Chancellor 40
    Shall contain statement of facts, and an argument 45
    Supreme Chancellor shall certify his decision on, to the parties
        in interest.. 45
    Supreme Lodge may adopt additional rules governing 47

WRITTEN WORK.
    May not be changed without lying over one session, and
        adopted by a four-fifths vote........................... 4

WRITTEN WORK—(Continued.)   SECTIONS.
   Appeals regarding, from the decision of the Chair, considered
      only while in the Third Rank 43
   Committee on, in the Supreme Lodge—duties of 150, 166
   Lodges may not change, alter or amend............ 548
   Supreme Chancellor authorized to transmit to foreign coun-
      tries 554
   Under the control of the Supreme Lodge.................... 635
   What constitutes.. 764

www.ingramcontent.com/pod-product-compliance
Lightning Source LLC
Chambersburg PA
CBHW032043230426
43672CB00009B/1450